P9-AGS-102

DATE DUE

OCT 22	MAY 28 '00		
NOV 12 '79			
DEC 3 '79			
MAR 3 '79			
DEC 14 '79			
JAN 30 '80			
NOV 1 '87			
JUN 7 '95			
OCT 30 '95			
NOV 13 '96			
FEB 26 '97			

APR 15 '81

100 Years of Emancipation

RAND McNALLY PUBLIC AFFAIRS SERIES

100 Years of

ESSAYS BY

HARRY V. JAFFA

ROY WILKINS

HERBERT J. STORING

JAMES BALDWIN

JAMES FARMER

JAMES JACKSON KILPATRICK

ABRAM L. HARRIS

LOUIS H. POLLAK

WALTER BERNS

Emancipation

EDITED BY

ROBERT A. GOLDWIN

RAND McNALLY & COMPANY · CHICAGO

RAND MᶜNALLY PUBLIC AFFAIRS SERIES

    America Armed: Essays on United States Military Policy
    A Nation of States: Essays on the American Federal System
    Why Foreign Aid?
    Political Parties, U.S.A.
    100 Years of Emancipation

To Dorothy Jones
who had the idea in the first place

PREFACE

●

The strong light by which an understanding of the past illumi-
nates the present is nowhere better exemplified than in the case
of race relations in the United States. Can anyone claim to
understand the staggering events of 1963, in Oxford and Birmingham and Washington and everywhere throughout our nation,
who is ignorant of their origins in the events of 1863 and before?
And is there hope that we as a nation can free ourselves from
our present dark plight if we fail to grasp its true source in the
long career of American slavery? The prospect is not bright,
because to understand slavery we must understand freedom.
Emancipation remains this nation's greatest unfinished task primarily because we have not yet been successful in learning the
true nature of freedom and the price of a national commitment to it.

If the Civil War was the greatest turning point in the
history of the American nation, which few deny; and if Lincoln
was our greatest national leader, which many certainly assert;
and if, as is the case, the *conduct* emancipation of the slaves was the
single act above all others for which Lincoln is most widely
remembered, is it not remarkable that there was no grand and
official national celebration of the hundredth anniversary of
the Emancipation Proclamation? The answer, which I suppose
thoughtful citizens, white and black alike, would give to my
question, is, simply, No. They might be puzzled by the asking
of the question, but not by the absence of celebration for, after
all, they would ask, what is there to celebrate? How much more
can we say than that one hundred years after emancipation
there is none among us who desires to return to the system of

human slavery? In a way, of course, that is a very great deal to say, but it is surely not enough to occasion patriotic speeches, brass-band parades, and dancing in the streets.

The prelude to the century of emancipation now completed was almost two and a half centuries of slavery, a slavery so dearly prized by some and so hotly despised by others that it could be terminated only by a civil struggle unmatched in the world's annals for ferocity and slaughter. And there lies the difficulty in even commemorating, let alone celebrating, emancipation; for, being the same nation, the same people adhering to the same principles, we cannot pronounce emancipation without stirring within ourselves the lingering presence of our past as slave-owners and slaves. The human inclinations and defects that made of us a slave nation still dwell within us, in company and in tension with those other human forces that willed and accomplished the destruction of slavery. Many Americans had hoped, therefore, for the sake of the quiet of our daily lives, public and private, to be able to continue to forget, or at least to ignore, the slave past—precisely because it cannot be denied. There may have been a wisdom in this general reluctance to be reminded, frequently and openly, of the extent to which our nation—the land of the free—has been shaped by the institution of slavery. But 1963 ended all hope of tranquility based on self-induced blindness, as effectively as 1863 ended slavery.

The race problem in America can no longer be hidden or disguised; the reticence that might have been prudent in general and for ordinary purposes can no longer be considered useful or possible. The simple and unavoidable truth is that this most vexatious American problem persists, and there is no prospect of melioration without tracing its origins back to the source in American slavery, and perhaps beyond, to those universal human qualities that underlie slavery anywhere, for slavery is not, as we know, an American, nor even a Western, invention.

The present essays are an effort to describe and understand this most awful aspect of our national being. In this manner, we observe, we acknowledge, we commemorate, we strive toward, emancipation.

R. A. G.

January, 1964

CONTENTS

●

THE EDITOR AND THE AUTHORS

●

ROBERT A. GOLDWIN

is Lecturer in Political Science and Director, Public Affairs Conference Center, The University of Chicago. He is the editor of *Readings in World Politics,* 5th ed., 1959; *Readings in American Foreign Policy,* 4th ed., 1959; and *Readings in Russian Foreign Policy,* 3rd ed., 1959.

HARRY V. JAFFA

is Professor of Political Science, The Ohio State University. His fields of specialization are political philosophy and American political thought. He is the author of *Thomism and Aristotelianism,* 1952; *Crisis of the House Divided,* 1959; and editor of *In the Name of the People,* 1960 (with R. W. Johannsen).

ROY WILKINS

is Executive Secretary of the National Association for the Advancement of Colored People. A former newspaperman, he was for many years the editor of *Crisis,* the official monthly magazine of the NAACP.

HERBERT J. STORING

is Associate Professor of Political Science, The University of Chicago, specializing in the study of public administration and constitutional law. He is co-author of *The State and the Farmer,* 1962 (with Peter Self), and editor and joint author of *Essays on the Scientific Study of Politics,* 1962.

The Editor and the Authors

JAMES BALDWIN

author, has written extensively on race problems. He is the author of three novels, *Giovanni's Room,* 1956, *Go Tell It on the Mountain,* 1961, and *Another Country,* 1962, and three volumes of essays, *Notes of a Native Son,* 1957, *Nobody Knows My Name,* 1961, and *The Fire Next Time,* 1963. His stories and articles have appeared in dozens of leading periodicals in the United States and abroad.

JAMES FARMER

is National Director and one of the founders, in 1942, of the Congress of Racial Equality (CORE). A former radio and television commentator, his articles on race relations and civil rights have appeared in many publications.

JAMES JACKSON KILPATRICK

Editor of *The Richmond* (Virginia) *News Leader,* is the author of *The Sovereign States: Notes of a Citizen of Virginia,* 1957, and *The Southern Case for School Segregation,* 1962.

ABRAM L. HARRIS

late Professor of Economics and Philosophy, The University of Chicago, was four times a Guggenheim Foundation Fellow and served as an elected member of the Executive Committee, American Economic Association. His books include *The Black Worker,* 1931 (with S. D. Spero); *The Negro as Capitalist,* 1936; and *Economics and Social Reform,* 1958.

LOUIS H. POLLAK

Professor of Law, Yale University Law School, began his legal career as Clerk for Justice Rutledge. He is Chairman of the Connecticut Advisory Committee to the United States Civil Rights Commission and a Director of the NAACP Legal Defense and Educational Fund. His articles have appeared in numerous legal journals.

WALTER BERNS

Professor of Government, Cornell University, specializes in the field of constitutional law. He is the author of *Freedom, Virtue and the First Amendment,* 1957, and many articles in various political science and legal periodicals.

Harry V. Jaffa

❀

THE EMANCIPATION PROCLAMATION

In Lincoln Park, Washington, D.C., is a monument that is perhaps not less notable than the great Lincoln Memorial itself. At its center is a statue of the standing figure of the Emancipator. His right hand, holding the Proclamation, rests upon a column displaying a bust in relief of George Washington. Lincoln's left arm and hand are extended, the index finger raised significantly. Beneath the extended arm is the crouched figure of a young Negro, the chain that joined the shackles upon his wrists broken. The face of the kneeling figure is almost expressionless; or perhaps one should say that the expression is that of one who is oblivious of everything present, whose vision is fixed upon a horizon that lies in the future. This scene embodies what most of us have been familiar with since childhood as the story-book version of how freedom came to the Negro slave in America. The extended arm and finger of the Emancipator, and the suppressed power of the rising bondsman whose chains have been shattered, are suggestive of Michelangelo's *Creation,* as they are of the tradition, expressed with surpassing dignity and beauty in the lore and music of the American Negro himself, of how the people of faith are set free by an act of divine power.

The tale told by the Freedman's Monument has, however, through the years achieved a standing not unlike other elements of popular mythology: for instance, that of George Washington and the cherry tree. It is said to be edifying, but hardly true. I cannot think of a better summary of recent historiography in regard to the actual episode than the following paragraph from Professor Richard Hofstadter's essay on Lincoln in *The American Political Tradition:*

1

Harry V. Jaffa

The Emancipation Proclamation of January 1, 1863, had all the moral grandeur of a bill of lading. It contained no indictment of slavery, but simply based emancipation upon "military necessity." It expressly omitted the loyal slave states from its terms. Finally, it did not in fact free any slaves. For it excluded by detailed enumeration from the sphere covered in the Proclamation all the counties in Virginia and parishes in Louisiana that were occupied by Union troops and into which the government actually had the power to bring freedom. It simply declared free all slaves in "the States and parts of States" where the people were in rebellion —that is to say, precisely where its effect could not reach. Beyond its propaganda value the Proclamation added nothing to what Congress had already done in the Confiscation Act.[1]

Hofstadter continues with the two contemporary comments which nearly every historical account records. The first, Seward's, that "We show our sympathy with slavery by emancipating the slaves where we cannot reach them and holding them in bondage where we can set them free"; and the second, that of the editorialist of the London *Spectator,* that "The principle [of the Proclamation] is not that a human being cannot justly own another, but that he cannot own him unless he is loyal to the United States."

Which view of the Emancipation Proclamation is the true one: that expressed in the memorial to the Great Emancipator by the grateful people who believed he had set them free, or that expressed in the sardonic accents of today's historical "revisionists"? I believe the only safe starting point is the recognition that the Emancipation Proclamation, like the policy of which it is the symbol if not the embodiment, is a thing of paradox. This much is recognized, to a degree, by Professor Hofstadter, who concludes, as do most historians, that "for all its limitations, the Emancipation Proclamation probably made genuine emancipation inevitable." It is sometimes even recognized that without its so-called limitations the Proclamation might not have been so efficacious to this end. This, however, does not decide the important question of whether or not "genuine emancipation" was its intended effect. There is even a school

[1] (New York: Vintage Books, 1948), p. 132.

of thought that maintains that the real purpose of the Proclamation was to forestall, possibly even prevent, "genuine emancipation." It holds that Lincoln issued a Proclamation that literally freed no one, while diverting attention from his non-enforcement of the Confiscation Act of July 17, 1862, which the radicals in Congress, who were sincere emancipationists, had foisted upon him. We must accordingly ask, was the emancipating effect of the Proclamation the result of Lincoln's statecraft, was it in spite of that statecraft, or was it the outcome of events which had controlled him, and over which he had no really independent influence at all? Lincoln did say later, "I claim not to have controlled events but confess plainly that events have controlled me." But this statement only reproduces the enigmas of the Proclamation: since Lincoln found the sole constitutional justification for his action in military necessity he could not have attributed what he did to a deliberate design—as distinct from necessity—without implicitly confessing disingenuousness. That Lincoln had a political motive for denying he acted for the sake of the freedom of the slaves, does not justify us in supposing that he attributed to military necessity what was in fact his personal inclination. Perhaps the truth is both subtler and simpler: perhaps Lincoln's "oft-expressed personal wish that all men everywhere could be free" disposed him to proclaim freedom, provided that such action might become his official duty, for reasons distinct from (although possibly inseparable from) his personal wish. What did lead to that coincidence of personal wish and official duty—if indeed we can finally say that it did occur—is what we must inquire into.

The two Proclamations, of September 22, 1862, and January 1, 1863, are generally regarded as marking a sharp change in Lincoln's policy, from a "conservative" to a "liberal" policy, and, indeed, as changing the character of the war. Allen Nevins accepts this view, while interpreting it in a way that represents a kind of compromise between the Freedman's Monument and revisionist historiography, when he writes:

> The stroke of his pen lifted the aims of the war to a higher level, infused a new moral meaning into the conflict, and gave our ideals of democracy far greater breadth and strength than they had previously possessed.

3

Harry V. Jaffa

> It is true that for an initial hour on New Year's Day in 1863 the proclamation freed slaves only where the Federal Government as yet possessed no authority. . . . But every southward march by Union troops thereafter was a liberating march. . . .[2]

But Nevins' attempt at compromise is not without difficulties. The preliminary Proclamation had promised that no slaves would be freed in any state, or part of a state, the people whereof were *not* in rebellion against the United States one hundred days hence; and the final Proclamation made good that promise. There is no question but that the presidential Proclamations treated as wrong only rebellion against the United States, as the London *Spectator* editorialist had observed. Whatever one credits the Proclamation with accomplishing, therefore, it is hard to see how it gave "a new moral meaning" to "our ideals of democracy."

In a remarkable interview with a group of Chicago clergymen on September 13, 1862, little more than a week before the first Proclamation was issued (and when it had been lying secretly in his desk for about two months), Lincoln was told that a proclamation of emancipation would add moral purpose to a conflict in which, it was alleged, "Europe and the whole civilized world . . . now saw no other reason . . . than national pride and ambition, [and] an unwillingness to abridge our domain and power." To which the President replied, "I think you should admit that we already have an important principle to rally and unite the people in the fact that constitutional government is at stake. This is a fundamental idea, going about as deep as anything." Lincoln at Gettysburg was to speak of "a new birth of freedom," and by this to imply that the cause of popular government required a deeper dimension of morality than it had hitherto possessed, but he never meant that there was a deeper cause than the cause of popular government, or that the cause of popular government differed in any sense from the cause of constitutional government. From the writer for the *Spectator* in 1863 until Professor Nevins in 1963, there has been an underestimation of how wrong it was, from Lincoln's point of view, to rebel against the United States. For Lincoln, as we shall

[2] "The Centenary of Emancipation," *Saturday Review*, January 5, 1963, p. 25.

4

see, the wrong of rebellion and the wrong of slavery were in point of principle identical. For this reason emancipation in itself could not give "new moral meaning" to a cause already possessed of that meaning in full measure.

The supposed "conservatism" of Lincoln's war policy from Fort Sumter, April 12, 1861, until the issuance of the preliminary Proclamation, September 22, 1862, is based upon an implicit downgrading of what Lincoln himself called the cause of constitutional government, a cause "going about as deep as any thing." Characteristically, the supposed "liberalism" if not "radicalism" of the emancipation policy, or of a policy which made the advance of the Union armies coincide with the abolition of slavery upon the soil of the rebellion, is regarded as elevating "human rights" over constitutional rights. There has been a tendency to see the two phases of the war as corresponding to the phases in which, first the Constitution, and then the Declaration of Independence, were looked to for the principles which needed to be vindicated. Needless to say, this implies a tension, if not contradiction, between these two documents, as sources and statements of moral and political obligation. But there is no evidence that Lincoln himself was ever aware of any such tension or contradiction.

It is true that Lincoln, in his major speeches before he became President, appealed more often to the principles of the Declaration, in vindication of the policy he proposed, than he did to the Constitution; and it is also true that, in the Inaugural Address of March 4, 1861, he proclaimed as his policy only the perpetuation of the Union under the Constitution, a policy which, he held, was nothing less than the fulfillment of his oath to execute the laws, and to preserve, protect, and defend the Constitution itself. To look at the war in terms of an early "conservative" phase and a later "liberal" one is to take too limited a view. If the words "conservative" and "liberal" mean anything at all in this connection then we must first see where Lincoln the candidate and President-elect stood. We must see if the wartime transition is not in some ways paralleled by a transition in the period when Lincoln's pronouncements passed from those of a private citizen to those of the head of a government.

Harry V. Jaffa

From the moment of Lincoln's return to active political life in 1854 until his election as President in 1860, he had but a single policy objective, and that objective, with nearly all the basic arguments in support of it, was stated in his "Peoria" speech. The burden of the speech can be given very simply: it was that the 1820 Missouri Compromise legislation, with its prohibition "forever" upon slavery in the remaining, unorganized Louisiana Territory (a prohibition which had just been repealed in the Kansas-Nebraska Act) must be restored. Every political speech which Lincoln delivered in the next six years had the restoration of this ban upon slavery as its leading purpose. All of Lincoln's arguments culminated in a plea that slavery not be permitted to *extend* itself into *new* lands, such as those from which it had been prohibited by the Missouri Compromise (and, earlier, by the Northwest Ordinance). Never did Lincoln argue for any political action against slavery in any state. Never did he argue for a construction of the Constitution which might have accomplished such interference indirectly, as by denying the competence of the federal government to pass fugitive-slave legislation, or by maintaining the competence of the federal government, under the commerce clause, to interfere with the interstate slave trade.

Of course, if slavery was evil—as Lincoln insisted—it was evil in a state no less than in a territory. But Lincoln insisted that the evils of slavery in states were subject to state jurisdiction alone. Since slavery was forbidden by Illinois, all direct interest which he, Lincoln, possessed in slavery as a state institution was exhausted. However, the territorial question, as presented by the Kansas-Nebraska Act and complicated by the *Dred Scott* decision, indirectly involved the domestic institutions of Illinois and of every other state. In the House Divided speech (June 16, 1858), with which he launched his celebrated campaign for the Senate, he said that he believed "this government cannot endure permanently half *slave* and half *free*." By this Lincoln indicated his conviction that slavery as an institution could not remain static, merely remaining upon the soil where it already existed. It would either expand or contract, either become lawful in all states, old as well as new, North as well as South, or be placed in course of ultimate extinction. The repeal of the Missouri

6

The Emancipation Proclamation

Compromise signaled a drive to open to slavery virgin territories, hitherto untouched by slavery, which might in time become additional slave states. The opinion of the Court in the *Dred Scott* decision held that neither Congress nor a territorial legislature had power to forbid any slave-owner from carrying into and holding his slave property in any United States territory. Lincoln pointed out that the reasoning of the Chief Justice supplied the premises of a syllogism whose conclusion would be that it was unconstitutional to forbid slave-owners to carry their peculiar property into free states no less than into territories. The decision would surely come, he said, when the political climate should so change as to make such a decision enforceable.

Lincoln insisted that in saying that the government could not endure permanently, half slave and half free, he was only making a prediction. But it followed from that prediction that if the people of the United States once took a firm and irrevocable decision against the extension of slavery, that the death-knell of the institution would be sounded, for slavery would then be "in course of ultimate extinction," although Lincoln confessed that that extinction might take another hundred years. The "radicalism" of Lincoln's speeches throughout this period consists in the absoluteness of the decision he demanded, *in principle,* to put slavery "in course of ultimate extinction." But the *only* political action which Lincoln asked for to accomplish this ultimate extinction was the prohibition of slavery in the territories or, more accurately, the restoration of the 1820 prohibition of slavery in the remaining Louisiana Territory. In the Cooper Union speech, of February 27, 1860, Lincoln presented a lengthy historical argument demonstrating that the policy of prohibiting slavery by federal legislation derived from the Founding Fathers, and that the "popular sovereignty" policy advocated by Senator Stephen Douglas, of allowing the settlers to decide the question for themselves, was a departure from that original policy. The position of the Supreme Court—or, rather, a narrow majority thereof—that Congress had no power to exclude slavery from a territory, he regarded as nothing less than subversive of the whole position of the Fathers. In this speech (and a number of others which preceded it, in which these arguments were first developed), Lincoln argued as a conservative:

> What is conservatism? Is it not adherence to the old and
> tried, against the new and untried? We stick to, contend
> for, the identical old policy on the point in controversy
> which was adopted by "our Fathers who framed the
> government under which we live"; while you with one
> accord reject, and scout, and spit upon that old policy,
> and insist upon substituting something new.

To repeat, Lincoln, in all the elaborate and passionate
rhetoric which he employed from 1854 to 1860, demanded but
one thing: the restoration of the Missouri Compromise. But he
demanded it *upon principle*, that is, upon the grounds that
slavery was wrong. It is difficult to realize today why, for Lincoln,
the reasons for excluding slavery from the territories were as
important as the exclusion itself. Suffice it to say that the arch-
enemy was Douglas' doctrine of "popular sovereignty," which
meant, in this context, decision by a vote of the first handful of
settlers who came to legislate for an organized territory on the
whole question of whether the territory should admit slavery and
whether the future state formed from the territory should be a
free or a slave state. It was an obvious absurdity, Lincoln
thought, to leave a decision which might shift the unstable
relation between the free and slave states, and hence determine
whether the government would become all slave or all free, to
such a tiny fraction of the whole United States. To leave to the
first few chance settlers the decision of the vast future of many
millions, both in the particular territory (and future state) and
in the United States, was a travesty of the idea of majority rule.

Still more fundamental, it was immoral and illogical to
leave a matter of fundamental human rights to the decision of
a mere numerical majority. Majority rule is not a principle, but
an inference from a principle, designed to implement the principle from which it is an inference. Because all men are created
equal, no man has the right to govern another without that
other's consent. Majority rule is nothing but a device for register-
ing consent, and rests upon a previous, implied unanimity to
have majority rule. The relation of master and slave is a total
violation of the principle of equality upon which majorities rest
their claim to respect. Douglas' so-called popular sovereignty
would, in effect, put to a vote the question of whether it is right

to be ruled by votes. Majority rule cannot, to repeat, vindicate itself, for it rests upon the truth of the proposition that all men are created equal. Slavery, as a denial of this proposition, is an evil, and must be recognized as such. This does not mean, however, that slavery ought never to be tolerated, or that to accept slavery, or participate in it in any way, is always and everywhere wrong. The human condition is full of evils, of which slavery is only one. But whatever extenuation there might be for slavery in the places where it already existed, there could be none for introducing it in places where it had never existed. And this was the condition of the territories for which Lincoln demanded a federal prohibition. To say, as Douglas was wont to say, that he "don't care" whether slavery was voted up or voted down, was as much as to say that he didn't care whether the principle of self-government was voted up or down.

According to Lincoln, the Founding Fathers erected the constitutional structure of the United States upon, and for the purpose of giving effect to, the principles of the Declaration of Independence. They recognized, and believed, that slavery was wrong, and it was one of their sharpest grounds of complaint against British rule that slavery had been introduced, and that the colonists had repeatedly been checked in their efforts to halt the importation of slaves. The compromises of the Constitution with respect to slavery were compromises with "necessity." They could not get rid of the Negroes, and they did not believe they could live safely with them, at least in those Southern states where their numbers were very great, upon any other footing than that of slavery. In Jefferson's words, they had the wolf by the ears, and could neither hold him nor let him go. Justice was in one scale and self-preservation in the other. But justice, as distinct from charity, as Lincoln and Jefferson knew, does not require that we check our own instincts of self-preservation. Whatever might be demanded from individual men, political societies are not obliged to practice suicide. Gradual emancipation, accompanied by voluntary deportation of the freedmen, was the only solution envisaged by either Jefferson or Lincoln, or by any notable statesman between them. And so slavery was ungrudgingly given all the guarantees by the Constitution that it required for its security in those states where it already existed. Its future, in all states, remained a matter for state jurisdiction alone, and in a few short years after the adoption of the Constitution all the states north of Maryland and Delaware adopted one or another plan leading to the abolition of slavery. In the earliest federal territorial legislation, said Lincoln, slavery was prohibited, and the Northwest Ordinance, adopted under the Confederation, was reaffirmed by the first Congress under the Constitution.

Such, in brief, was the main reasoning of Lincoln's pre-election speeches. That it was representative of the main line of thinking of his party is shown by the following key planks in the platform of the convention which nominated Lincoln for the Presidency, and upon which he was elected:

> 2. That the maintenance of the principles promulgated in the Declaration of Independence and embodied in the Federal Constitution,—"that all men are created equal; that they are endowed by their Creator with certain unalienable rights; that among these are life, liberty, and the pursuit of happiness; that, to secure these rights, governments are instituted among men, deriving their just powers from the consent of the governed,"—is essential to the preservation of our republican institutions; and that the Federal Constitution, the rights of the States, and the Union of the States, must and shall be preserved.

> 4. That the maintenance inviolate of the rights of the States, and especially the right of each State to order and control its own domestic institutions according to its own judgment exclusively, is essential to that balance of power on which the perfection and endurance of our political power depends. . . .

> 7. That the new dogma that the Constitution, of its own force, carries slavery into any or all of the Territories of the United States, is a dangerous political heresy, at variance with the explicit provisions of that instrument itself, with contemporaneous exposition, and with legislative and judicial precedent; is revolutionary in its tendency, and subversive of the peace and harmony of the country.

> 8. That the normal condition of all the territory of the United States is freedom; that as our Republican fathers, when they had abolished slavery in all our national

territory, ordained that no person should be deprived of life, liberty, or property without due process of law, it becomes our duty, by legislation, whenever such legislation is necessary, to maintain this provision of the Constitution against all attempts to violate it; and we deny the authority of Congress, of a territorial legislature, or of any individual, to give legal existence to slavery in any Territory of the United States.

Lincoln thus came to office upon a platform and program that was exceedingly "liberal" in its uncompromising insistence upon the Declaration of Independence as the source of the principles embodied in the Constitution; but it was exceedingly "conservative" in its rejection of "new dogmas" at variance with the precedents of the Fathers in the interpretation of the Constitution, and no less so in its insistence that all guarantees given slavery by the Constitution, in its reservation to the states of all rights of legislation upon domestic questions, must be faithfully observed. Only in its broadening of the demand for the prohibition of slavery in "*any* Territory of the United States" (italics added), and in its silence upon the question of fugitive slaves, did the Republican platform seem less conservative than Lincoln himself in his earlier speeches. We must remember, however, that Lincoln made no public statements from the time of his nomination until after his election. All the "campaigning" Lincoln did consisted in the publication and circulation of the volume of the debates with Douglas and a pamphlet edition of the Cooper Union speech.

Lincoln's election was the signal for secession in South Carolina, and before his inauguration five other states also seceded. Buchanan, Lincoln's predecessor, while opposed to the Southern actions, and believing them unconstitutional, could find no political or constitutional justification for taking effective steps to oppose them. The election had made Lincoln's policy of opposing, *upon principle,* the spread of slavery the policy of the government of the United States. It guaranteed that there would be no new slave states *if* the Union endured. If the Union were broken up, apart from infinite other evils, there must have been some division of the national territories; and slavery would have gone into the southern portion, not to mention the consequences if Manifest Destiny had resumed its march in Mexico, the Caribbean, and Central America, under the stars and bars.

It is important, however, to realize how limited immediate Republican objectives would have been had secession not occurred. In the Thirty-Seventh Congress, elected at the same time as Lincoln, Republicans could have mustered only 108 votes, to the opposition's 129, and they would have had only 29 in the Senate as opposed to 37. They would not have been able to pass the act outlawing slavery in all federal territories, as they did on June 19, 1862, nor would they have been able to abolish slavery in the District of Columbia, as they did on April 16, 1862, had the Southern members of Congress kept their seats. But the supreme political fact was that Northern free-soilers could control the White House, and this meant that there could not be another slave state. Given even a large Republican minority in Congress, slave-owners would not make the attempt to colonize the existing organized territories for, apart from all other obstacles, Lincoln would almost certainly veto any bid for admission of a slave state. All the dynamics of the existing situation pointed to a long procession of free states, with no slave states to balance them. At some point in the future, there would be enough free states to amend the Constitution in a way that could lead to direct federal interference with slavery in the slave states. So the Southerners opined, and I think opined truly, and they acted in accordance with this opinion. It is worth mention that even today there would not be sufficient "free" states to pass an amendment of the Constitution over the opposition of the former slave states, which number fifteen. It requires thirty-eight states to amend the Constitution, and thirteen is sufficient to veto an amendment. However, since territorial legislation, and legislation to admit new states, require only bare majorities in Congress, many more new states could have been carved out of the territories if antislavery majorities had controlled Congress, and had wished to amend the Constitution. The behavior of the radicals in Congress, both during the war and in reconstruction, suggests that they would have proceeded with legislation to abolish slavery without much concern with its constitutionality. It would have taken no amendment, however, to have passed a law abolishing the interstate slave trade: this, as we have noted, could have been justified under the commerce clause, and would have very quickly made the institution of slavery economically unsupportable. The Southerners were quite well aware of this, and the course of the war suggests that they were not far wrong in their apprehensions of Republican radicalism, although it is impossible to say how influential this would have been in the absence of the dynamics of war.

To understand Lincoln's "conservatism" in the first great phase of the war, it is necessary to realize that everything he had fought for politically, from 1854 on, was now assured *if,* but only *if,* the Union was preserved. The greatest danger, after the election, that the fruits of victory might be lost came during the four months that separated his election and his inauguration. Lincoln made no public statements during this period, but it was not true, as some historians have alleged, that he did nothing except grow a beard! As the secession movement proceeded apace, desperate efforts were made to arrest the process, to find some compromise that would avert the dread conflict of arms that was almost sure to come if the Union could not be preserved peacefully. The most famous of these was the so-called Crittenden Compromise, which would have extended the Missouri Compromise line to the Pacific. But Lincoln would have none of it. "Entertain no proposition for a compromise in regard to the *extension* of slavery" (italics by Lincoln), he wrote a Republican Congressman, on December 11, 1860. "The instant you do, they have us under again; all our labor is lost, and sooner or later must be done over. . . . The tug has to come and better now than later." And on December 15 he assured a Southern Congressman that on the main point upon which he had been elected there would be no shifting of position, no hesitation, no reason for doubting where he stood. "Is it desired that I shall shift the ground upon which I have been elected? I can not do it. . . . It would make me appear as if I repented for the crime of having been elected, and was anxious to apologize and beg for forgiveness." He then recommended the exact passages in the book containing the debates with Douglas which gave his position on points about which the Congressman had questioned him, at the same time explaining why he did not feel any new pronouncements were called for. "On the territorial question, I am inflexible." Thus Lincoln took his stand until his inauguration. If his Inaugural Address, which initiated what has been regarded as his most "conservative" phase, has no reference to the Republican platform, except the assurance with respect to the right of the states to control slavery, it was because the cause symbolized by the platform had already triumphed through the ballot box. From that point on nothing but disunion could endanger the fruits of victory in the long political struggle against slavery, as Lincoln had understood and fought that battle.

Both in the pre-inaugural period, and in the opening stages of the conflict, the danger of disunion, now the paramount danger, did not come from the forces of slavery alone. It came as well from the abolitionists. Now the name "abolitionist" was applied to a number of shades of opinion, although it is usually identified with the most extreme among them. However, there was a spectrum of opinions, beginning with those who insisted upon instant emancipation of all slaves, by any means, without regard to existing legality, without regard to the disruption and injury it would cause among both whites and blacks, and without indemnity or compensation of any kind. To the "right" of these were those who recognized some force in the legal securities to slavery in the Constitution, some danger in emancipation that was too general, too sudden, and for which too little preparation had been made, either among whites or blacks. Finally, there were those who recognized that, although in the abstract there could be no right of property in human beings, that the titles to the slaves were acquired, for the most part, in good faith, and there was a constitutional command that the obligation of contract be not impaired. As the spectrum proceeded from left to right, at some point the name "abolitionist" ceased to apply, and that of free-soiler replaced it. Lincoln was always a free-soiler, never an abolitionist, and in some respects Lincoln agreed with his Southern brethren that the abolitionists were a curse and an affliction. Of the abolitionists on the extreme left were those who, because the Constitution gave some protection to slavery, denounced it as "a covenant with death and a league with hell," and raised the cry, "No union with slaveholders." These extremists, always a tiny minority before the war, strangely resembled their opposite numbers below Mason and Dixon's line. Both saw political salvation in the separation of the sections and the destruction of the Union. One side wished to be freed of all obligation to return fugitive slaves, the other to be freed of all restraint from extending slavery or reopening the slave trade. It was a classic case of extreme political opposites coming to a kind of practical agreement.

In the spectrum of antislavery opinions sketched above, Lincoln himself would have to be placed at the farthest limit of the extreme right. He was the most conservative of antislavery men. He did not, in any campaign, urge any form of emancipation other than that implied in the exclusion of slavery from the territories. First privately, later publicly, he favored gradual emancipation, and in the plan he recommended to Congress in December, 1862, the state action which he envisaged might have been extended over thirty-five years, until 1900. In the plan he put forward while a Congressman, in 1848, for emancipation in the District of Columbia, three factors were crucial: it had to be gradual, voluntary (it had to be approved by a referendum in the District), and compensated. But Lincoln's task, as war came, was to preserve the Union. All the emancipation Lincoln desired, and probably a good deal more, was assured *if* the Union endured. If it did not endure, all the lets and hindrances exerted upon slavery by the free states in the Union would be removed. The extreme abolitionists, in the supposed purity of their principles, would have abandoned the four million slaves to their fate. As the secession crisis developed, however, the attitude of the border states trembled in the balance. Virginia did not cast its lot with the Confederacy until after Sumter, and when it did so the western counties broke away, eventually to form a new state, a case of secession from secession. Tennessee went with the South, although Unionist sentiment was strong; many a Tennesseean marched with the Federal armies, and many a family was divided. But Missouri and Kentucky were slave states which, with Maryland and Delaware, remained faithful to the Union cause, as they might not have done had a man they trusted less, whom they regarded as less one of their own, occupied the presidential chair. The strategic importance of Kentucky and Missouri can be seen by a glance at the map. Lincoln himself thought that the military task of conquering the South would not have been possible without them. "Neutrality" by Kentucky would have denied the Union armies vital communications. If we think then of the range of Unionist opinion, and not merely of anti-slavery opinion, we will begin to appreciate the political task Lincoln faced. Border-state Unionists, supported by large and powerful elements of conservative Democrats and old-line Whigs throughout the free states, would fight for the Union but not against slavery. Abolitionists, on the other hand, would not fight for the Union, but would fight against slavery. When we realize that these extremes were about as willing to fight each other as to fight secession, we realize that preserving the Union meant, for Lincoln, first of all, creating an effective political coalition. Fighting the war was always secondary to keeping alive the political coalition willing to fight the war. The military problem was at every point complicated by the dual character of the functions which the commander-in-chief had to perform.

It is fair to say that, in the early months, everything depended upon the border states. It was in this period that Lincoln said nothing, or almost nothing on the subject of slavery. It was in this period that he revoked the emancipation edicts of Generals Fremont and Hunter. Yet a very far-seeing Englishman, of a very radical persuasion in regard to American politics, understood what Lincoln was doing far better than most American radicals. John Stuart Mill (in December, 1861), made these observations:

> The present government of the United States is not an Abolitionist government. Abolitionists, in America, mean those who do not keep within the Constitution; who demand the destruction (as far as slavery is concerned) of as much of it [i.e., the Constitution] as protects the internal legislation of each State from the control of Congress; who aim at abolishing slavery wherever it exists, by force if need be. . . . The Republican party neither aim nor profess to aim at this object. . . . But though not an Abolitionist party, they are a Free-soil party. If they have not taken arms against

slavery, they have against its extension. *And they know,
as we may know if we please, that this amounts to the
same thing. The day when slavery can no longer extend
itself, is the day of its doom.* The slave-owners know
this, and it is the cause of their fury. [Italics added.][3]

Now mark well Mill's interpretation of the "conservatism" of
Lincoln's leadership in this period:

> The Republican leaders do not talk to the public
> of these almost certain results of success in the present
> conflict. . . . The most ordinary policy teaches them to
> inscribe on their banner that part only of their known
> principles in which their supporters are unanimous.
> The preservation of the Union is an object about which
> the North are agreed; and it has many adherents, as
> they believe, in the South generally. That nearly half the
> population of the Border Slave States are in favor of it
> is a patent fact, since they are now fighting in its de-
> fense. It is not probable that they would be willing to
> fight directly against slavery. The Republicans well
> know that if they can reëstablish the Union, they gain
> everything for which they originally contended; and it
> would be a plain breach of faith with the Southern
> friends of the Government, if, after rallying them round
> its standard for a purpose of which they approve, it
> were suddenly to alter its terms of communion without
> their consent.

But Mill saw from the distance what Lincoln, of course, must
have seen with at least equal certainty, that the middle ground
that marked the nearest common denominator of Union opinion
could not long remain the ground of policy.

> But the parties in a protracted civil war almost
> invariably end by taking more extreme, not to say
> higher grounds of principle, than they began with. . . .
> Without the smallest pretension to see further into
> futurity than other people, I at least have foreseen and
> foretold from the first, that if the South were not
> promptly put down, the contest would become distinctly
> an antislavery one. . . . In one of his recent letters [the
> *Times'* correspondent, Mr. Russell] names the end of
> next summer as the period by which, if the war has not

[3] *The Contest in America* (Boston: Little, Brown & Co., 1862). Reprinted from *Fraser's Magazine,* February–May, 1862.

sooner terminated, it will have assumed a complete anti-slavery character.

It is breath-taking to realize that these keen-eyed observers from England could virtually name the month that emancipation would become the policy of Lincoln's government, and that they could do so almost a year in advance of the fact. Let us, from this perspective, follow Lincoln's almost pathetic attempts to prepare the border-state Unionists for the fate which, if they would not prepare for it, would only come the more harshly upon them. In a message to Congress of March 6, 1862, Lincoln recommended the adoption of a joint resolution in these words:

> Resolved, That the United States, in order to cooperate with any State which may adopt gradual abolition of slavery, give to such State pecuniary aid, to be used by such State, in its discretion, to compensate it for the inconvenience, public and private, produced by such change of system.

Lincoln explained to the Congress, which adopted his proposed resolution a month later (April 10), that if the border slave-states would make *any* beginning toward emancipation, it would strike an almost mortal blow at the hopes of the rebellion, which believed that if they could force any kind of recognition of any part of their Confederacy, they would eventually be joined by the loyal slave-states. Lincoln realized this resolution had no practical effect in itself; it was "merely initiatory." But it is also exemplary of Lincoln's cautious, step-by-step way of moving to change the basis of policy from plain, unqualified Unionism, to a Unionism that recognized the necessity of antislavery dynamism. Two months later, on May 9, Lincoln issued his famous proclamation countermanding the emancipation order of General David Hunter, who had declared that as Georgia, Florida, and South Carolina were under martial law, and as martial law and slavery were incompatible, that the slaves in these states were free. Lincoln said that "neither General Hunter, nor any other person has been authorized . . . to make proclamation declaring the slaves of any state free . . . [and] whether it be competent for me, as Commander-in-Chief . . . to declare the slaves of any State or States free; and whether at any time, or in any case, it shall become a necessity indispensable to the maintenance of the government to examine such power, are questions which I reserve to myself. . . . " Here, written upon the wall, for all to see who would see, was the shadow of the Emancipation Proclamation. But Lincoln did not stop here. In this masterful document, while with one hand he revoked a proclamation that was loudly acclaimed by the radicals, as Fremont's had been before, with the other he moved to prepare the public for a policy of emancipation that would mean infinitely more, when it came, than any which might have proceeded from overly-enthusiastic radical generals. He reminded the nation of the joint resolution which Congress had recently passed upon his recommendation. Then he addressed to the border-state men these words:

> The resolution . . . was adopted by large majorities in both branches of Congress, and now stands an authentic, definite, and solemn proposal of the Nation to the States and people most interested. . . . To the people of these States now, I mostly appeal. I do not argue—I beseech you to make the arguments for yourselves. You cannot, if you would, be blind to the signs of the times.
>
> This proposal makes common cause for a common object, casting no reproaches upon any. It acts not the Pharisee. The change it contemplates would come gently as the dews of Heaven, not rending or wrecking anything. Will you not embrace it? So much good has not been done by one effort in all past time, as on the Providence of God, it is now your high privilege to do. May the vast future not have to lament that you have neglected it.

Alas, the vast future has much cause to lament. The majority of the border-state men, loyal Unionists though they were, would not accept the implicit condemnation of slavery which in their hearts they felt would be implied even if they themselves took a single step to abolish slavery upon their soil. Though Lincoln, with words of beauty, turned away every possible reproach such as they had been accustomed to hear from abolitionists, there was a mark of *hubris* upon them, as upon all men touched by slavery in that period, as indeed it was upon the radical abolitionists. Lincoln was to address the border-state delegations in Congress in July, before they left for home, and in majestic and pathetic language, rang every change upon the foregoing theme. But to no avail. In their reply to him they said:

> Confine yourself to your constitutional authority; confine your subordinates within the same limits; conduct this war solely for the purpose of restoring the Constitution to its legitimate authority; concede to each State and its loyal citizens their just rights, and we are wedded to you by indissoluble ties.

Lincoln had told the border-state Congressmen that, if the war continued, "the institution in your states will be extinguished by mere friction and abrasion. . . . It will be gone, and you will have nothing valuable in lieu of it. . . . How much better . . . to take the step which, at once shortens the war, and secures substantial compensation for that which is sure to be wholly lost in any other event." By friction and abrasion, Lincoln meant that, as Federal armies moved forward upon the soil of slave states, rebel or loyal, the problems of dealing with the Negroes became ever larger and ever more complicated. Obviously, the fugitive-slave law, which Lincoln had so carefully pledged himself to enforce in his Inaugural Address, could not be enforced in the midst of war. For example, the task of distinguishing the fugitives of loyal masters from the fugitives of rebels, was administratively insuperable. But as the war placed greater and greater strains upon the human and material resources of the sections, there loomed ever larger the fact that the slave population of the deep South nearly equalled that of the whites, and was little less than half of the white population in the upper South. One reason why the Confederacy could put so high a proportion of its white male population under arms was that Negro labor did the drudging tasks which every society requires, and which must be done by one set of hands if not by another. Slavery was what the rebel states were fighting for, and slavery enabled them to fight for slavery. Lincoln's cautious, constitutional conservatism was the necessary stabilizing factor while he bound up the loose ties of Unionism, as he organized the Union to fight for its life. But once the fight was organized, and became increasingly desperate, once abolitionists and border-state Unionists, neither of whom would fight for the other, had been committed to the same cause by their blood in battle, the

The Emancipation Proclamation

policy had to change. The task was no longer to make them pull in harness together, but to strike blows that would kill the rebellion. And of all these blows, none held such power as that directed against slavery by the two proclamations.

Although the two proclamations were, as Lincoln insistently described them, war measures, measures of military necessity, and justified under the Constitution only as such, Lincoln's political (as distinct from military) emancipation policy, continued to occupy his thoughts; indeed, nothing occupied him more. There is no place here to consider the many measures that Congress had passed before the proclamations. Most important was the second Confiscation Act, of July 17, 1862. This was, as J. G. Randall says, primarily a treason and confiscation act. It enacted that all slaves of persons hereafter engaged in rebellion, or the slaves of persons who in any way gave aid and comfort to rebellion, and all slaves captured or deserted from such persons, should be forever free. Although Lincoln signed this act, he undoubtedly considered it neither constitutional nor wise. But he was having enough trouble with the radicals without vetoing a law which could not have any greater effect than he wished it to have. In any case, Lincoln always held to the conviction, finally expressed with surpassing majesty in the Gettysburg Address and the Second Inaugural, that slavery was the sin of the whole nation, not of a section. If for the remission of that sin, the Lord in His infinite justice might exact a price in blood from the whole nation, was it less the duty of a wise statesmanship ultimately to share the money cost among the whole nation? Lincoln's Emancipation Proclamations, unlike the Congressional measures, were not a punishment for anything; they were rather a summons to the slaves, not to rise against their masters, but to shift the power of their labor from the oppressors to their liberators. And so they presently did. But for the nonmilitary settlement of the slavery question, Lincoln pressed on with his plan for voluntary, compensated emancipation.

Space does not permit a full consideration of the plan that Lincoln presented to Congress in his annual message of December 1, 1862, a message which came after approximately two-thirds of the one hundred days had passed, in which the rebellion had warning of the impending final proclamation of emancipation.

Harry V. Jaffa

Lincoln recommended that his plan be embodied in articles amendatory of the Constitution, so that no question could arise as to its constitutionality. The first feature of the plan was the offer of United States bonds, in an amount that would be a multiple of the number of slaves in each emancipating state, and a fair average evaluation for each slave. What this would be, Lincoln did not attempt to determine in the message. Next, the adoption of emancipation schemes by each state would be a matter of state action. There was no federal coercion contemplated; it was a pure "grant-in-aid" scheme, such as Congress now enacts in every session, and any state could leave it as well as take it, as far as the law was concerned. Finally, emancipation was to be gradual, and might extend until the year 1900. Lincoln then proposed, in a distinct article, that Congress provide compensation for loyal masters whose slaves had either escaped, or otherwise gained their freedom by the chances of war. Finally, in still another article, he sought definite authorization for Congress to appropriate money for the colonization abroad of the freed slaves. As we review Lincoln's plan we must be struck by the almost Jeffersonian fundamentalism wherewith he sought constitutional authority for policies which carried the federal government into a wholly new sphere of legislation; and how, while exercising the leadership of the President of the whole United States, for a national plan, he tried to secure the sanction of the people in the states, acting through state authority, to carry it into effect. Even as, years before, in proposing compensated emancipation for the District of Columbia, he had made the proposal dependent upon a vote of the citizens of the District, he here proposed that an amendment to the Constitution be passed, not to emancipate the slaves, but to authorize the federal government to pay the states, *if they wished* to emancipate the slaves. But behind this Lincolnian "voluntarism" lay the fact so starkly insisted upon by Mill: no matter what action the states did or did not take, slavery was doomed. Lincoln's plan, which never passed from Congress to the states, remains as a model of that charity which he preached and practiced but which, like the counsels of perfection, was beyond the capacities of the men for whose sake he devised it.

Let us then, with this incomplete account of the movement

of policy, opinion, and events, which culminated in the Emancipation Proclamation, whose centennial we now observe, ask again the questions with which we began. In my opinion, the Freedman's Monument is a true account, not of an isolated event of the war, but of Lincoln's whole policy. Lincoln *is* the Great Emancipator, not because of what he did on January 1, 1863, but because of everything he did, and said, from his first speech against the Kansas-Nebraska Act, until his Second Inaugural, and indeed until the last day of his life. In a sense, it is true that Lincoln never intended to emancipate the Negro: what he intended was to emancipate the American republic from the curse of slavery, a curse which lay upon both races, and which in different ways enslaved them both. This might have happened "gently as the dews of Heaven, not rending or wrecking anything," if the slave power had accepted his election, and settled slowly and seriously to deal with the gradual and peaceable "ultimate extinction" implied in the containment of slavery. It might have still come with much gentleness, if the border states had started the process of voluntary emancipation, which would have broken the hopes of the Confederacy. It came instead with the hard and pitiless hand of war. Lincoln's message was always peace, but like other messengers of peace, he brought not peace but a sword. In the last analysis, it is absurd to characterize Lincoln's policy as either "liberal" or "conservative," if by these terms we imply a mere party or sectarian position. His policy encompassed everything that was viable in every element of opinion, by which, of course, we exclude the proslavery and antislavery extremists, because there was nothing viable in what they proposed. As the proslavery extremists utterly disregarded the primordial fact of human equality, so did the abolitionists disregard utterly the element of consent required for the just acts of government. In fact, the two were more akin than opposed, even in principle, for what both disregarded was at bottom the same thing—the thing whose disregard is of the essence of tyranny.

In Lincoln's works there is a draft of a joint resolution for the Congress, dated February 5, 1865, which apparently never was submitted because the Cabinet advised him that it would be hopeless to do so. The resolution was one which would have empowered him to give $400 million to the slave states, then in rebellion, one half if they ceased their resistance to the national authority by April 1, 1865, the other half if they ratified the pending Thirteenth Amendment. Although the war was even then nearly won, and although there were bayonets enough to see that the amendment was "ratified," Lincoln still sought to keep alive as much of the true spirit of the Constitution as the temper of the time would admit. Of course, he failed again.

Or did he fail? Perhaps the power of the word is still greater than the power of the deed. Even among the cold hearts and muddy understandings that could not comprehend the meaning of Lincoln's magnanimity to the defeated South, there were those who thrilled to hear, "With malice toward none, with charity for all. . . ."

ROY WILKINS

•

EMANCIPATION AND
MILITANT LEADERSHIP

In strict accuracy, it may not be said that in 1963 we can look back on "one hundred years of emancipation," since a respectable case can be made for the contention that Negro citizens in the United States have had their basic constitutional status affirmed only since May 17, 1954.

The Emancipation Proclamation was signaled in September, 1862, and actually signed and issued by President Abraham Lincoln January 1, 1863, but the newly freed slaves did not, then and there, begin life as free men. The Texas Emancipation Day is known far and wide as "Juneteenth," a convenient contraction of June 19th. The Thirteenth, Fourteenth, and Fifteenth Amendments to the Constitution were not to become a part of that document until 1865–1870.

But the Black Codes, the Hayes-Tilden Compromise of 1876, and the *Plessy* v. *Ferguson* "separate but equal" ruling by the United States Supreme Court in 1896[1] constituted such official nullification of the verdict at Appomattox and of the Amendments themselves that no careful student of the period can treat it as a span "of emancipation."

If the unofficial and more gross compulsions be added—that is, the Klan, lynchings, the prostitution of the administration of justice, and the system of plantation peonage—the spread of emancipated living is further reduced. Dr. Rayford Logan, the historian, in *The Negro in American Life and Thought,* labels the quarter century beginning in 1877 as "the nadir" as far as Negro gains were concerned.[2]

---

[1] *Plessy* v. *Ferguson,* 163 U.S. 537 (1896).
[2] *The Negro in American Life and Thought: the Nadir, 1877–1901* (New York: Dial Press, 1954).

Roy Wilkins

We can observe, then, the struggle which occupied most of the years following the issuance of the Emancipation Proclamation. It was a struggle of a people in a position of legal inferiority to emerge into the equality which was the mark of first-class citizenship. Mr. Justice Harlan, the lone dissenter in the 1896 *Plessy* decision, prophesied with deadly accuracy what the ruling was to do to dark Americans:

> If laws of like character [i.e., racial segregation laws like the Louisiana separate railway car statute] should be enacted in the several states of the union, the effect would be in the highest degree mischievous. Slavery as an institution tolerated by law would, it is true, have disappeared from our country, but there would remain a power in the states, by sinister legislation, to interfere with the full enjoyment of the blessings of freedom; to regulate civil rights common to all citizens upon the basis of race; and to place in a condition of legal inferiority a large body of American citizens. . . .

Thus, for 58 of the 100 years, the Negro was in the *Plessy* prison. His full enjoyment of the blessings of freedom was interfered with, indeed, and on a scale so broad, in detail so minute, and in regulation so harsh that emancipation became a mockery. For two generations he was to batter at the walls of segregation and restriction, step by heartbreaking step, to inch forward to the place he thought he had won as a result of the Civil War.

Because the struggle against the second-class, separate-but-equal status was spearheaded almost completely by the people who were physically or philosophically allied with or under the banner of the National Association for the Advancement of Colored People (NAACP), this paper will deal largely with the leadership and the history of that organization.

The leadership against the degradation which slavery imposes and the leadership against the re-enslavement of the *Plessy* doctrine was militant in nature. It was not accommodationist. Such adjustments as it made were forced upon it and were endured only until counterforces could be mustered and brought to bear.

There were accommodationists, of course, and there were escapists. Both have had their pages in history and both have had impacts of sorts on the problem. There have been the extremists: those unwilling to bow physically even to overwhelming force, those willing to die.

The militant wing of the Negro movement traces its beginnings to the insurrectionists, Gabriel Prosser, Denmark Vesey, Nat Turner, and lesser known ones. It has its roots even farther back—in the "bad" slaves who fought on shipboard and attempted to take over the slave ships. Richard Bardolph, in *The Negro Vanguard,* classifies six of sixteen Negro notables for the period 1801–1831 as being "remembered principally as militant champions of Negro rights."[3] One of these was David Walker, whose pamphlet, *Walker's Appeal,* issued in 1829, was described as "incendiary."

Ten were associated with the founding and development of the Negro church, but this did not exclude all of them from the ranks of the militants, for Richard Allen, in founding the African Methodist Episcopal Church in 1816 in Philadelphia, denounced segregation within and without the church. The AME Zion Church under Founder James Varick had a similar philosophy. (It may be of interest, in passing, to note here that one of the sixty signers of a Call to organize the NAACP in 1909 was Bishop Alexander Walters of the AME Zion Church, and that today the chairman of the National Board of the NAACP is AME Zion Bishop Stephen Gill Spottswood.)

In the generation, 1831–1865, the emerging prominent Negroes who stirred the struggle in increasingly militant fashion were those, says Bardolph, "who found economic and social disabilities increasingly intolerable precisely because they had assimilated so much of America's civilization and had come to share its values and expectations."[4] The NAACP is a lineal descendant of the men of 1831–1865. Benjamin Brawley in his *Social History of the American Negro* quotes an NAACP spokesman:

> We have dreamed of an organization that would work ceaselessly to make Americans know that the so-called "Negro problem" is simply one phase of the vaster

[3] *The Negro Vanguard* (New York: Rinehart and Co., 1959), p. 30.
[4] *Ibid.,* p. 42.

problem of democracy in America, and that those who wish freedom and justice for their country must wish these for every black citizen.[5]

The official Call to organize the NAACP, issued on Lincoln's birthday in 1909, posed the questions which stirred Negro and concerned white citizens then as now:

How far has it [the nation's progress since 1865] lived up to the obligations imposed upon it by the Emancipation Proclamation? How far has it gone in assuring to each and every citizen, irrespective of color, the equality of opportunity and equality before the law, which underlie our American institutions and are guaranteed by the Constitution?[6]

THE ARCH ACCOMMODATIONIST

Before that desperate cry was raised there had been a period in which accommodationist leadership had functioned—the Age of Booker T. Washington. This age brought to Southern whites a time of relative quiet which they used to the full to consolidate their economic, political, and social positions of dominance. The age brought a kind of relief to the North which gave ear, even more attentively, to the racial themes of the South.

To the Negro, the Washington era brought new restraints, fresh persecutions in the form of riots and lynchings, a wave of propaganda against his citizenship and even his status as a human being, almost complete disfranchisement, and a type of economic exploitation hardly distinguishable from slavery.

In his excellent text, *From Slavery to Freedom,* Dr. John Hope Franklin, a softer commentator than many on Mr. Washington, concludes his pages on the leader with this observation: "During his lifetime lynchings decreased only slightly, the Negro was effectively disfranchised and the black workers were systematically excluded from the major labor organizations. . . ."[7]

The principal indictment, as might be expected, came from W. E. B. Du Bois in his memorable essays, *The Souls of Black Folk,* in 1903.

[5] *Social History of the American Negro* (New York: Macmillan, 1921), p. 339.
[6] Mary White Ovington, *How the NAACP Began* (New York: NAACP, 1914), p. 3. (Pamphlet)
[7] *From Slavery to Freedom* (New York: Alfred A. Knopf, 1948), p. 390.

Mr. Washington represents in Negro thought the old attitude of adjustment and submission. . . . [His] program practically accepts the alleged inferiority of the Negro races. . . . In the history of nearly all other races and peoples the doctrine preached at such crises has been that manly self-respect is worth more than lands and houses, and that a people who voluntarily surrender such respect, or cease striving for it, are not worth civilizing. . . .

Mr. Washington distinctly asks that black people give up, at least for the present, three things, (a) political power, (b) insistence on civil rights, (c) higher education of Negro youth and concentrate all their energies on industrial education, the accumulation of wealth and the conciliation of the South. . . . As a result of the tender of this palm-branch, what has been the return? In these [fifteen] years there have occurred: (1) the disfranchisement of the Negro, (2) the legal creation of a distinct status of civil inferiority for the Negro, and the steady withdrawal of aid from institutions for the higher training of the Negro. . . .

The question then comes: Is it possible, and probable, that nine millions of men can make effective progress in economic lines if they are deprived of political rights, made a servile caste and allowed only the most meagre chance for developing their exceptional men?[8]

Du Bois concluded that those who answered the question in the negative could no longer be silent; they had to ask the nation for the right to vote, for civic equality, and for the education of youth according to ability.

The reaction to the darkness of these years which Brawley calls "The Vale of Tears," was to be the formation of the NAACP. "[T]he period," he says, "became one of bitter social and economic antagonism. . . ."[9] Logan's classification of the era as "the nadir" has already been noted. Onto this forbidding and tension-torn stage stepped the resolute new effort at organized militant leadership, strong in little else but moral conviction.

[8] *The Souls of Black Folk* (New York: Blue Heron Press, 1953), pp. 50–51.

[9] Brawley, *op. cit.*, p. 297.

Roy Wilkins

THE CONSTITUTIONAL FOUNDATION

The NAACP, in more ways than can be recorded in this short paper, cleared the underbrush and laid the legal and political foundation, so that desegregation and first-class, responsible, participating citizenship for the Negro are now only a matter of time.

The 1954 school desegregation decision capped a long series of legal rulings won by the NAACP. Through the flat repudiation of the "separate but equal" concept of 1896, this decision became, in effect, a new Emancipation Proclamation. The Supreme Court of 1954 had unanimously affirmed the lone dissenter of 1896, Mr. Justice Harlan, and had made the Constitution color-blind. The NAACP, after thirty-nine years (its first appeal went to the highest court in 1915), had indeed set the legal and political status of the Negro unmistakably.

Three hundred eminent Americans of both races met in a two-day conference in New York in May, 1909, and eventually became the National Association for the Advancement of Colored People. The tone that was to come down through the years to penetrate even into the Deep South was set during those 1909 meetings. Charles Edward Russell, who was to become a director of the new association, read a set of principles at the first conference, committing it to "a union of the races in the public schools as against segregation of the Negroes as is now the case in the South."

Hope that the conference "will utter no uncertain sound on any point" was expressed in a message from William Lloyd Garrison, son of the abolitionist, who added: "The republican experiment is at stake, every tolerated wrong to the Negro reacting with double force upon white citizens guilty of faithlessness to their brothers. . . . Safety lies in an absolute refusal to differentiate the rights of human beings."

The NAACP, through the years, has been dedicated to erasing the differentiations between the rights enjoyed by the white and colored citizens of the United States of America. No one today who deplores "going too fast," or advises leaving the problem to the Southern states, or condemns what is termed federal "coercion," can understand the impatient mood of the

Negro of the sixties unless he knows something of the history that has gone before.

Anyone who hopes for any accuracy in predicting what will develop in the next decade or in the next quarter century cannot ignore the sweep of events since the turn of the century. In the shaping of those events the NAACP has had a major role.

The NAACP program is not confined to one technique or to one aspect of the struggle or to one section of the country. Every sort of method has been used since the earliest days—picketing, mass meetings, demonstrations, marches, court cases, legislative lobbying, sit-ins, persuasive education through all media, and selective-buying campaigns. Among the early picketing and arrests were those in connection with the NAACP campaign across the nation against the showing of the Klan film, *The Birth of a Nation,* in 1917.

The Crude Oppression

The new NAACP crusaders faced first not so much ideological tasks (though these abounded and demanded attention), but the crude and cruel oppressions that menaced human beings physically: lynching, riots, activities of the Ku Klux Klan, punitive acts by individuals (including police), and peonage.

Unceasingly, the young and financially weak NAACP hammered at the crime of lynching. Its published study of the crime, covering the years 1889–1918, was the first such survey and furnished ammunition which enabled speakers and writers at last to make a dent in the all-pervading propaganda that lynching occurred only to punish the crime of rape. It was found that in less than 20 per cent of all cases was any sort of sex charge involved and in a much smaller percentage was rape even charged, much less proved.

In a campaign spread over thirty years, lynching was beaten back. Every device to appeal to the nation and the world was employed, the chief political and propaganda weapon being the annual effort to have the Congress enact a Federal antilynching law. Books, magazines, newspapers, and the stage—even an art exhibit—all played parts in the drama.

Among the first of the many "marches" of the Negro population took place in 1917 when 15,000 men, women, and children, headed by the officers and staff members of the NAACP, marched down New York's famed Fifth Avenue in a silent protest against mob murders. Walter White's antilynching novel, *Fire in the Flint*, was translated into more than a dozen foreign languages, including Japanese, Norwegian, and Russian. During World War I the Kaiser's troops gave an assist to the antilynching fight by dropping leaflets among the American Negro soldiers asking why they were fighting the Germans in France "while your people are being lynched back home." Walter White's magazine articles, pamphlets, and lectures, based on his personal, on-the-spot investigations, were a powerful force in stamping out the crime. His testimony before Congressional committees and his indefatigable one-topic lobbying in Washington, in state capitals, and in city halls aroused both the conscience of the nation and the concern of the hard-boiled politicians.

The moral and political pressure won out eventually and the annual lynching rate (which had been as high as one hundred) shrank to below ten, then to three (in 1955 in Mississippi) and finally to nothing.

In 1959 the State of Mississippi revived its reputation as the leader of the lynch league by staging an old-fashioned, uncamouflaged mob killing of a Negro truck driver in Poplarville. It then added some sort of record by having its county grand jury completely ignore a report by the Federal Bureau of Investigation which named the lynchers and set forth the evidence against each.

Riots, too, persisted, with mobs in Northern centers like Chicago, Detroit, and New York indulging in violent racial outbursts. Police brutality and killings of Negroes by police became even more numerous. There has been improvement here and there in punishment of white persons for individual violence against Negroes, but further progress apparently will have to await the increased participation of Negro citizens in the politics of the South.

WITHOUT CONSENT OF THE GOVERNED

A close second on the NAACP agenda, to the atrocities and other physical violence, was disfranchisement. The denial of a vote and a voice in government to persons solely because of their color was (and is) a cardinal element in the Southern way of life.

The NAACP filed its very first brief in the United States Supreme Court in 1915 as a friend of the court in a case arising in Oklahoma challenging the grandfather clause, then a popular method of disfranchisement incorporated in the constitution of many Southern states.

The Supreme Court outlawed the grandfather clause as unconstitutional. The NAACP thus had its initial small victory in the long heartbreaking crusade to resurrect the Thirteenth, Fourteenth, and Fifteenth Amendments to the Constitution. Even the friendly observers of the 1960's tend to forget the tremendous, almost insuperable odds against the Negro as he sought to establish his constitutional citizenship. He could make the emotional and moral appeal with some success. He could get a kind of help against bestial violence and poverty and unfairness. But this aid was rendered him by conscience-stricken benevolents who shied from the hard-core, bedrock task of establishing rights.

Deprived of the grandfather clause, the Southern states promptly employed other devices, notably the white Democratic Primary with its simple, bald declaration that only white persons could participate in the Democratic party primary elections. More difficult registration procedures were enforced, and new emphasis was placed on the dependable poll tax.

It was not until 1944 that the Supreme Court finally outlawed the White Primary after the NAACP had brought three cases from Texas. The poll tax still remains in five states—Virginia, Texas, Mississippi, Alabama, and Arkansas—but in 1962 Congress resolved to outlaw the poll tax by constitutional amendment, which now awaits the ratification of the states. Today, the South has had to fall back upon literacy tests, interpretation-of-the-Constitution tests, trickery by local registrars, complex registration procedures, and old-fashioned threats and intimidations.

Two civil-rights laws (1957 and 1960), the first in eighty-odd years, were enacted to protect the right to register and vote. The Congress also set up a Civil Rights Commission, whose findings bid fair to stimluate further legislation. In the first year of the Kennedy Administration, more than a dozen voter-registration suits were filed by Attorney General Robert F. Kennedy. Top

Roy Wilkins

figures in the Administration, from Presidents Kennedy and Johnson on down, have emphasized their interest in this phase of civil rights.

While the campaign was being pressed in the South, the area of the greatest and most callous deprivation, developments were taking place in the North. World War I shut off the tide of immigration from Europe and sent labor agents from Northern industry into the South. Over the objections of the South (which passed labor laws similar to the old fugitive-slave laws) the great migration from plantations to plants began.

By the time of the presidential campaign of 1928 the migrants had become a significant political factor in some big-city machines, Republican in Cleveland and Chicago, and Democratic (Pendergast) in Kansas City. Tammany in New York was angling for the Negro vote. The Republican Vare-Penrose machine in Pennsylvania included Negroes.

The NAACP's Walter White felt in 1930 that there was enough Negro voter strength in the North and West to challenge a nominee of President Hoover's to the United States Supreme Court. The basis of the protest was a sentence or two in a political campaign speech of the nominee in North Carolina to the effect that neither party desired the Negro in politics in this country. Contending that this view would endanger any appeals of Negro citizens to the Supreme Court on voting rights, the NAACP carried on an intensive nationwide campaign during the month between the nomination and the Senate vote on confirmation. When the nominee failed of confirmation by a single vote, it was evident to all political observers that the Negro vote in the North had become a factor not to be ignored. When in subsequent Senate elections, eight Senators who had voted for confirmation were defeated for re-election, the political chiefs—never sentimental—knew that a turning point had arrived.

After the pendulum of Negro voting had swung from Abolitionist Republicanism to New Deal Democracy in the thirties, the day of maturity arrived in 1948. Under NAACP stimulation and with the revolt of the Young Turks, a mild (then regarded as strong) civil-rights plank was pushed through the Democratic national convention in Philadelphia, causing four Southern states to walk out and set up a separate party.

Emancipation and Militant Leadership

Harry Truman won despite the Southern bolt. The November election validated both the action at Philadelphia and President Truman's sending of a civil-rights legislative program to the Congress the previous February, for the Negro vote in strategic Northern urban centers played a key role in the Truman victory. From that time on, the civil-rights issue has been squarely in the national political picture of both major parties (not around the fringes as in the old days), and the non-Southern Negro voting power is now balanced (in the Democratic party) against the Deep South white vote.

This confrontation is important because it makes infinitely more difficult the anti-Negro hocus-pocus of the Southern bloc entrenched in the Congress (courtesy the lily-white ballot box back home) and of other Southerners dug into scores of Federal departments and agencies.

The Dixie bloc has had to give on appointments of Negroes to areas where none had ever trod before, except as messengers. It has had to give on confirmations of prestige appointments. It has swallowed desegregation of schools on military posts and of civilian services at all military installations. It had to take desegregation of the armed services as a policy and very largely as a practice. It acquiesced in a much stiffer no-discrimination policy in Federal civil service. It accepted with varying degrees of grace the desegregation of public accommodations in the nation's capital.

Negro state legislators, city councilmen, state and local board of education members, commissioners, judges, assistant attorneys-general, and other elected and appointed officials represent formidable components of Northern party segments necessary to national party victory. The Southerners cannot do as they did in the good old days. The perceptive ones are doing a rear-guard minuet. It sounds harmless, but because of their skill and seniority, because of the immaturity and insularity of their constituents, and because of the weaknesses of their Northern "opponents," the largely meaningless ritual is postponing government by consent of the governed and contributing to the restlessness of the Negro.

The NAACP's two-fisted attack upon voiceless citizenship, while not complete as yet, has gone far toward relieving the evils

35

set forth in 1909 and has cleared the channels for the surge to final success.

EQUAL JUSTICE UNDER LAW

The action in the Preston Cobb case in which a fifteen-year-old Georgia boy was sentenced to death in 1961 is thoroughly in the pioneer tradition of the NAACP as a rescuer in time of need and proves that the Association, for all its expanded activity across the civil-rights field, is still the counsellor and defender of those in dire trouble because of their color.

The NAACP has restricted its legal aid generally to those cases where a person has been or is in danger of being deprived of his constitutional rights because of his color and to those court actions likely to establish or to re-emphasize or broaden a constitutional principle.

Exclusion of Negroes from the jury was the basis of the reversal of a conviction won by NAACP attorneys in the Arkansas Supreme Court in 1920 in the Phillips County share-cropper cases. The United States Supreme Court reversed an Oklahoma conviction in 1935 (*Hollins* v. *Oklahoma,* 295 U.S. 394) on the same ground.

The customary use of confessions extorted by torture to con-vict prisoners of a crime without further evidence was outlawed as unconstitutional by the United States Supreme Court in a case brought from Mississippi in 1936 (*Brown, Ellington and Shields* v. *State of Mississippi,* 297 U.S. 278), Chief Justice Hughes de-claring, "the rack and torture chamber may not be substituted for the witness chair."

Residential segregation by municipal ordinance was declared unconstitutional in 1917 in a case (*Buchanan* v. *Warley,* 245 U.S. 60) arising in Louisville, Kentucky, and successfully argued by NAACP attorneys. Twenty-seven years later the popular and widespread covenants between individuals to restrict the owner-ship and occupation of property because of race or religion were declared by the Supreme Court to be unenforceable in the courts.

The equal protection clause of the Fourteenth Amendment was successfully invoked in a series of cases brought by Negro teachers with the assistance of NAACP attorneys to erase the salary differential, based upon race and color, which had been in effect in several of the Southern and border states.

The Arkansas sharecropper cases (*Moore* v. *Dempsey,* 261 U.S. 86) produced the vital ruling in 1923 that a trial dominated by mob sentiment is not due process of law. Subsequently all seventy-nine defendants were set free by the state.

Latter-day students of race relations know the NAACP for its activity in the court cases directed against segregation and discrimination in public education, capped, of course, by *Brown* v. *Board of Education,* 347 U.S. 483, decided May 17, 1954. The Southern plaint that this decision outlawing racial segregation in the public schools was "sudden" ignores the fact that NAACP attorneys had won in 1938 the action (*Lloyd Gaines* v. *University of Missouri,* 305 U.S. 337) which was the handwriting on the wall to all who chose to read.

The University of Texas case, decided twelve years later, finished what the Missouri case had begun. After the Texas ruling it was only a question of time before a decision on elementary and secondary schools would be forthcoming. It came down three weeks short of four years later.

BREAD AND SHELTER

The Negro has had to fight for bread ever since the day of emancipation. In the South he was confined to "Negro" jobs at "Negro" wage rates. In the North, with rare exceptions, only certain types of jobs were open to him. The unions, largely craft, joined the employers in restricting the opportunities and earning power of the Negro worker.

Changes have occurred since the industrial unions were organized in the thirties and since World War II, but as late as 1960 the median annual income of white families was $5,835 and that of Negro families $3,323. This was the picture despite state fair employment practice laws, federal government policy against job discrimination in the federal establishment and in firms holding government contracts. It is there despite increases in white-collar, technical, and supervisory jobs for Negroes and some upgrading in skilled and semiskilled industrial categories.

Conference on Economic Progress figures reveal that in 1960 60.6 per cent of Negro families were earning less than $4,000 a year, whereas only 28.5 per cent of white families were in this bracket. In the $6,000–$7,500 bracket were 11.2 per cent of the Negro families and 20.4 per cent of the white families. Only six-tenths of one per cent of the Negro families were in the $15,000 and up group.[10] These figures tell the story of the deprivation on a racial basis in the employment field, irrespective of the relatively few luxurious homes, the increased number of middle-class families, and the automobiles, clothes, fur coats, and other articles of conspicuous consumption which meet the eye of the casual observer.

Though there has been some spotty improvement, an astonishing number of methods of discriminating against Negro workers is still in vogue in the organized labor movement, including (a) exclusion from membership, (b) separate categories of work and separate lines of progression toward separate senority ratings, (c) discriminatory assignment of members to available jobs through hiring halls, shape-ups, and similar union-operated devices, (d) exclusion from or sharp restriction in apprenticeship training, and (e) restriction in upgrading and promotion to better paying and supervisory posts.

Industrial unionism opened opportunity to Negro workers in the automobile, steel, and rubber industries. The United Mine Workers under John L. Lewis long had had a no-bias policy. In the textile industry the two unions benefitted Negroes not a whit, never quarreled with the industry's exclusionist, segregationist policies. There are black spinners in the textile mills of the African Congo, but precious few—in small, scattered spots—in the United States. A South Carolina law prohibits Negroes and whites from working on the same floor in industrial plants and this has drawn no fire from the unions.

A formidable roadblock to the future economic well-being of the entire Negro community is presented by automation and other technological changes in the economy. Negro workers, through enforced restriction and exclusion, have been concentrated in disproportionate numbers in the unskilled and semi-skilled job occupations. It is in these categories that automation and other changes are wiping out jobs at an estimated rate of

[10] *Poverty and Deprivation in the United States* (Washington: Conference on Economic Progress, April, 1962), p. 59.

35,000 a week. For the bulk of Negro workers, the Jim Crow barriers must be breeched speedily. The alternative is occupancy, in increasing degree, of the frightening status of America's hard-core, permanently unemployed.

Of all the new housing built with FHA mortgage insurance in the United States since World War II, *less than 2 per cent* has been made available to Negro purchasers.

The tradition of the slave cabins behind and away from the "big house" has been carried forward in the Negro ghetto pattern, and with variations (and some deviations) this has flourished in the North as well as in the South. The Negro citizen does not have a free market when renting or purchasing. He must take what he can get at the price charged. The real-estate agents, landlords, bankers, and other financiers (of both races) are a combine against which he has been able to fling only indignation.

In late years the urban redevelopers have joined the army of tormentors that plagues him. Since the developers of lily-white suburbs and real-estate and mortgage firms aided the landlords of ancient central-city properties in penning the Negro in-migrants into these areas, the present occupants are, naturally, the first to be ousted by redevelopment projects. Slum clearance has become Negro clearance. The new civic centers, parkways, malls, parks, and luxury apartments that have replaced the profitable ruins have no room for the dark former residents. These are either crammed into already overflowing ghettos where unconscionable tribute continues to be exacted, or shunted to odd corners, or even into other towns and cities.

It is no wonder, then, that the Negro citizen voices loud demands that his Federal government refuse to assist any housing program which discriminates between citizens on the basis of race, color, or religion. It seems little enough to ask that his government not finance his blood-letting with public funds.

Housing remains one of the most difficult areas in so-called race relations. A vast collection of myth, emotions, and blatant falsehoods constitutes a barrier that is yielding but slowly to fact and reason. Churches, civic groups, human-relations agencies, and Negro and white individuals (including some bankers,

39

builders, white homeowners, and real-estate men) are making forays into the complex. There is every indication that new patterns can be set if truth, integrity, and persistence are permitted to take over, backed up by the full use of the powers of government. Fair housing laws in eighteen states are helping, and Kennedy's executive order of November 20, 1962, against discrimination in Federally-assisted housing is also helping, but on a disappointingly limited scale.

PURSUIT OF KNOWLEDGE AND HAPPINESS

Unquestionably, one of the principal controls employed by the Southern states to keep the Negro "in his place" has been the segregated public school system. In order to become a functioning citizen, the newly emancipated Negro desperately needed knowledge.

At one time (1929–1930) during the "separate but equal" era, Mississippi was spending a few pennies less than *eight times* as much per capita on public education for white children as it spent on Negro children—$35.29 white, $4.44 Negro. The same year South Carolina's per capita ratio was $154 white, $24 Negro, roughly six to one.

Negro adults who are now thirty-six years of age got their basic public schooling in the named states in the facilities afforded by these expenditures. Those now forty-six years of age fared even worse. In the school year 1956–1957, three years after the Supreme Court decision, Mississippi was spending $187.33 on the education of each white pupil and $107.34 on that of each Negro pupil.

The South has wailed that Negroes and integrationists want to go "too fast" and are forcing desegregation suddenly "down the throat of the South," but the truth is that in the seven years since the decision slightly less than 7 per cent of the Negro children in the affected states have been integrated. Nearly 2,500,-000 are still attending segregated schools. Although token steps in 1961 were taken without upheaval or violence in such cities as Atlanta, Dallas, and Memphis, they constituted just that—token integration.

The NAACP is proud of its record in combatting Jim Crow education. As was noted at the outset of this paper, the goal of unsegregated schools was set at the opening of the preliminary conference in 1909 at which the NAACP was born. The Association has pounded away over the years until the victory in *Brown* v. *Board of Education.*

As might have been expected, the new Emancipation Proclamation set forth in *Brown* v. *Board of Education* stunned the South and set off a campaign to defy the Court. The resistance to the school ruling may well have spurred the pursuit of dignity embodied in the Negro student sit-in movement at lunch counters, libraries, and other public places during 1960–1961.

On February 1, 1960, four Negro college students in Greensboro, North Carolina, sat down in a "no-service" lunch counter and the movement spread on a wave of spontaneous enthusiasm from the eastern seaboard to El Paso, Texas. This South-wide movement followed successful pilot sit-in projects by NAACP youth groups in 1958 and 1959 in Oklahoma City, Oklahoma; Wichita, Kansas; and at Washington University in St. Louis, Missouri. A widely accepted estimate in the fall of 1960 was that desegregation had been effected in some lunch counters in 112 cities. The number grew. Dallas changed its policy without any large scale demonstration. Atlanta changed peacefully in the fall of 1961 after the pressure of demonstrations in the spring. Even Macon, Georgia, changed, as did the one-time capital of the Confederacy, Richmond, Virginia.

Fully as important as the actual desegregation achieved was the signalling of the basic message that Negro citizens were finished with segregation. The myth that Negroes were satisfied with the old system was shattered. From here on in the planning has to be only on "how and when," not on "whether" segregation shall go. The answer of Negro youth and its elders is "Now!"

Hard on the heels of the lunch-counter campaign, personal dignity was brought to interstate travel by the Freedom Riders in 1961. The clean-up is not complete (even as with lunch counters), but the point has been made, an ICC order has been secured, and many communities are complying, although Mississippi, Alabama, and Louisiana are offering their usual stubborn resistance.

Unhampered travel, of course, is necessary to the precious pursuit of happiness set forth in the Declaration of Independence. And places in which to be relaxed and happy are also a requirement. Jim Crow railroad accommodations, made legal by *Plessy* v. *Ferguson* in 1896, were on their way out in the forties.

Numerous other decisions down through the years pushed back exclusion from or discriminatory treatment in amusement parks, theaters, restaurants, hotels, motels, beaches, parks, playgrounds, golf courses, tennis courts, excursion steamers and affiliated parks, and picnic grounds. Enactment of state civil-rights laws and their subsequent expansion and strengthening helped to correct many conditions in the Northeast, Middle West, and Far West. No sweeping generalizations can be made about any region, but access and service are now much more the rule than the exception outside the South. The non-Southern city with completely closed hotel doors is rare today.

Happiness, always elusive, may never be completely captured, but it is now possible to pursue it with zest rather than with foreboding.

THE END IN VIEW

Any impartial observer (which the writer is not) would be forced to agree that the record of militant, integrationist civil-rights leadership during the last half of the one hundred years since the Emancipation Proclamation is impressive.

Two world wars gave the alert Negro population opportunity to ask the embarrassing question: If we make war to save democracy in Europe and Southeast Asia, why not act to save and guarantee democracy in our own race relations? Both wars stimulated changes, the last one bringing in its wake the end of the galling segregated armed services.

The so-called new activities are really not new, as any reviewer of the long struggle knows readily enough. Protest and agitation and demonstration have been a part of the militant program for generations. If legal activity seemed, by virtue of its dramatic decisions, to be the chief weapon employed by the NAACP, it was only that the legal, constitutional position of the Negro had to be established if anything were to come of any other effort.

The centennial of Abraham Lincoln's Emancipation Proclamation finds the Negro American in a mood to claim without further delay all the rights and privileges he should have begun to enjoy after the adoption of the three post–Civil War Amendments to the Constitution. He has been kept back, to use a school promotion expression, but he now proposes to take his place according to the standards applied to all others.

He is driven by his knowledge of the manifold ways in which he and his have been cheated, frustrated, and violated over the decades. He knows that this was no passing harassment as it was with some other ethnic groups, to be replaced in time with grudging respect, even honor. He knows it in its Dixie origins for a deep, persistent animus, fed by a greed and a fear and a guilt that sought not only to restrict and use him for present advantage, but diabolically to fabricate a "history" and a body of "science" that would snare him for yet decades more, even though he managed, somehow, to escape the crude corrals of segregation.

He knows all this as he rounds out nearly a century of fighting for a freedom that came bit by dribbling bit, literally torn by him and a handful of allies from the tight hands and hard hearts of the overlords.

The Southern white people, too, carry the virus of the slave period in their blood, from the policeman who notches his gun with Negro killings on through the muscle supremacists, the petty scavengers, the editors, the judges, the Pharisees of the cloth, and up to those in the Congress and in Governors' mansions who rear like fire horses to every racial gong. With a few brave exceptions, their insulated children utter the creed of their grandfathers and great grandfathers, blissfully unaware of the anachronism.

They share a common prison, these black and white Americans, in different cell blocks, perhaps, but confined, nevertheless; and the drive of the one for freedom cannot help but free the other also.

The Negro American is driven, too, by the swift events of the second half of the twentieth century. Black men in Africa are becoming prime ministers, presidents, cabinet members, generals, and ambassadors of new, independent nations. Black men are voting—some by symbols of fish, birds, animals, and plants—

and are sitting in the councils of government in African lands still in transition. Black men are at work in the banks, industries, offices, and transportation systems of their part of the world. Brown, black, and yellow men of Asia and the islands of the sea are similarly on the march.

In Mississippi, U.S.A., however, less than *4 per cent* of the eligible Negro citizens are permitted to register to vote. No black engineers hold the throttle of a locomotive in the United States as they do in the Congo. In all the states of the South where eleven million Negro Americans live there is no Negro Congressman or mayor or judge or sheriff and only one state legislator. A Negro doctor of medicine is still not a doctor in the eyes of the Georgia Medical Association which, in 1961, voted to maintain its ban against his membership, thus barring Negro doctors from Georgia from membership in the American Medical Association as well.

Under these conditions, made clear to even the uneducated through mass communication in plain words and plainer pictures, it is safe to predict that the pressure from American Negroes for their full citizenship rights will increase. Under the influence of world trends, the restraints imposed upon so irrelevant a basis as race and color will spur even greater impatience with a gradualism whose every hesitant half-step is inordinately hailed as a Bunyan leap.

They present themselves and their demands in much the same manner as do the Africans:

"Here we are, ready or not. In a very real and demonstrable sense you retarded us, man, son, grandson. Now you want us to wait for the adjustment of your mistakes, for the rectification of your course, chosen so deliberately generations ago. We say the price is too great. We alone cannot pay for both. Let us both go free and together pay our debt to ourselves, to our country, and to our Western world of individual liberty under law."

In his drive, the Negro citizen will use every available weapon short of violence. No sector of race relations, North or South, will escape the pressures. As with any other population of its size there will be differences on methods, on priorities, and on the degree of concentration. There will be no differences on objectives, except for that minute minority which rejects integration into American life.

44

Emancipation and Militant Leadership

The current is now so strong and so broad that those Negroes who have a financial stake in segregation, those who have made individual pacts with the white world, and those few who have been converted by the brain-washing cannot influence the course of events.

The forward movement will include increased attention to problems within the group: more effective pooling and use of finances and other money-making resources now being dissipated or spent thoughtlessly with others; improved family and community discipline as the wrenching transition from deprived rural to deprived urban environments is eased; restoration of excellence as a goal; and further inculcation of citizenship responsibility for the general welfare beyond the boundaries of group, race, religion, or class.

Unfinished though the NAACP's task is in these sixties, the imprint of its declarations and its deeds is sharp and clear in the history of the United States in the twentieth century. As that century dawned, William E. Burghardt Du Bois, the voice of the militant heretics against the "worthy serf" doctrine, opined, "the problem of the twentieth century is the problem of the color line."

In goading, cajoling, and driving our nation toward a just solution of its segment of the century's problem, the NAACP has remained true to Garrison's message to the 1909 organizing meeting. As its opponents attest, it has uttered no uncertain sound. It has proclaimed the republican democratic experiment and the well-being of white citizens to be endangered by the toleration of wrongs done the Negro. With the slingshot of faith and skill and everlasting work it slew the Goliath of divided citizenship, pointing up the Garrison truism that safety (and peace and mutual respect) lies "in an absolute refusal to differentiate the rights of human beings."

That there is now wide acceptance of that position, as well as broad concurrence in the militant integrationist argument, is indicated in *Goals for Americans,* the 1960 report of the President's Commission on National Goals:

> Democracy, let us remember, has a fundamental commitment to equality in the best and most realistic senses of that word: to equality before the law, equality of political voice, equality in constitutional rights, equality

of opportunity, and equality of consideration. Somehow we must push farther and faster than we have in the past—through education, persuasion, example, and, where clearly necessary, force of law—to honor this commitment. Somehow we must eliminate the sordid or timid techniques of unequal treatment that still leave millions outside the circle of first-class citizenship in which most Americans are privileged to go about their affairs. . . . We have no more pressing task in the decade before us than to see that the promise is made in good faith to all who live among us.

If this means that some men must renounce old privileges in order that other men may enjoy new liberties, then that is the way the knife of democratic aspiration will have to cut.

HERBERT J. STORING

•

THE SCHOOL OF SLAVERY:
A RECONSIDERATION OF
BOOKER T. WASHINGTON

> You ask that which he found a piece of property and turned into a free American citizen to speak to you tonight on Abraham Lincoln. I am not fitted by ancestry or training to be your teacher tonight for, as I have stated, I was born a slave.
> —Booker T. Washington, an address before the Republican Club of New York City, February 12, 1909

"One hesitates," wrote W. E. Burghardt Du Bois in 1903, "to criticise a life which, beginning with so little, has done so much. And yet the time is come when one may speak in all sincerity and utter courtesy of the mistakes and shortcomings of Mr. Washington's career, as well as of his triumphs, without being thought captious or envious, and without forgetting that it is easier to do ill than well in the world."[1] It is the premise of this essay that these words apply now to the very movement of which Du Bois's critical essay, "Of Mr. Booker T. Washington and Others," was one of the first major documents and of which the National Association for the Advancement of Colored People is the major instrument. Is it not time to "speak in all sincerity and utter courtesy of the mistakes and shortcomings," not of this man or this organization, but of the understanding they represent of the principles that govern or ought to govern the conduct of American citizens and free men, white and black, in their relations with one another?

[1] W. E. Burghardt Du Bois, *The Souls of Black Folk* (Chicago: A. C. McClurg & Co., 1903), pp. 43–44. This book is available in a paperback edition (Greenwich, Conn.: Fawcett Publications, Premier Americana, 1961).

Herbert J. Storing

Although the movement headed by the NAACP has never enjoyed the same degree of unity of purpose or widespread support that characterized the leadership of Booker T. Washington, it is scarcely less pre-eminent in its day and in its chosen field than Washington was in his. Here too is a life, albeit an institutional one, that began with little and has done much; and one hesitates to criticize it for fear, not so much of seeming captious and envious, as of seeming infected with one or another of the forms of bigotry through which the NAACP and its allied groups have had to steer and to which no respectable man would resort. Yet unwillingness to speak on these grounds can hardly be justified if there is reason to think, as Du Bois thought of Washington, that the standard to which men are invited to repair is false or in important respects defective.

Our concern is not, any more than Du Bois's was, with particular mistakes or superficial shortcomings. We are not concerned with tactics; we are somewhat more concerned with broad strategy, where means and ends mix; and we are above all concerned with the ends sought and the reasons for thinking them good. But why approach these questions through Booker T. Washington instead of looking at present-day leaders addressing themselves to present-day problems? A strong historical justification may be found in the fact that the Negro "protest" movement of the twentieth century, of which the NAACP is still the major exponent, took form very largely in response to and rejection of Washington's policy of "accommodation." It was not a thoughtless response; it was surely not merely captious and envious. But it was heavily dependent on its picture of what it was against; it was against Booker T. Washington. Not that Washington plays much part in the rhetoric of the "protest" movement today. Yet it may be suggested, without here trying to prove, that the movement, understandably preoccupied today with specific policies, relies heavily for its higher justification on its early leaders and they, in turn, defined their position against the background that Washington provided.

We have used the customary terms, "accommodation" and "protest," in referring to Washington's position and that of his opponents. But although the terms are now common in the histories, they are the product of the anti-Washington movement; they convey, without explaining or justifying, the anti-Washington argument. The terms imply that the difference was a difference in strategy, or approach, or style. The question was *how* to go about promoting the advancement of colored people, to adopt the terminology of the new organization. Washington's answer to that question was summed up by many, not without some justification, as "accommodation"; and the "protest" movement was born out of and rests upon a rejection of that answer. Of course all questions of strategy point to the ends served, and the higher principles of strategy are determined by the order of the ends, in principle and in time. Problems of higher strategy and questions about ends become more pressing when tactics at the lower levels are successful. Such is the condition of the "protest" movement today, and in this condition lies the need to speak of Washington again. For Washington always kept in central position the question that his successors push to the periphery: what constitutes the "advancement" of colored people, or any people?

Since the ranks of the "protest" movement were so largely formed in opposition to Washington and since that movement, for all its variety of forms and objectives, still finds its definition in that original protest, it is well to begin with the bill of particulars drawn against Washington's leadership. This was a bill drawn by men who felt deeply and reasoned well, men who concluded, often slowly and reluctantly, that the future of the Negro in the United States lay in a rejection of the position of the most powerful, most loved, and most feared Negro leader the country has ever seen. Their passion, reason, and organizational and political skill have prevailed. What was the indictment?

> First, that Washington advocated, successfully, that the Negro should enter into a compromise with the dominant white community, North and South, in which the Negro would in effect give up his claims for equal political, civil, and social rights and accept a position of indefinite tenure at the bottom of the ladder, in return for the opportunity to be left to earn and consume his crust of bread and, if he should work very hard, to enjoy the modest material comforts of a dutiful dependent class.

Second, that Washington acceded to the disfranchisement of the Negro and to the use by the Negro of his vote, in the rare cases where he was permitted to vote, under the tutelage of his former masters, thus accepting and accelerating the withdrawal of the only weapon with which the Negro could enforce his civil rights, his economic opportunity, and his dignity as a human being.

Third, that Washington insisted on the fundamental need for the Negro to secure and retain the good will and co-operation of the Southern whites and strengthened white prejudice and gave countenance to indignities practiced against the freedman by his counsel of silent submission.

Fourth, that Washington practiced and encouraged a form of education designed to keep the Negro in the South and on the land, designed to fit the Negro for menial labor and to content him with a more or less permanent position as a hewer of wood and a drawer of water; that in consequence he neglected and even deliberately stifled the efforts of others to further higher educational opportunities for Negroes, thus further contributing to their permanent depression.

Fifth, that Washington taught a mean materialism, mitigated only by the delusive hope that as the Negro succeeded in his pursuit of material well-being he would lay the foundation for increased acceptance by his white neighbors and for his own higher aspirations; that he adopted in fact the prevailing business philosophy of Northern businessmen with whom he came into increasing contact, sacrificing the best interests of Negroes to Northern Avarice as he sacrificed them to Southern Prejudice.

Sixth, that Washington was perennially and unreasonably optimistic about the improvement of the condition of the Negro and his acceptance by the white community, and that he used his enormous influence, cultivated with so much care and at so great a cost, to frustrate or suppress a more vigorous and varied Negro leadership, precisely at the time when his own program, however understandable or even justifiable it may have been as the best bargain that a people just emerging from slavery could make, proved increasingly narrow and insufficient.[2]

[2] I have omitted one count from this list, the soft indictment much favored by historians, that Washington was, after all, merely a "man of his

The School of Slavery

The Tuskegee movement was not a separatist or nationalist movement. It rested emphatically on the fact of "integration," although not the kind of integration that first comes to mind today. In the same year that Justice Harlan said, in his dissent in *Plessy* v. *Ferguson,* that "the destinies of the two races in this country are indissolubly linked together," Washington said: "We rise as you rise; when we fall you fall. When you are strong we are strong; when we are weak you are weak. There is no power that can separate our destiny."[3] Washington sought to work out that destiny within the limits set by the primitive condition of the Negro and the prejudice of the white. But whereas Harlan stressed the need to protect the Negro against irrational prejudice, Washington argued—can it have been seriously, we ask today?—that "the Negro can afford to be wronged; the white man cannot afford to wrong him," and that unjust laws directed by whites against Negroes harm the former but only inconvenience the latter. Whereas Harlan's underlying theme is race hate, Washington's is "the question of the highest citizenship." The inconveniences suffered by the Negro would diminish and diminish in significance to the extent that he could measure up to this highest citizenship. "This country demands that every race measure itself by the American standard. By it a race must rise or fall, succeed or fail, and in the last analysis mere sentiment counts but little."

But is not the American standard the Declaration of Inde-

---

times," sharing the widespread opportunism, accepting current notions of Negro education (and even Negro inferiority), moved by the fashionable currents of Social Darwinism and the Gospel of Wealth. We need not pause here to inquire whether this does not attempt to explain what is reasonably clear—what Washington said and did—by viewing it as a reflection of what is cloudy and vague—the "times" in which he lived; or whether these "times" were not formed out of the ideas of men, men like Washington. Our concern is more down to earth. If we are to presume that he is merely a "man of his times" (and treat him with the patronizing tolerance he would then deserve) are we not to presume (and to treat) similarly Washington's opponents and their successors? And have we not therefore cut away any ground upon which we might stand in addressing ourselves, as all of these men thought to address themselves, to questions about the "times" in which we live? The hard indictment is much preferable, because on that basis we can confront Washington, and thus his successors.

[3] 163 U.S. 560 (1896); E. Davidson Washington (ed.), *Selected Speeches of Booker T. Washington* (Garden City, N.Y.: Doubleday, Doran & Co., 1932), pp. 75–77.

pendence? And is it not the Negro's task to act as the thorny, relentless conscience of America by demanding the equality, the rights, the freedom that American whites, professing adherence to the national standard, refuse to grant to American Negroes? So indeed Du Bois and his colleagues and successors argued. Washington speaks of duty; yet surely, they insisted and continue to insist, the language of America is rights. This is both the strongest case against Washington and the way to an understanding of his deepest justification; for Washington found in the pages of slavery—full of injustice and degradation as they were— instruction in freedom and in the highest citizenship.

There is irony in the condition of the American Negro, a hard irony but, Washington thought, a noble one. The white slave-trader violated the fundamental principles of his own civilization and thereby degraded himself, even in comparison with the black slave-traders with whom he had commerce; yet he introduced those slaves and their descendants to the civilization that he served so badly. The fact provides him no defense, as it provides no defense of those who bought from him and used men as animals; but it is a fact that few American Negroes would wish to see undone.

> Think of it: we went into slavery pagans; we came out Christians. We went into slavery pieces of property; we came out American citizens. We went into slavery without a language; we came out speaking the proud Anglo-Saxon tongue. We went into slavery with slave chains clanking about our wrists; we came out with the American ballot in our hands.[4]

This is not an argument that "all's for the best," nor is it an apology for injustice past or present, but Washington constantly sought to draw American Negroes' attention to the fact that slavery was their road to freedom and civilization and to explain the past and present implications of that fact. The Africans' very struggle against slavery was their first lesson in freedom; "the fugitive slaves learned in the United States, in their very efforts to be free, something about the nature of freedom that they could not have learned in Africa."[5] Washington often

[4] *Selected Speeches*, p. 37.
[5] Booker T. Washington, *The Story of the Negro: The Rise of the Race from Slavery* (London: T. Fisher Unwin, 1909), I, 231.

argued that, notwithstanding all the cruelty and moral wrong of slavery, "the ten million Negroes inhabiting this country, who themselves or whose ancestors went through the school of American slavery, are in a stronger and more hopeful condition, materially, intellectually, morally, and religiously, than is true of an equal number of black people in any other portion of the globe."[6] This is not, to repeat, to justify slavery, the net result of which is bad—"bad for the enslaved, and perhaps worse for the enslaver."[7] But Washington thought that the American Negro could not understand or improve his present condition without remembering that as he suffers arbitrarily indignities and injustice, so he came arbitrarily into possession of "the American standard" by which he measures the behavior of others and himself.

Washington often spoke of the contrast between the history of the Negro and the American Indian in their relations with the white man. The Indian, proud, free, ungovernable, refused to wear the yoke of slavery and when he was forced to do so rarely made a good slave; he elected to remain the noble savage or to die. The Negro, on the other hand, uprooted to an alien land, submitted mildly to being tamed, trained, and worked; he survived and even prospered. Observe the result. The Indian became increasingly merely savage, a despicable cur surviving (when he did survive) on scraps from the white man's table. The Negro became increasingly civilized; so that in 1879 the young Negro students at Hampton, only a very few years removed from slavery, agreed only with some muttering to accept among themselves a group of uncouth, evil-smelling, tobacco-smoking Indians so that the blacks might help to civilize the reds.

There is a good deal to be said, Washington suggests, for the noble savage in preference to the submissive slave—the stigma of slavery cuts deep and stays long. But that was not really the choice. The Negro seems to have been the only race, he repeatedly points out, to look the white man in the face and live. The Indian chose the way of degradation and destruction, while

---

[6] Booker T. Washington, *Up From Slavery: An Autobiography* (1st ed.; New York: Doubleday, Page & Co., 1901), p. 16. This book is available in a paperback edition (New York: Bantam Books, 1963).

[7] Booker T. Washington and W. E. Burghardt Du Bois, *The Negro in the South* (Philadelphia: George W. Jacobs & Co., 1907), p. 16.

the Negro chose, not merely survival, but "the only method that existed at that time for getting possession of the white man's learning and the white man's civilisation."[8] The irony of the history of the American Negro—heightened by the fact that he was the only man who did not choose to come to the New World but was brought unwillingly because he was needed there—did not end with Emancipation. As he suffered the degradation and violence of his slavery as the price of his entry into the land of freedom, so he suffered and continues to suffer the discrimination and injustice of his partial freedom as the price of freedom itself. No one has a "right" to exact this price of him, and he might at any time refuse to pay it, as the Indian did. The Negro bent his back and lowered his eyes, not out of dumb submission or for the sake of mere survival, but to learn to stand straight and hold his head high.

With this as background, let us turn to Washington's much criticized policy with respect to the civil and especially the political rights of Negroes. Washington did seek to promote the rights of Negroes. He spoke out against lynching; he emphasized that the Negro must be dangerously dissatisfied until he gets equal justice; he argued against segregation laws; he criticized the grossly unequal educational facilities for Negroes; he helped to finance the test case against the "grandfather clause"; he sought to secure adequate accommodations for Negroes on Southern railroads; and he used his influence, often quietly and even under cover, to combat specific cases of injustice and discrimination. He insisted that "no question is ever permanently settled until it is settled on the principles of highest justice";[9] and he left no fair doubt of his opinion that the highest justice so far as the Negro was concerned included (but was not exhausted by) full civil and political rights. Yet Washington never made the active pursuit of these rights a major part of his policy, and he sought deliberately to turn Negroes' minds in other directions. "Brains, property, and character for the Negro will settle the question of civil rights," he argued in his first address in 1884.

---

[8] *The Story of the Negro*, I, 136.
[9] *Selected Speeches*, pp. 82–83.

"The best course to pursue in regard to the civil rights bill in the South is to let it alone; let it alone and it will settle itself." Thirty years later, when growing discrimination caused Washington to speak out more sharply on questions of civil and political rights, he nevertheless adhered to the view that "no law of Congress or of the State Legislature can help us as much, in the last analysis, as things that we can do. . . ."[10]

So far as political rights are concerned, we have Theodore Roosevelt's plain-spoken testimony that no one was more alive than Washington to the threat "contained in the mass of ignorant, propertyless, semi-vicious Black voters, wholly lacking in the character which alone fits a race for self-government, who nevertheless have been given the ballot in certain Southern States." Roosevelt estimated that half of the considerable time that he spent in consultation with Washington was spent "discussing methods for keeping out of office, and out of all political power, the ignorant, semi-criminal, shiftless Black Man who, when manipulated by the able and unscrupulous politician, Black or White, is so dreadful a menace to our political institutions."[11] It is the duty of the Negro, Washington taught, "to deport himself modestly in regard to political claims, depending upon the slow but sure influences that proceed from the possession of property, intelligence, and high character for the full recognition of his political rights."[12] A heavy burden of justification lies on a Negro leader who spent so considerable a portion of his energy discouraging the exercise by Negroes of political rights that were legally theirs.

Before considering that justification, however, it is necessary to engage in the somewhat academic exercise of recalling and attempting to take seriously some distinctions, once generally accepted in the United States and implicit in Washington's program, which successive waves of the "protest" movement have caused to be almost forgotten. The three post–Civil War Amendments to the Constitution are concerned with three distinct stages in the emancipation of the Negro. The Thirteenth Amendment

[10] *Ibid.*, pp. 3, 243.
[11] Preface to Emmett J. Scott and Lyman Beecher Stowe, *Booker T. Washington, Builder of a Civilization* (Garden City, N.Y.: Doubleday, Page & Co., 1917), pp. xiii–xiv.
[12] *Up From Slavery*, p. 235.

granted him legal freedom; the Fourteenth made him a citizen and provided a Constitutional guarantee of basic civil rights; the Fifteenth gave him the vote. No later one of these guarantees is necessarily implied in any earlier one. According to the principles of American law and political theory, a man (or a woman) might be a citizen enjoying full civil rights, for example, and yet not be permitted to vote or to hold office or to sit on juries. Participation in the political life of the community has always been thought to depend on qualifications, however minimal, set by the present citizenry or their representatives, acting according to their best judgment.

As a man might enjoy full civil rights and even be a citizen without being permitted to vote, so a man might be legally free, not a slave, without enjoying full civil rights; he might, for example, be subject to special regulations so far as the ownership of property or the making and enforcing of contracts or his personal liberty of movement are concerned. Admittedly this is a harder case. But if, as many have thought, a native-born free American who is not a citizen in possession of full civil rights is an anomaly, it is an anomaly suffered in recognition of the impossibility of transforming a man, much more a large body of men, from slave to citizen overnight. Indeed, the Fourteenth Amendment, following hard upon Emancipation, although it removed the anomaly in law, did not remove, and at that time could not have removed, the anomaly in fact. We need not engage in loose talk about the Negro's "virtual re-enslavement" after Reconstruction or ignore the degree of legal protection which even the notorious black codes provided, and which large numbers of Negroes actually enjoyed, to see that the freedman was just that—no longer slave, not yet truly free. Washington describes the conditions of the freedman as a kind of serfdom, a natural and even necessary serfdom, which was "merely one of the stages through which a society, in which slavery has existed, has usually worked its way to freedom."[13]

It must immediately be said that freedom in the fullest or highest sense depends, and has always been understood to depend, on the enjoyment of all three of these degrees of freedom —bare legal freedom, civil rights, and political responsibility.

[13] *The Story of the Negro*, II, 50.

Moreover, it is obvious that the actual enjoyment of the status legally guaranteed at one of the lower stages may in practice be impossible without the protection of a higher stage; for example, legally guaranteed civil rights may in practice be withheld from a group without political power. (That this is not necessarily the case is testified by the experience of many groups, for example women and aliens at various times and places.) But before entering into these important considerations, let us proceed academically a bit further and engage in an exercise of the imagination about the introduction of the freedmen to the full privileges and responsibilities of American citizenship. Our purpose is not to sigh about what might have been or to attempt to lay the blame for what is—to put such questions in any prominent place would violate the whole spirit of Washington's enterprise—but to see if we can thus understand Washington's policy.

Let us suppose that the doubts of men like President Andrew Johnson about the wisdom of admitting the Negro quickly into full political participation had prevailed. Suppose that a constitutional amendment had been passed opening the franchise only to individual Negroes who could meet reasonable but rather strict property and literacy qualifications to be set by Congress and administered by the states under federal supervision. What would have been some of the consequences? First, there is some reason to expect that the provisions, even though administered largely by Southern whites, would have been administered fairly and that Negro political participation, just because it was to be slow and limited, would have come to be accepted. Second, it is reasonable to expect that the groundwork would have been laid for a gradual but steady extension of the franchise, both by giving the white Southerner time to make the drastic adjustment required of him and by removing the basis of his fear, or alleged fear, of the sudden rise to political power of an unprepared group with many reasons to use its power against white interests. Third, it might be expected that, introduced to politics in this way, the Negro would have learned to use political power more independently and wisely than in fact he did. Fourth, it seems possible that such a policy, based on genuine American principles and directed to conditions and interests as they actually existed, might have led to a more harmonious development of relations between the races in the South. Finally, however, this policy would certainly have done injustice to many individual Negroes and in a sense to the whole race, for whites were not held to such standards. The freedman would have been required, before entering fully into citizenship, to show himself better prepared than many, perhaps most, whites.

When Booker T. Washington imagined that such a policy, despite its essential element of injustice to Negroes, would have been the least unsatisfactory way of integrating Negroes into American political life, he was standing in an eminently respectable line of statesmen, at the head of which, had he lived, we might have found Abraham Lincoln. Du Bois himself entertained similar speculations; but he thought that once federal protection of the Negro was withdrawn and he was handed back to the guardianship of those who were determined to thwart his freedom, the Negro's only defense lay in the ballot. Du Bois concedes "that it is possible, and sometimes best, that a partially undeveloped people should be ruled by the best of their stronger and better neighbors for their own good, until such time as they can start and fight the world's battles alone." These conditions would be fairly well fulfilled "if the representatives of the best white Southern public opinion were the ruling and guiding powers in the South to-day"; but "the best opinion of the South to-day is not the ruling opinion." Consequently, "to leave the Negro helpless and without a ballot to-day is to leave him, not to the guidance of the best, but rather to the exploitation and debauchment of the worst. . . ."[14] "This truth," Du Bois says elsewhere, "the great Thaddeus Stephens saw, and with a statesmanship far greater than Lincoln's he forced Negro suffrage on the South."[15] "No one thought, at the time, that the ex-slaves could use the ballot intelligently or very effectively; but they did think that the possession of so great power by a great class in the nation would compel their fellows to educate this class to its intelligent use."[16]

Behind Washington's desire to see the Negro take up only slowly the exercise of his political rights lay his view that the

[14] *The Souls of Black Folk*, pp. 172–77.
[15] Washington and Du Bois, *The Negro in the South*, p. 89.
[16] *The Souls of Black Folk*, pp. 173–74.

Negro had been pushed too fast through the several stages of emancipation. Washington was not blind to the force of arguments like Du Bois's; but he was neither so sure as Du Bois that the best opinion in the South was, or could be assumed to be, beyond restoration, nor so hopeful about the educational effects upon Negroes of the possession of the ballot. Washington thought that the Negro's premature assumption of political power and responsibility found him so ill-prepared that he aroused legitimate fears and measures of self-defense in the white community and that he was unable to use his political power intelligently even to protect his own interests, to say nothing of exercising well the responsibilities of full citizenship.

Regarding white fears of a black political assault, it might be said that the Negroes were not to blame for what they were and that no harm done by their political activity could exceed the measure of just retribution. Washington saw that this kind of reasoning, however true, is a poor basis for any positive policy. In the history of the relations between Negro and white in the South there is scarcely any wrong on one side that cannot be shown to proceed from some prior wrong on the other. Washington's aim was to break out of the chain of mutual fear and injustice and to make, to the extent conditions permitted, a new beginning. To make a policy of protesting injustice, laying the blame for it at the white man's door, and forcing that growth of Negro political power which was the very thing most feared by the whites was, he thought, only to lengthen the chain of mutual harm. The new beginning required the Negro to concede that the Southern whites (despite all their past and present guilt) had some legitimate reason to fear large-scale political participation by the Negro. Conceding this, Washington also conceded the necessity of applying special qualifications to Negro voters. He adhered to the principle that "whatever tests are required, they should be made to apply with equal and exact justice to both races."[17] Yet he was sufficiently realistic to know that such tests would in fact be applied more strictly, to say the least, to Negroes than to whites; and he was sufficiently statesmanlike to recognize that justice may be poorly served by a blind determination to do justice in every individual

[17] *Up From Slavery*, p. 237.

case—to insist on no tests or on tests applied strictly to all, even to those parts of the population not previously thought to need them. There was some unfairness in this policy, as there would have been in the better policy we have imagined, since the Negro is held to stricter requirements than the white. But while an individual white may be just as poor and ignorant as an individual Negro, it is of the utmost political relevance if the ignorant white is the exception and the ignorant Negro the rule.

Washington was willing to make substantial concessions to prepare for a new beginning, but that did not imply any concession or compromise so far as the *end* was concerned. In the end, he insisted, the only safe course for the South was also the right one: to admit the Negro to full citizenship when he should have become fit for it.

> It ought to be clearly recognised that, in a republican form of government, if any group of people is left permanently without the franchise it is placed at a serious disadvantage. I do not object to restrictions being placed upon the use of the ballot, but if any portion of the population is prevented from taking part in the government by reason of these restrictions, they should have held out before them the incentive of securing the ballot in proportion as they grow in property-holding, intelligence, and character.[18]

This was the duty of the South, and it was the course of both justice and policy.

The Negro's duty was to make himself fit, and that is the basis of Washington's efforts to turn Negroes from political to economic activity. His aim, he said, was not "to give the people the idea that political rights were not valuable or necessary, but rather to impress upon them that economic efficiency was the foundation for every kind of success."[19] Washington saw more clearly than Du Bois ever did the relation of politics and economics so far as the American Negro was concerned. Economics is fundamental; it is not sufficient. The most immediate lesson the Negro had to learn was the former, because the intelligent use of the vote requires a foundation that he did not have. "Show me a race that is living on the outer edges of the indus-

[18] *The Story of the Negro*, II, 370.
[19] *Ibid.*, II, 192.

trial world, on the skimmed milk of business, and I will show you a race that is the football for political parties, and a race that cannot be what it should be in morals and religion."[20] Unquestionably a race, even though permitted a considerable degree of economic opportunity, is at a disadvantage without the vote (although Washington pointed out that a prosperous man is seldom without political influence, whether or not he can vote) ; but so is a race that is ignorant, untrained, and poverty-ridden at a disadvantage even if it has the vote. The questions are which of these disadvantages is the more fundamental, which can be removed, and which is it the business of Negroes to remove? Washington argued that, under existing conditions, if the Negro placed major emphasis on political activity he offered himself up as a pawn in the political struggles of others. There is something to be got out of being a pawn, and there is a kind of education in it; but it is not the kind of reward or the kind of education that the Negro ought to strive for.

Washington's famous policy of "accommodation" was based on the belief that political wisdom, and political courage too, consists in removing the evils that can be removed and doing the good that can be done rather than crying out against all the injustice there is. But Washington did more than trim his sails to the wind. He recognized that the progress of the Negro depended on the receptivity and co-operation of the white, as well as on the efforts of the Negro. And while he was, in the nature of the case, in a better position to influence the latter, he also did what he could to influence the former. If the Southern white was so intransigent that he simply would not permit the Negro to lay the economic foundation for his higher aspirations—if Negroes could not get contracts enforced, if they were not permitted in any significant numbers to own property, if they were forced to live in constant terror of violence—then Washington's policy collapses. Under such circumstances a resort to political power in sheer self-defense—mean and doubtful as the outcome must have been—would have been the only course open to the Negro short of abject submission or violent

[20] *Selected Speeches*, p. 44.

rebellion. The exact degree to which opportunities were, or are, open must remain a matter of debate; but it will be generally agreed that the Negro did not and does not confront such desperate extremity.

Washington was, by deliberate choice, an "optimist." "There is no hope for any man or woman, whatever his color, who is pessimistic; who is continually whining and crying about his condition. There is hope for any race of people, however handicapped by difficulties, that makes up its mind that it will succeed, that it will make success the stepping stone to a life of success and usefulness."[21] Again and again Washington insists on "the great human law, which is universal and eternal, that merit, no matter under what skin found, is, in the long run, recognized and rewarded." "The individual who can do something that the world wants done will, in the end, make his way regardless of his race." "Say what we will, there is something in human nature which we cannot blot out, which makes one man, in the end, recognize and reward merit in another, regardless of colour or race."[22] Washington was sufficiently in contact with the life of the Negro in the South to know that "the long run" might be very long indeed, that there is also something in human nature that refuses to recognize merit, and that Negro success in economic matters might result immediately in further repression rather than in acceptance. (But before quoting Southern history too quickly to prove this point it would be necessary to consider how that history might have been different if the fear of Negro political power had been removed by the Negro.) His optimism was genuine but it was not simple-minded. It was meant, of course, to stimulate the Negro; but it was also an attempt, by stating as a fact what was, in part, only what ought to be the fact, to stimulate the Southern white, in the best way that a Negro could do it, to the exercise of his better nature. Washington sought to strengthen the "best opinion" among the Southern whites which Du Bois admitted, or almost admitted, ought to rule.

In his first speech in 1884 Washington observed that Southerners have "a good deal of human nature"; they like to receive

[21] *Ibid.*, p. 207.
[22] *Up From Slavery*, pp. 40–41, 155, 235, and *passim.*

praise for doing good deeds and they resist outsiders who tell
them to abandon the customs of centuries. He advocated no
unmanly stooping to satisfy unreasonable whims but thought it
prudent as well as charitable to remember what the South had
to overcome.[23] "I early learned that it is a hard matter to con-
vert an individual by abusing him, and that this is more often
accomplished by giving credit for all the praiseworthy actions
performed than by calling attention alone to all the evil done."[24]
Washington kept in the forefront the consideration that reform,
wherever it might begin and whatever means it might use, is
the making of just men, and that is rarely done by bitterness
and abuse. Whether treating history or current affairs, Washington chose to see and to tell the Southern white side of the
story as sympathetically and hopefully as was consistent with
historical truth and fundamental principles of right. He found
and praised Southern abolitionists, he assigned ample credit to
the numerous Southerners who freed or wished to free their
slaves, and he gave a balanced explanation of the fears that many
white Southerners had of a large class of freedmen. He found
it significant, in one of his last speeches, that the opinion in
the *Guinn* case (1915), which outlawed the "grandfather clause,"
was written by a native-born Southerner, a former Confederate
soldier, and a former slave-holder. He emphasized the good
relations of individual whites and individual Negroes. He
stressed the openness of many Southerners to straightforward
criticism. Part of this same policy was Washington's careful
avoidance of giving cause for irritation or resentment among
Southern or other white people in the matter of the law and
custom of segregation. Though necessarily involved in white
society in the North, and to a considerable extent even in the
South, Washington sought to avoid giving the impression of
seeking social intercourse with whites, typically refusing invita-
tions to purely social functions or attending doubtful ones without his wife and, we may be sure, wrapped in an aloof, busi-
nesslike dignity.

This policy was saved, not from boot-licking, for only bitter
or ignorant opponents could see that in it, but from a mere

[23] *Selected Speeches*, pp. 6–7.
[24] *Up From Slavery*, p. 201.

calculation about how to retain the co-operation of the Southern whites, by the fact that it was a policy also meant to minister to the whites. Washington is usually represented as a bridge between the white and the Negro communities, a broker making forays into the North and returning laden with money, a few political offices, and good wishes, and making humble explanation to the white South in return for at least bare tolerance and some modest support. For instance, Gunnar Myrdal says: "Washington's main motive . . . was accommodation *for a price*. . . . [H]e promised Negro patience, boosted Negro efforts, begged for money for his school and indulgence generally for his poor people."[25] He was a bridge, but he bargained with the whites not only for money and support for the Negro but also for the sake of the white's own souls. One of the remarkable characteristics of Washington is the extent to which he succeeded in living as well as mouthing the rule "that I would permit no man, no matter what his colour might be, to narrow and degrade my soul by making me hate him."[26] He knew the hates and hurts of racial difference and strife; but he succeeded where so many other Negro leaders and writers have tried but failed, in wiping away all traces of bitterness and its accompanying corruption. Perhaps this was easier for Washington, who had experienced, even though as a mere child, the emergence from slavery into freedom, than it was for a man like Du Bois, born and reared in New England and scarcely part of the people he sought to lead; or for Walter White whose features and complexion permitted him to live in both worlds; or for the other members of the Negro elite, largely Northern-born and Northern-educated, far from slavery yet not free of it. One of Washington's aims, indeed, was to keep alive that recollection of slavery, the source of the American Negro's instruction in and contribution to American freedom.

It was the school of slavery that gave Washington his deep understanding of and sympathy for the burden of the whites— a burden of guilt for past wrongs; of fears for the future, reasonable and unreasonable; of hate and prejudice. He took care not to add to that burden unnecessarily and to lighten it when he

[25] Gunnar Myrdal, *An American Dilemma: The Negro Problem and Modern Democracy* (New York: Harper & Brothers, 1944) , p. 726.

[26] *Up From Slavery*, p. 165.

could. Washington did not give major emphasis to the wrongs done to Negroes, not fundamentally out of prudent reticence, but because Negroes were not the sufferers of the deepest wrong. It is on the side of the masters that the net disadvantage of slavery is to be countd. Through slavery, the Negro found or had thrust upon him freedom and civilization; his master betrayed them. And the price continues to be paid. The most harmful effect, Washington reiterated, of Southern efforts to deprive the Negro of the ballot is not the wrong done to the Negro, which is temporary (and which, like slavery itself, may prove a net advantage by forcing the Negro to give his attention to more lasting methods of betterment) but in the permanent injury to the morals of the white man. In possession of this understanding, Washington could urge the ignorant black, bruised and maimed by the white man's boot, to let his heart go out to his tormentor, who condemned himself to stay in the ditch in order to keep the black man there. If the white man's guilt is greater, so is his hurt, because his contact with the black tends to pull him down, whereas the black can scarcely do anything but rise. But in his rise, Washington thought, he can help the white man up.

Speaking in Chicago on the duty owed by "the great and prosperous North" to "your less fortunate brothers of the white race South who suffered and are still suffering the consequences of American slavery," Washington spoke of Our New Citizen.

> Surely, surely, if the Negro, with all that is behind him, can forget the past, you ought to rise above him in this regard. When the South is poor you are poor, when the South commits crime you commit crime, when the South prospers you prosper. There is no power that can separate our destiny. Let us ascend in this matter above color or race or party or sectionalism into the region of duty of man to man, American to American, Christian to Christian. If the Negro who has been oppressed, ostracized, denied rights in a Christian land, can help you, North and South, to rise, can be the medium of your rising to these sublime heights of unselfishness and self-forgetfulness, who may say that the Negro, this new citizen, will not see in it a recompense for all that he has suffered and will have performed a mission that will be placed beside that of the lowly Nazarine?

Let the Negro, the North, and the South do their duty with a new spirit and a new determination during this, the dawning of a new century, and at the end of fifty years a picture will be painted—what is it? A race dragged from its native land in chains, three hundred years of slavery, years of fratricidal war, thousands of lives laid down, freedom for the slave, reconstruction, blunders, bitterness between North and South. The South staggers under the burden; the North forgets the past and comes to the rescue; the Negro, in the midst, teaching North and South patience, forbearance, long-suffering, obedience to law, developing in intellect, character and property, skill and habits of industry. The North and South, joining hands with the Negro, take him whom they have wronged, help him, encourage him, stimulate him in self-help, give him the rights of man, and, in lifting up the Negro, lift themselves up into that atmosphere where there is a new North, a new South—a new citizen—a new republic.[27]

The most famous expression of Washington's accommodation to segregation is his speech at the Atlanta Exposition in 1895: "In all things that are purely social we can be as separate as the fingers, yet one as the hand in all things essential to mutual progress." "The wisest among my race understand that the agitation of questions of social equality is the extremest folly, and that progress in the enjoyment of all the privileges that will come to us must be the result of severe and constant struggle rather than of artificial forcing."[28] These statements, called by Myrdal "the makeshift compromise with white society in the South,"[29] have been often discussed and criticized as leading to the strengthening of segregation. Justice Brown's opinion in the notorious Supreme Court case of *Plessy* v. *Ferguson,* which came the next year, does represent the judicial stamp of approval on the Washington policy. To avoid misunderstanding, even at the cost of straying for a bit from the immediate question, let me state what I understand to be the rationale of the *Plessy* decision and of Washington's policy.

[27] *Selected Speeches,* pp. 47–50.
[28] *Ibid.,* pp. 34–36. This speech is also printed in *Up From Slavery,* pp. 218–25.
[29] *An American Dilemma,* p. 641.

The School of Slavery

First, it is not a violation of the equal protection clause of the Fourteenth Amendment—or of any standard of good law—for the law to make discriminations, provided they are reasonable, provided, that is to say, they are reasonably related to some legitimate end of the law. One legitimate end of the law is to preserve the peace and order and to promote the general convenience of the community. Distinctions of race may be reasonably related to such ends, as for example where two races (or two generally discernible groups of people) possessing significantly different habits (however caused) with respect to, say, hygiene, social behavior, and criminality, come into contact. Given conditions in the South forty years after emancipation, it was not unreasonable to require segregation of the races in certain public places. It may not have been necessary or even wise, but it was not unreasonable; that is, an argument can be made for it that would have weight in the mind of an intelligent, informed, and unbiased man.[30]

Second—and now I enter into interpretation and attribute a silent argument or assumption to Justice Brown which I concede is open to debate—it may be admitted that in practice the "separate" facilities are not likely to be "equal." Nor is that inequality without some reason, for the specific relations being regulated are those between a superior and an inferior race, not intrinsically but in fact. Nevertheless, the standard of the law must be equality (and the standard of equality was set, not by the Supreme Court, but by the Louisiana statute, which put "equal" before "separate"). Whenever the law touches the actual conditions, it moves them in the direction of equality, not the equality of men, because that the law cannot provide, but the

[30] The fact that Jim Crow legislation was fairly late in coming is certainly relevant but it does not prove its unreasonableness or even that it was not a response to a deeply felt and legitimate need. A regulation of the relations between the races (if that be granted to be a legitimate end) at one time by the force of economic and political and moral superiority of one race might not suffice at another time when the progress of the second race had been sufficient to threaten the old methods of regulation but not yet sufficient to abolish the need for regulation. I repeat: it is not necessary to this argument that these Jim Crow regulations should have been wise or necessary (Washington argued that they were neither); it is only necessary that such an argument might have been seriously made by a reasonable man. See Booker T. Washington, "My View of Segregation Laws," *The New Republic,* December 4, 1915, pp. 113–14.

equality of civil rights: that platform on which every man in the United States is entitled to a place in his stretching out for true freedom.

Third, when Justice Brown says that if enforced separation is regarded as stamping the colored race with a badge of inferiority, "it is not by reason of anything found in the act, but solely because the colored race chooses to put that construction upon it"[31]—a remark so often subject to derision today and (rightly) put in contrast with Chief Justice Warren's reasoning in *Brown* v. *Board of Education* (1954) —he was, I believe, not purporting to state the literal fact of the case but the higher truth of it. The literal fact is, as argued above, that the law finds its reason in an actual (although not inherent) inferiority and in that sense is a stamp of inferiority. The higher truth may be seen by comparing the reactions to segregated travel of Martin Luther King and Frederick Douglass. King reports that the first time he was seated behind a curtain in a dining car, "I felt as if the curtain had been dropped on my selfhood." He could never "adjust" to separate accommodations, not only because the separation was always unequal, but "because the very idea of separation did something to my sense of dignity and self-respect."[32] Washington reports that Frederick Douglass told how he was traveling in Pennsylvania and was forced to ride in the baggage car, despite having paid the same fare as other passengers. Upon receiving apologies for being "degraded in this manner" from some of the white passengers, "Mr. Douglass straightened himself up on the box upon which he was sitting, and replied: 'They cannot degrade Frederick Douglass. The soul that is within me no man can degrade. I am not the one that is being degraded on account of this treatment, but those who are inflicting it upon me.' "[33] Such a man is not stamped with inferiority by separate (and manifestly unequal!) accommodations, because he does not choose to put that construction on it.

Finally, neither Justice Brown nor Washington looked upon social integration as an end or even as a necessary means to an

---

[31] 163 U.S. 551 (1896).

[32] Martin Luther King, Jr., *Stride Toward Freedom: The Montgomery Story* (New York: Harper & Row, 1958), pp. 20–21.

[33] *Up From Slavery*, p. 100.

end; they both reject the argument "that equal rights cannot
be secured to the negro except by an enforced commingling of the
two races."[34] It is for this reason that Washington is often criticized. Admittedly, it is said, Washington did well enough for
his time, but he tended to ignore and to obstruct others who
wanted to hold up before Negroes the great end or ideal, which
is a world without race-consciousness and willing, even anxious,
to accept each man as an individual. As Dr. King says, "our
ultimate goal is integration which is genuine intergroup and
interpersonal living."[35] Washington was indeed silent about this
great ideal, or only spoke to deny that the Negro hankered to
mingle socially with whites. "I have never at any time asked or
expected that any one, in dealing with me, should overlook
or forget that I am a Negro."[36] He took the sensible view that
racial differences and racial feelings would continue for as long
as men could foresee, and perhaps did not even wholly deserve
being wiped out. The problem was not to obliterate a sense of
racial difference, surely not by forcing one race on another, but
to enable the races to live side by side in peace and mutual
assistance. That would require some separation, as it required
some integration. Above all, Washington refused to accept social
integration as an end or even as a major means, because he saw
that it would be fatal to the dignity of the Negro if he were to
measure—as the standard of social integration inevitably encouraged him to measure—his own manhood (or "selfhood") according to the degree of his acceptance into every phase of white
society.

Two major obstacles stood and stand between the status
actually held by the American Negro and the status that he
ought to enjoy: his own deficiencies and the unwillingness of his
white fellows to admit him to his rightful place. Washington
argued that both of these handicaps harmed both groups, that
both required sympathetic understanding to be overcome, that
the Negro's opportunity and duty lay mainly in overcoming the

[34] 163 U.S. 551 (1896).
[35] *Stride Toward Freedom*, p. 220.
[36] Booker T. Washington, *My Larger Education* (Garden City, N.Y.:
Doubleday, Page & Co., 1911), p. 49.

former, and that in doing that he would go far to help to overcome the latter.

> There is but one salvation for our country, and that is obedience to law, whether this law relates to human life, to property, or to our rights as citizens. For us, however, in our present condition, I believe that our greatest hope for salvation and uplift is for us to turn our attention mainly in the direction of progressive, constructive work. Let construction be our motto in every department of our lives North and South. Pursuing this policy, we will convince the world that we are worthy of the best treatment.[37]

While often reminding his audiences, colored and white, that there was neither justice nor policy in depriving the Negro of basic civil rights and the qualified Negro of political rights, he consistently and more emphatically tried to turn the Negro's attention from rights withheld to rights unwisely exercised or poorly prepared for, from limited opportunities to neglected opportunities, from social discrimination to social misbehavior. The protesters argued that the whites did the Negro a double wrong, causing his present situation and then blaming him for it. The NAACP insisted, in an early declaration, that the responsibility for the conditions of the Negro "rests chiefly upon the white people of the United States [and] that it is their duty to change them. . . ."[38] "If they accuse," Du Bois argued bitterly, "Negro women of lewdness and Negro men of monstrous crime, what are they doing but advertising to the world the shameless lewdness of those Southern men who brought millions of mulattoes into the world? . . . Suppose today Negroes do steal; who was it that for centuries made stealing a virtue by stealing their labor?"[39] Washington did not deny these facts—they are undeniable—but he quietly insisted upon what is also a fact, that "in spite of all that may be said in palliation, there is too much crime committed by our people in all parts of the country. We should let the world understand that we are not going to hide crime simply because it is committed by black people."[40] The

[37] Selected Speeches, p. 207; cf. Booker T. Washington, Working With the Hands (New York: Doubleday, Page & Co., 1904), pp. 245–46.
[38] The Crisis, May, 1911, p. 24.
[39] Washington and Du Bois, The Negro in the South, pp. 181–82.
[40] Selected Speeches, p. 237.

task of Negro leadership, in Washington's view, was to hold the Negro American rather than the white American to the American standard, or rather to hold the white American to the American standard by holding the Negro to it.

The chief instrument of this task of leadership was the program of "industrial education," which Washington himself had learned, broom in hand, at the Hampton Institute. During Reconstruction, Washington says, two ideas agitated the minds of colored people, a desire to hold public office and a craze to learn Latin and Greek (both of which passions also gripped Washington). The instincts of the colored people toward the higher regions of freedom could scarcely have been better; their preparation for reaching them could not easily have been worse. One of the saddest things Washington saw traveling through Alabama when he first came to Tuskegee in 1881 was "a young man, who had attended some high school, sitting down in a one-room cabin, with grease on his clothing, filth all around him, and weeds in the yard and garden, engaged in studying a French grammar."[41] Du Bois, the defender of higher education and the higher life, insisted, in some of his most powerful early writing against the Tuskegee movement, on "the rule of inequality:— that of the million black youth, some were fitted to know and some to dig; that some had the talent and capacity of university men, and some the talent and capacity of blacksmiths. . . ."[42] Washington and Du Bois agreed, of course, that both industrial education and higher education were needed, but Washington emphasized, with a wisdom Du Bois appreciated only later, the need to put first things first. Here as elsewhere Washington took the responsibility, which the protesters shun, of stating priorities: "Where the want of time and money prevents this broader culture (and a choice must be made by most), let us choose to give the student that training in his own language, in the arts and sciences that will have special bearing on his life and will thus enable him to render the most acceptable worship to God and the best service to man."[43] There is no need to deny Du Bois's affirmation (Washington emphatically asserted it) that "life [is]

[41] *Up From Slavery,* p. 122.
[42] *The Souls of Black Folk,* p. 84.
[43] *Selected Speeches,* pp. 18–19.

more than meat, and the body more than raiment"[44] to come to the conclusion that the Negro would be predominantly concerned for many years with food and clothing.

Washington's argument, then, was that the Negro was at the bottom and that his education had to begin there. He had to prepare to meet conditions as they were, to make a living, to learn the dignity of labor. He was building the foundations of his civilization so that later he might erect noble arches and elegant spires or study those put up by others. While insisting that as the industrial condition of a race improved, in the same degree its intellectual, moral, and religious life would improve, Washington did not take this to be an automatic process. He was in fact constantly exhorting Negroes to remember that material improvement was only the first step, and no pupil at Tuskegee, no member of the National Negro Business League (which he organized), no Negro within the range of his influence was allowed to forget it. It can certainly be said of Washington's program that it ran the risk of having people fix their attention on material comforts at the expense of higher things —it is hard to see how that risk could have been avoided under the circumstances. But it is unmerited to imply that Washington was careless in guarding against such a result or that he ever tacitly encouraged it. Du Bois's allegation that Washington's program was "a gospel of Work and Money to such an extent as apparently almost completely to overshadow the higher aims of life"[45] will not stand up to a fair examination of what Washington said and what he did.

Those who criticize Washington's industrial education on the grounds that it was intended to make the Negro a permanent peasant preoccupied with material things or that it did not keep pace with the onrush of the industrial revolution too often forget that, despite its name, industrial education was not merely or even basically a system of technical training.[46] It was

[44] *The Souls of Black Folk*, p. 94.

[45] *Ibid.*, p. 50.

[46] Washington did sometimes call his system "industrial training." On the relation between training and education and the liberating effects of good vocational training, see *Working With the Hands*, p. 82 and *passim*. This volume is a sequel to *Up From Slavery* and contains a more detailed description of Washington's educational program.

aimed at the intellectual and moral improvement of the Southern Negroes, beginning where they were; it was the vehicle for instruction in the rudiments of civilization and true freedom. The goal, Washington reiterated, was to educate the hand, the head, and the heart. Washington taught skills and the love of labor, not only because his pupils needed to earn a living, but "for the independence and self-reliance which the ability to do something which the world wants done brings."[47] He taught neatness and personal cleanliness, the latter carried to such lengths that he insisted on his daily bath even under the most awkward circumstances, thus teaching those around him the value of the bath, "not only in keeping the body healthy, but in inspiring self-respect and promoting virtue."[48] He taught and vigorously insisted on the use of the toothbrush in the belief that "there are few single agencies of civilization that are more far-reaching."[49] He taught system, order, and regularity, and Tuskegee was operated according to a strict discipline. "A race or an individual which has no fixed habits, no fixed place of abode, no time for going to bed, for getting up in the morning, for going to work; no arrangement, order, or system in all the ordinary business of life, such a race and such an individual are lacking in self-control, lacking in some of the fundamentals of civilization."[50]

Washington aimed to start "the Negro off in his new life in a natural, logical, sensible manner instead of allowing him to be led into temptation to begin life in an artificial atmosphere without any real foundation."[51] Civilization begins with the things of most immediate importance, food, clothing, and shelter; it extends to skills, trade, commerce; and it leads finally to the broadest and most complete knowledge of the arts and sciences. The oft-told story of the rise of Tuskegee was meant to illustrate this natural development. "All the industries at Tuskegee have been started in natural and logical order, growing out of the needs of a community settlement. We began with farming, because we wanted something to eat." With few ex-

[47] *Up From Slavery*, p. 74.
[48] *Ibid.*, p. 58.
[49] *Ibid.*, p. 75.
[50] From a talk to the students of Tuskegee, quoted in Scott and Stowe, *Booker T. Washington*, p. 231.
[51] Washington and Du Bois, *The Negro in the South*, p. 51.

ceptions the buildings were reared by the students themselves, and although they were often crude and defective, "I felt that it would be following out a more natural process of development to teach them how to construct their own buildings." "It means a great deal, I think, to start off on a foundation which one has made for one's self."[52]

This same idea of a natural development was involved in Washington's emphasis on the soil as the place for Negroes, or for most Negroes. It was not merely that most Negroes were in fact on the soil, for Washington might have urged them to get into the towns (and into the North), as Du Bois and others did. He thought that the Negro was better off on the land; and he said of the aimless, foolish, foppish Negroes that he had observed in Washington that he wished he could remove the bulk of them "into the country districts and plant them upon the soil, upon the solid and never deceptive foundation of Mother Nature, where all nations and races that have ever succeeded have gotten their start,—a start that at first may be slow and toilsome, but one that nevertheless is real."[53] Washington thought that the Negro was at his best in the rural districts and at his worst in the cities, and the great migration from the former to the latter does not itself disprove this judgment. It is not correct, as John Hope Franklin claims, that Washington "failed to see . . . that the industrial urban community was infinitely more attractive to Negroes as well as to whites."[54] He saw that quite well, but he thought that it was a superficial and harmful attraction which it was the duty of a Negro leader to resist. Perhaps it is true, as Franklin suggests, "that nothing represented more vividly the Negro's reflection of a typical American reaction than his inclination to move from the country to the city in the late nineteenth and early twentieth centuries," but Washington's point was that the Negroes were not typical Americans but unusually primitive and inexperienced ones and unusually open to the harmful effects of the products of high industrial civilization.

It may be, of course, that the pull of economic forces was

[52] *Up From Slavery*, pp. 138, 149, 162, and *passim*.

[53] *Ibid.*, p. 90.

[54] John Hope Franklin, *From Slavery to Freedom: A History of American Negroes* (New York: Alfred A. Knopf, 1947), p. 390.

so strong that the Negro was inevitably drawn to the cities and to the North, quite apart from what men like Washington or Du Bois might do to discourage or encourage him. In any case it is clear that, in general, the Negro today cannot be remade into a simple country toiler, even if that were desirable. Yet insufficient as the old Tuskegee system is now in its details, the principles of that education are as relevant in, say, Chicago or Washington, D.C., today as they were in Alabama a half century and more ago. "There is no position, however high, in science, or letters, or politics, that I would withhold from any race, but I would have the foundation sure."[55]

"After Emancipation," Du Bois writes, "it was the plain duty of some one to assume [the] group leadership and training of the Negro laborer," and Du Bois means that it was the duty of someone *other* than the Negro, as unquestionably it was.[56] It is characteristic that Washington was less concerned to point to the unfulfilled duties of others in the past than to discover and to take up the present duties of himself and his race.

> We have a right in a conservative and sensible manner to enter our complaints, but we shall make a fatal error if we yield to the temptation of believing that mere opposition to our wrongs, and the simple utterance of complaint, will take the place of progressive, constructive action, which must constitute the bedrock of all true civilization. The weakest race or individual can condemn a policy; it is the work of a statesman to construct one.[57]

Did Washington ask the Negro to carry a burden that was too heavy for him? Perhaps he did. Was it any wonder that

[55] *Selected Speeches*, p. 45. Discussing a student's commencement oration on cabbages, Washington says: "As a matter of fact, there is just as much that is interesting, strange, mysterious, and wonderful; just as much to be learned that is edifying, broadening, and refining in a cabbage as there is in a page of Latin. There is, however, this distinction: it will make very little difference to the world whether one Negro boy, more or less, learns to construe a page of Latin. On the other hand, as soon as one Negro boy has been taught to apply thought and study and ideas to the growing of cabbages, he has started a process which, if it goes on and continues, will eventually transform the whole face of things as they exist in the South to-day." *My Larger Education*, pp. 142–43.
[56] *The Souls of Black Folk*, p. 168.
[57] *Selected Speeches*, p. 98.

many Negroes, bewildered and sorely tried, screamed out their bitterness and demanded their legal rights, and even more than their legal rights, often regardless of the consequences? It was not. Yet when the harsh words have been said, when the blame is assigned, when many rights have been granted and are actually enjoyed, Washington's soft, tough words still speak. Opportunities are limited. How well have we used those that are open? Rights are still curtailed. Have we prepared to exercise those we have? The Negro is blamed for too much of American crime. Are we nevertheless responsible for too much of it? The Negro is less than completely free. Do we know what freedom is? The Negro is a second-class citizen. Are we fit for first-class citizenship? The Negro can find deficiencies, in these respects and countless others, in every phase of American life, but his own deficiencies are not one whit removed by pointing out those of others. The Negro can serve himself, as he can serve his country, only by learning and thereby teaching the lesson that Theodore Roosevelt said was "more essential than any other, for this country to learn, . . . that the enjoyment of rights should be made conditional upon the performance of duty."[58]

In a speech in 1903, on the occasion of the birthday of George Washington, Booker Washington drew, as he often did, upon the history of the United States and the Negro's servitude and freedom in it to teach the meaning of freedom. Raising the question, "What is liberty for a race, and how is it to be obtained?" he warned against superficial or apparent freedom, the play that the child thinks is freedom, the spending that one man, the debauchery that another, the loafing that still another, mistakes for freedom.

> And so, all through human experience, we find that the highest and most complete freedom comes slowly, and is purchased only at a tremendous cost. Freedom comes through seeming restriction. Those are most truly free today who have passed through great discipline. Those persons in the United States who are most truly free in body, mind, morals, are those who have passed through the most severe training—are those who have exercised the most patience and, at the same time, the most dogged persistence and determination.[59]

[58] Preface to Scott and Stowe, *Booker T. Washington,* p. x.
[59] *Selected Speeches,* pp. 108–11.

The School of Slavery

The Negro's problem is to transform the restrictions and the discipline that were and are imposed upon him into the inner restrictions and discipline of the truly free man—to learn to work, Washington often said, having in the past only been worked. "It is a mistake," Washington said elsewhere, "to assume that the Negro, who had been a slave for two hundred and fifty years, gained his freedom by the signing, on a certain date, of a certain paper by the President of the United States. It is a mistake to assume that one man can, in any true sense, give freedom to another. Freedom, in the larger and higher sense, every man must gain for himself."[60] There is, as Washington said, "nothing new or startling in this. It is the old, old road that all races that have got upon their feet and have remained there have had to travel."[61]

It was more than a policy of making the best of a bad situation that led Washington to stress, again and again, the advantages of having difficult obstacles to overcome, for that was intrinsic to his basic teaching about the nature of freedom. Here again, Washington found an ironical but real advantage to the Negro in his very disadvantages. "With few exceptions, the Negro youth must work harder and must perform his tasks even better than a white youth in order to secure recognition." The protester sees the unfairness of such a situation; Washington saw its high opportunity. "But out of the hard and unusual struggle through which he is compelled to pass, he gets a strength, a confidence, that one misses whose pathway is comparatively smooth by reason of birth and race."[62] No doubt it is true that the training in civilization offered the Negro by his hard and unfriendly environment is only to be won by extraordinary patience, persistence, and labor. Many individuals, and perhaps the whole race, will succumb—and no one can blame them. Nevertheless, Washington's conclusion is hardly avoidable: "Standing as I do today before this audience, when the very soul of my race is aching, is seeking for guidance as perhaps never before, I say deliberately that I know no other road. If I knew how to find more speedy and prompt relief, I should

[60] *The Story of the Negro*, II, 47–48.
[61] *Selected Speeches*, p. 111.
[62] *Up From Slavery*, p. 40. See *My Larger Education*, pp. 1–7 and *passim*.

77

be a coward and a hypocrite if I did not point the way to it."[63]

But does not Washington simplify? Doubtless he does; he was speaking to and for a simple people. But his simplification, particularly when taken with his actual policy, points more surely to the truth than those of the protesters. Du Bois contends that "in a world where it means so much to take a man by the hand and sit beside him, to look frankly into his eyes and feel his heart beating with red blood; in a world where a social cigar or a cup of tea together means more than legislative halls and magazine articles and speeches,—one can imagine the consequences of the almost utter absence of such social amenities between estranged races, whose separation extends even to parks and streetcars."[64] Washington would argue that the importance that this world, to which Du Bois and his successors accommodate themselves, attaches to sentimental social good fellowship is an indication of the extent to which this world has lost its sense of priority. Martin Luther King, for example, says of the Negroes of Montgomery, Alabama:

> Their minds and souls were so conditioned to the system of segregation that they submissively adjusted themselves to things as they were. This is the ultimate tragedy of segregation. It not only harms one physically but injures one spiritually. It scars the soul and degrades the personality. It inflicts the segregated with a false sense of inferiority, while confirming the segregator in a false estimate of his own superiority.[65]

It was the allegedly lamblike and submissive Washington who, a half century ago, stated what is surely the only manly response to this complaint:

> Character, not circumstances, makes the man. It is more important that we be prepared for voting than that we vote, more important that we be prepared to hold office than that we hold office, more important that we be prepared for the highest recognition than that we be recognized.[66]

[63] *Selected Speeches*, p. 111.
[64] *The Souls of Black Folk*, p. 185.
[65] *Stride Toward Freedom*, p. 37.
[66] *Selected Speeches*, p. 76.

The School of Slavery

The hardships and injustice faced by the Negro in America are not tragic or even exceptional. "On the contrary, they are common, and every race that has struggled up from a lower to a higher civilisation has had to face these things. They have been part of its education."[67] There was for Washington no tormented introspection; no fondling of his psychological hurts; no wallowing, now in pride, now in shame, in the mysteries within the "Veil" of color; no self-conscious, self-pitying search for "identification." Washington had no need to repudiate white civilization, because he saw that, with all its faults, it *is* civilization; he had no need to repudiate his Negro heritage, because he saw in it a source of strength with which he and other Negroes might enter into civilization, earn the higher freedom, and through their example even help their former masters to recover it. It is not Washington who is the accommodationist.

It is much, perhaps it is too much, to ask the Negro to set himself as an example of devotion to duty, when his fellow Americans clamor for rights. It is much to ask the Negro to affirm that dignity and self-respect are not within the gift of any man or any law and to deny that a man consists of his psychological reactions to the psychological prejudices of those around him, when more and more whites look for themselves in the opinions of others. It is much to ask the Negro leader to teach his own people that a man is, finally, responsible for himself, when the other members of his society hanker to place the responsibility elsewhere. That is what Washington asked and taught. Could any lesson more noble or more needed issue from the school of slavery?

[67] *The Story of the Negro*, I, 15.

JAMES BALDWIN

●

THE WHITE PROBLEM*

I should say two things before I begin. One: I beg you to hold somewhere in the center of your mind the fact that this is a centennial year, that we are celebrating, this year, one hundred years of Negro freedom. Two: we are speaking in the context of the Birmingham crisis. And in this attempt to speak to you, I am going to have to play entirely, as they say, by ear. I want you to reconsider, or really to listen to, for the first time, the last two lines of an extremely celebrated song, as though you were an actor, and you were on the stage, under the necessity to deliver Hamlet's soliloquy, "To be or not to be," etc., as though these lines had never been heard before. These two lines could be considered extremely corny, but I ask you to take them seriously. They are a question. The two lines I want you to pretend you are delivering on some stage, somewhere in the world, as though these lines had never been heard before, are these:

> Oh, say, does that star-spangled banner still wave
> O'er the land of the free and the home of the brave?

And now please try to make a certain leap with me. I have one more quotation I want to give you, which comes from Nietzsche—it has been on my mind all week long. At some point, the man says:

> I stand before my highest mountain, and before my
> longest journey, and, therefore, must I descend deeper
> than I have ever before descended.

There are several thousand things one must attempt to suggest, due to the context in which we are speaking. In the

* Adapted by the author from a speech made in Los Angeles, May 10, 1963. Copyright © 1963 by James Baldwin.

life of a woman, in the life of a man, in anybody's life, there are always many elements at work. The crucial element I wish to consider here is that element of a life which we consider to be an identity; the way in which one puts oneself together, what one imagines oneself to be; for one example, the invented reality standing before you now, who is arbitrarily known as Jimmy Baldwin. This invented reality contains a great number of elements, all of them extremely difficult, if not impossible, to name. The invented reality has struck a certain kind of bargain with the world: he has a name, we know what he does, and we think, therefore, that we know who he is. But it is not that simple. The truth, forever, for everybody, is that one is a stranger to oneself, and that one must deal with this stranger day in and day out, that one, in fact, is forced to create, as distinct from invent, oneself. Life demands of everyone a certain kind of humility, the humility to be able to make the descent that Nietzsche is talking about.

Life does not offer one as many choices as one would like to believe. In my life, and in your life, too, I am sure, when young one supposes that there is some way to avoid disaster. Let me try to spell that out a little. When I was a little boy, for example, I used to tell my mother, "I'm going to do this, I'm going to do that, I'm going to go here and I'm going to go there. I'm going to be a writer—I'm going to *do, do, do, be* this." Mama would look at me and say, "It's more than a notion."

It took me a long time, a very long time, to begin to realize that she was right, and begin to realize what she meant. I, like all of us, thought I knew what I wanted, and I thought I knew who I was, and—like all of us—I thought that whatever it was I wanted and wherever I wanted to go, I could achieve without paying my dues. For one of the things that one cannot imagine, especially when one is young, is how to pay your dues. You don't even know that there are dues to be paid. Later on, one begins to discover, with great pain, and very much against one's will, that whatever it is you want, what you want, at bottom, must be to *become yourself*: there is nothing else to want. Whatever one's journey is, one's got to accept the fact that disaster is one of the conditions under which you will make it. (The journey, I mean, not "make it" in the American sense.) And you will learn a certain humility because the terms that you have invented, which you think describe and define you, inevitably collide with the facts of life. When this collision occurs—and, make no mistake, this is an absolutely inevitable collision—when this collision occurs, like two trains meeting head-on in a tunnel, life offers you the choice, and it's a very narrow choice, of holding on to your definition of yourself, or saying, as the old folks used to say, and as everybody who wants to live has to say: *Yes, Lord.*

Which is to say, Yes, to life. Until you can do that, you've not become a man or a woman. Now, in this country this inability to say, Yes, to life is part of our dilemma, which could become a tragic one; it is part of the dilemma of being what is known as an American. The collective effort until this moment, and the collective delusion until this moment, has been precisely my delusion when I was a little boy, that you could get what you wanted, and become what you said you were going to be, painlessly. Furthermore, if one examines for a second, or if one tries to define the proper noun, *American,* one will discover that the noun equates with a catalogue of virtues, and with something called, plaintively enough, "I-Am-An-American Day." To be an American means, I gather—check me out, you think about it—that, though Greeks, Armenians, Turks, Frenchmen, Englishmen, Scots, Italians, may be corrupt, sexual, unpredictable, lazy, evil, a little lower than the angels, Americans are not. Quite overlooking the fact that the country was settled by Englishmen, Scots, Germans, Turks, Armenians, etc. Every nation under heaven is here, and not, after all, for a very long time.

I think that it might be useful, in order to survive our present crisis, to do what any individual does, is forced to do to survive his crisis, which is to look back on his beginnings. The beginnings of this country (it seems to me a banality to say it, but, alas, it has to be said) have nothing whatever to do with the myth we have created about it. The country did not come about because a handful of people in various parts of Europe said, "I want to be free," and promptly built a boat or a raft and crossed the Atlantic Ocean. Not at all, not at all. In passing, let me remark that the words liberty and freedom are terribly misused words. Liberty is a genuine political possibility, in spite of the fact that the word is so often used as a slogan, and freedom, which as I understand it, is beyond politics, though affecting politics and affected by it, may be the very last thing that people want. The very last thing. Anyway, the people who settled the country, the people who came here, came here for one reason, no matter how disguised. They came here because they thought it would be better here than wherever they were. That's why they came. And that's the only reason that they came. Anybody who was making it in England did not get on the Mayflower. It is important that one begin to recognize this because part of the dilemma of this country is that it has managed to believe the myth it has created about its past, which is another way of saying that it has entirely denied its past. And we all know, I think, what happens to a person who is born where I was born, say, in Harlem, and goes into the world pretending that he was born in Sutton Place. And what happens to a person, however odd this may sound, also happens to a nation, a nation being, when it finally comes into existence, the achievement of the people who make it up. And the quality of the nation being absolutely at the mercy of, defined and dictated by, the nature and the quality of its people.

Let me point, if I may, to another thing, which is really the same thing. The Italian immigrant arriving from Italy, for example, or the son of parents who were born in Sicily, makes a great point of not speaking Italian because he's going to become an American. And he can't bear his parents because they are backward. This may seem a trivial matter. But it is of the utmost importance when a father is despised by his son, and this is one of the facts of American life, and is what we are really referring to, in oblique and terrible fashion, when we talk about upward mobility.

In this extraordinary endeavor to create the country called America, a great many crimes were committed. And I want to make it absolutely clear, or as clear as I can, that I understand perfectly well that crime is universal, and as old as mankind, and I trust, therefore, that no one will assume that I am indicting or accusing. I'm not any longer interested in the crime. People treat each other very badly and always have and very probably always will. I'm not talking about the crime; I'm talking about denying what one does. This is a much more sinister matter. We did several things in order to conquer the country. There existed, at the time we reached these shores, a group of people who had never heard of machines, or, as far as I know, of money—which we *had* heard about. We promptly eliminated them, we killed them. I'm talking about the Indians, in case you don't know what I'm talking about. Well, people have done that for centuries, but I'm willing to bet anything you like that not many American children being taught American history have any real sense of what that collision was like, or what we really did, how we really achieved the extermination of the Indians, or what that meant. And it is interesting to consider that very few social critics, very few, have begun even to analyze the hidden reasons for the tremendous popularity of the cowboy-Indian legend in American life, a legend so powerful that it still, in 1963, dominates the American television screen. I suspect that all those cowboy-Indian stories are designed to reassure us that no crime was committed. We've made a legend out of a massacre. In which connection, if I may digress for a moment, there used to be an old joke going around among Negroes. If you remember the Lone Ranger, he was white, of course, and he had a side-kick called Tonto, an Indian. There's always a good Indian. He rode around with the Lone Ranger, and according to my memory of the story, Tonto and The Lone Ranger ran into this ambush of nothing but Indians. And the Lone Ranger said, "What are we going to do, Tonto?" And Tonto said, "What do you mean, *we?*"

Well, I tell that joke in order to point out something else. It's a Negro joke. One of the other things we did in order to conquer the country, physically speaking, was to enslave the Africans. Now slavery, like murder, is one of the oldest human institutions. So we cannot quarrel about the facts of slavery. That is to say, we could, but that's another story. We enslaved them because, in order to conquer the country, we had to have cheap labor. And the man who is now known as the American Negro, who is one of the oldest Americans, and the *only* one who never wanted to come here, did the dirty work, hoed the cotton —in fact, it is not too much to say that without his presence, without that strong back, the American economy, the American nation, would have had a vast amount of trouble creating that capital of which we are now so proud, and to which we claim Negroes have never contributed anything. If the Negro had not done all that totin' of barges and liftin' of bales, America would be a very different country and it would certainly be a much poorer country.

The people who settled the country had a fatal flaw. They could recognize a man when they saw one. They knew he wasn't, I mean *you can tell,* they knew he wasn't anything *else* but a man; but since they were Christian, and since they had already decided that they came here to establish a free country, the only way to justify the role this chattel was playing in one's life was to say that he *was not* a man. For if he wasn't a man, then no crime had been committed. That lie is the basis of our present trouble. It is an extremely complex lie. If, on the one hand, one man cannot avoid recognizing another man, it is also true then, obviously, that the black man in captivity, and treated like an animal, and told that he was, *knew* that *he* was a man being oppressed by other men who did not even have the courage to admit what they were doing. When the African, in Africa, enslaved other men, he did not pretend that he was merely breaking in oxen.

Let me tell you a small anecdote. I was in Dakar about a year ago, in Senegal, and just off Dakar there is a very small island, which was once the property of the Portugese. It is simply a rock with a fortress; from Africa, it is the nearest point to America. My sister and I went to this island to visit something called The Slave House. The House was not terribly large. It looks a little like houses you see in New Orleans. That's the truth. It's got two stories and a courtyard and a staircase on each side, sweeping stone staircases. I assume that the captains and the slavers lived upstairs; downstairs were the slave quarters. You walked through a kind of archway, very dark, very low, made of stone, and on either side of you were a series of cells, with stone floors and rusted bits of iron still embedded in the walls. This may be my imagination, but it seemed to me that the odor was still there, that I could still smell it. What it must have smelled like, with all those human beings chained together, in such a place. I remember that they couldn't speak to each other because they didn't come from the same tribe. In this corridor, as I say, there are the cells on either side of you, but straight ahead, as you enter the archway, or corridor, is a very much smaller doorway, cut out of the stone, which opens on the sea. You go to the edge of the door, and look down, and at your feet are some black stones and the foam of the Atlantic Ocean, bubbling up against you. The day that we were there, I tried, but it was impossible, the ocean is simply as vast as the horizon, I tried to imagine what it must have felt like to find yourself chained and speechless, speechless in the most total sense of that word, on your way *where?*

There were some French tourists around and I confess that for a moment I almost hit one of them on the head. They wouldn't have known why.

Anyway, it was the black man's necessity, once he got here, to accept the cross; he had to survive, to manage somehow to outwit his Christian master; what he was really facing when he got here was the Bible and the gun. But I'm not complaining about that now, either. What is most terrible is that American white men are not prepared to believe my version of the story, to believe that it happened. In order to avoid believing that, they have set up in themselves a fantastic system of evasions, denials, and justifications, which system is about to destroy their grasp of reality, which is another way of saying their moral sense.

What I am trying to say is that the crime is not the most important thing here. What makes our situation serious is that we have spent so many generations pretending that it did not happen. Ask yourself on what assumptions rest those extraordinary questions which white men ask, no matter how politely. On what assumption rests the question, "Would you let your sister marry one?" It's based on some preoccupation in the minds of white men. God knows I'm not interested in marrying your sister. I mean that. On what assumption, again, rests the extraordinary question, "What does the Negro want?" The question betrays a flight from reality which is absolutely unimaginable: if we weren't dealing with what, in the public mind, is a *Negro*, the question could never be asked, we'd know damn well what he wanted. We know very well that *we* would not like to live the way we compel Negroes to live. Anyone who asks, "What does

the Negro want?" is saying, in another way, that he does not
wish to be told, is saying that he is afraid to change, is afraid
to pay his dues.

Let's go back, for a minute, to where I started. Let's go
back to Nietzsche: *I stand before my highest mountain, and
before my longest journey, and, therefore, must I descend deeper
than I have ever before descended.* And we spoke a little earlier
about the necessity, when the collision between your terms and
life's terms occurs, of saying, Yes, to life. That's the descent. The
difference between a boy and a man is that a boy imagines there
is some way to get through life safely, and a man knows he's
got to pay his dues. In this country, the entire nation has always
assumed that I would pay their dues for them. What it means
to be a Negro in this country is that you represent, you are the
receptacle of, and the vehicle of, all the pain, disaster, sorrow,
which white Americans think they can escape. This is what is
really meant by keeping the Negro in his place. It is why white
people, until today, are still astounded and offended, if, by some
miscalculation, they are forced to suspect that you are not happy
where they have placed you. This is true; and I'm not talking
about the Deep South. People finally say to you, in an attempt
to dismiss the social reality, "But you're so bitter!" Well, I may
or may not be bitter, but, if I were, I would have good reasons
for it: chief among them that American blindness—or cowardice
—which allows us to pretend that life presents no reasons, to say
nothing of opportunities, for being bitter.

In this country, for a dangerously long time, there have
been two levels of experience. One, to put it cruelly, but, I
think, quite truthfully, can be summed up in the images of
Doris Day and Gary Cooper: two of the most grotesque appeals
to innocence the world has ever seen. And the other, subterra-
nean, indispensable, and denied, can be summed up, let us say,
in the tone and in the face of Ray Charles. And there has never
been in this country any genuine confrontation between these
two levels of experience. Let me force you, or try to force you,
to observe a paradox. Though almost all white Americans come
from Europe, Europe understands the American Negro better
than they understand the white American. White Americans find
it extremely difficult to establish any dialogue between themselves

87

and Europeans for the very good reason, no doubt, that they have yet to break into communion with themselves; but black Americans and Europeans know what it is to suffer, and are far beyond any hope of innocence. A bill for the American endeavor to get from the cradle to the grave looking like Eisenhower has now come in.

White people are astounded by Birmingham. Black people aren't. White people are endlessly demanding to be reassured that Birmingham is really on Mars. They don't want to believe, still less to act on the belief, that what is happening in Birmingham (and I mean this, and I'm not exaggerating; there are several thousand ways to kill or castrate a man) is happening all over the country, and has been for countless generations; they don't want to realize that there is not one step, one inch, no distance, morally or actually, between Birmingham and Los Angeles.

Now it is entirely possible that we may all go under. But until that happens, I prefer to believe that since a society is created by men, it can be remade by men. The price for this transformation is high. White people will have to ask themselves precisely why they found it necessary to invent the nigger; for the nigger is a white invention, and white people invented him out of terrible necessities of their own. And every white citizen of this country will have to accept the fact that he is not innocent, because those dogs and those hoses are being turned on American children, on American soil, with the tacit consent of the American republic, those crimes are being committed in your name. Black people will have to do something very hard, too, which is to allow the white citizen his first awkward steps toward maturity. We have, indeed, functioned in this country in precisely that way for a very long time—we were the first psychiatrists here. If we can hang on just a little bit longer, all of us, we may make it. We've got to try. But I've tried to outline what I take to be some of the conditions for our survival.

JAMES FARMER

●

THE NEW JACOBINS AND
FULL EMANCIPATION*

It is a poetic touch of history that the Emancipation centennial
year saw the Negro masses, for whom emancipation had been
fraudulent, spring alive and, to the staccato of marching feet,
demand that the promise of freedom become an immediate and
complete reality. The wakening may have seemed sudden, like
a Birmingham bomb blast, but the century of slumber had all
along been a fitful one and the arousing did not come all at
once.

It came in stages. The abolitionists, Du Bois and the post–
Civil War militants, and the NAACP never ceased nudging a
quiescent people. Another and important stage came in the
spring of 1942. While the "separate but equal" doctrine was very
much alive, and when it was still respectable to seek as a goal
the equalization of segregated facilities and jobs, a new organization came into being. If its nonviolent direct-action methods
have now become the property of animate masses, its beginnings
were small and inauspicious.

A little band of men and women of both races founded
CORE, the Congress of Racial Equality, with characteristic
youthful zeal, "not to make housing in ghettos more tolerable,
but to destroy residential segregation; not to make racial discrimination more bearable, but to wipe it out; . . . effectively
[to] repudiate every form of racism . . . [and to] forge the in-

* The last portion of this essay was begun in jail in Donaldsonville,
Louisiana, after arrest in Plaquemine, Louisiana. It was completed in New
Orleans, following the author's escape by hearse from a lynch mob in Plaque-
mine, on the night of September 1, 1963.

89

strumentalities through which that nationwide repudiation can be effected!"[1]

There was no rejection of already existing groups in the formation of CORE. It was more an affirmation of an unmet need: total individual involvement—and an assertion of a new method: nonviolent resistance and noncooperation. Following Pearl Harbor only by months, it was a wartime development. Almost all of its thirteen founders were pacifists, and the method they fostered was in a way the strategem of conscientious objectors: removal of oneself from support of and participation in a system believed to be evil. In that case it was war; in this case, racial segregation. Tolstoy, Thoreau, and Gandhi had provided the philosophical framework for this brand of principled noncooperation.

The act of not patronizing or being part of segregated facilities, if white, and not allowing oneself to be segregated, if black, was seen as basic. Segregation had persisted so long, reasoned these pioneers, precisely because people who claimed by words to be opposed to it had, in deeds, complied with its requirements and abided by its folkways. Negroes had, in fact, acquiesced, out of fear or conditioning or helplessness. Whites who disliked the system acquiesced, too, for few perceived it within their power to extricate themselves from the social, economic, and cultural web, if, indeed, they were aware of being involved in any web whatever. "How long are you white people going to keep pushing us around?" asked a Negro. "How long are you black people going to let us?" came the reply. It was the testimony of this new group that a widening circle of Negroes would stop "letting them," and a burgeoning band of whites, working with them, would cease, actively or tacitly, being part of the "pushing around" process. Such a bold commitment would, of course, draw reprisals from society, and this band of wartime radicals were prepared to accept, without violence, whatever consequences their actions evoked, and to risk livelihood and lives where necessary in the endeavor.

This was *nonresistance* only in terms of response to attack.

---

[1] Quotation from *Provisional Plans for Brotherhood Mobilization*, a memorandum circulated by the writer in 1941, which served as the basis for the establishment of CORE.

The New Jacobins and Full Emancipation

Along with the Tolstoian negative of noncooperation went an aggressive Gandhian positive of *direct action* as epitomized by the sit-in. Even in the decade of the forties, unheralded CORE sit-ins by small interracial groups removed barriers in restaurants and theaters, amusement places and recreation centers in Chicago, St. Louis, Detroit, Denver, and a dozen other northern cities. The tactic which became widely known in the sixties was hammered out in the forties. And for CORE, nonviolence was precisely that, an effective tactic, a pragmatic method, though for many of its members it was more—a philosophy, a way of life. To require as a basis for membership that we *love* all men, and to seek to build a movement on the practical adherence to that demand would be to try to succeed where all good-will religions have failed. One should have good will toward everyone, including his opponents, said these young pioneers, but if he could not rid himself of hate, at least he must control and discipline and dominate his feelings and avoid overt manifestations of hostility. That was the base ground on which CORE hoped to build a viable movement.

None but the most visionary of the original founders dreamed of a mass movement. Most expected it to remain small, a tight, disciplined cadre of nonviolent shock troops, all wholly involved themselves, not relying on the leaders, the professionals, the technicians, the skilled, the talented, relying only on themselves, on their bodies—sitting, standing, walking, marching, and absorbing whatever abuse might come, and on their dollars—not spending or allowing them to be used where they sustain segregation.

Few thought that so demanding a pact could find many adherents. Those who doubted the appeal of such a movement did not take into account the impact of World War II on the emotions of Negroes who, like other Americans, had sacrificed much in a fight "for freedom" and against the Nazi master race theory. Having helped win that battle, the similar theory back home loomed more intolerable and less impregnable. Nor did they reckon with the cumulative effect of increasing education among Negro youth. The more young men and women learned about themselves and the world and the American creed, the louder became their demands for full emancipation.

Nor could those who in the forties doubted the possibility of mass disobedience to segregation laws and customs have foreseen the impact upon American Negroes of Africa's emergence. As proud black men regained their long-lost freedom, and began to rebuild nations as they strode—with the lone exception of the Congo—unhaltingly, onto the stage of the contemporary history, American Negroes took another look at themselves and had much less dislike for what they saw. No longer were they a folk who had slammed the door on their historical past. Similarly, the future ceased being something too fearful, or too doubtful, to clamor toward.

So after the war Negroes stood prouder than before, angrier than before, and, perhaps, for the first time, held continued patience to be a vice, not a virtue. Angry men walked the streets, shorn of wartime jobs in industry or in the armed forces. They bristled anew at once-accepted insults, after having experienced, actually or vicariously, the relative acceptance of European and Asian lands. They were ready for anything. Frustrations deepened, and violence would have come easily.

Not many had ever heard of CORE or nonviolence. What they lacked was a method. The Montgomery bus boycott and Martin Luther King, Jr., offered that in 1956. Negroes collectively saw Negroes *en masse* sticking together, staying off buses, walking to work or using efficiently organized car pools, enduring hardships and suffering, and, with the aid of federal courts, winning. And they claimed, under King's tutelage, to love their tormentors. It was an impressive performance and people, almost universally, admired the lofty principles which Dr. King advocated. Angry young Negroes, though, were more impressed with the utilitarian method of direct action than with the philosophy of love for one's enemies.

If men everywhere applauded Montgomery, they cheered largely as spectators, saluting the valor of an embattled people and reveling in a forceful new leader. But they themselves, outside of Montgomery, were not yet individually involved.

Wider involvement came with the southern student sit-ins of 1960. Young militants who heretofore had accepted segregation by rote, suddenly called a halt. As their dramatic movement swept across the South, any town where one lived could, and hundreds did, become a nonviolent battleground inviting personal participation. Tens of thousands accepted the invitation—by sitting-in or by going to jail, by picketing or by marching. Hundreds of thousands more all over the nation found a minimal, though decisive, role by doing more than giving money: by withholding patronage from the offending stores, for the movement accidentally and happily had focused on a target of national leverage—the chain stores. This was all quite new and developmentally significant.

CORE's Freedom Rides, a year later, carried the developmental process another step or two. They provided *mobility,* establishing the thesis that where one happens to live in this country sets no boundaries on his responsibility to right wrongs.

The Freedom Rides did more than that: they helped to focus the role of creative conflict and tension in a nonviolent struggle. As every student of social change knows, no entrenched order like segregation ever gives way without conflict. The absence of tension in such an order is the absence of resistance. To put it in the religious terms of Gregory Vlastos: "He who preaches love in a society based upon injustice can purchase immunity from conflict only at the price of hypocrisy." Thus the tension created by the Rides was quite deliberate; the alternative was acquiescence.

Their limitations, in retrospect, were less obvious. No real effort was made, either in advance or simultaneously, to mobilize the Negro populace for support in towns along the route. As a result, the attempt to use a Gandhian "fill the jails" device, relying upon people who had to travel to reach the point of contact, became, through prohibitive expense, somewhat abortive.

Further, while most of the more than three hundred Freedom Riders came out of jail only at the deadline which Mississippi laws set for posting an appeal bond—forty days—none but a handful served their full sentences, which ranged from two to six months. This was a tactical mistake, allowing the Riders to drift out, after the first few weeks, faster than others could ride in. It thwarted the "fill the jails" strategy, even though the city of Jackson did have to rent the Maximum Security Unit at the State Penitentiary to house the overflow from its city and county jails.

The coming out of jail to file appeals also provided Mississippi with a heavy weapon—escalating cash bond requirements—to use against CORE and its Freedom Rides. Needless to say, the Magnolia State wielded that tool with a vengeance, tripling the bond, originally set at five hundred dollars, on each Rider as his case went to appeal.

Such a war of attrition most certainly would have ground the Freedom Rides to a halt short of desegregating anything except, perhaps, a few hearts, had not the positive aspects greatly outweighed the negative. The daring, the drama, the boldness of their challenge to clearly illegal forms of segregation—in seating on the buses and in the terminals—and the hysterical nature of the segregationist response, electrified the nation. The lines of tension on segregation were so tightly drawn, and the issue placed in such clear focus, that the Federal government could not ignore the situation. The Interstate Commerce Commission, responding to a request from the Attorney General, issued an order banning segregation in seating on interstate buses and outlawing racial discrimination in bus terminal facilities used by interstate passengers.

This order, which went into effect on November 1, 1961, had enforcement teeth. CORE test teams, set in motion immediately after the effective date of the ICC order, found compliance the rule rather than the exception. Incidents of non-compliance were confined to southern Georgia, northern Florida, Mississippi, and a part of Louisiana. Affidavits on these exceptions were turned over to the appropriate authorities in the Federal government for action, and in less than two years the pockets of resistance had shrunk, it appears, to less than the full state of Mississippi.

It remained for Birmingham and, before that, its dress rehearsal, Albany, Georgia, to learn from the Freedom Rides' mistakes, and launch massive demonstrations and jail-ins, wholly involving thousands, not hundreds, of Negroes—local citizens, not transients—and mobilizing the respective Negro communities *in toto*. A score of Birminghams followed the first. Birmingham thus set the stage for a full-scale revolt against segregation in this nation. Such a mass movement was possible because of the magic name of Martin Luther King, Jr. It was possible, in a more basic sense, because of an historical merger of two social forces.

What hapened after World War II, or really after Montgomery, was a kind of wedding of two forces, both bred by the war: the means-oriented idealists of pacifistic turn of mind, for whom nonviolence was a total philosophy, a way of life, and the ends-oriented militants, the postwar angry young men who saw in direct action a weapon and viewed nonviolence as a tactic.

Without such a fusion, no revolutionary mass movement could have emerged. Without the young Turks, the movement never could have grown to mass proportions, and without the idealists it could not have developed revolutionary dimensions. The anger of one without the disciplined idealism of the other could have produced only nihilism. Without the indigenous anger of the Negro masses, the idealists, for all their zeal, would have remained largely irrelevant, socially speaking, and would have gone on talking to themselves and whispering through an occasional keyhole to another human heart.

As in any viable marriage, each party speaks much truth to the other. The idealists warn that the ends do not justify the means, and the militants assert with equal validity that means are worthless which do not achieve desired and verifiable ends. Each tempers the other, and out of the creative tension between the two has come a third position which, I believe, more accurately reflects the movement. Nonviolence is neither a mere tactic, which may be dropped on any occasion, nor an inviolable spiritual commitment. It is somewhere between the two—not a philosophy, not a tactic, but a strategy involving both philosophical and tactical elements, in a massive and widening direct action campaign to redeem the American promise of full freedom for the Negro.

This does not mean that all of the hundreds of thousands of Negroes involved in the street campaigns for equality accept nonviolence as strategy or tactic or anything else. It is only the leaders, members, and close associates of the nonviolent movement who accept it in any way as an integral part of the struggle. The masses who now join the determined folks on picket lines

and sit-ins and protest marches share only a new-found willingness to become individually, physically involved and to risk
suffering or jail for common goals. The masses have no commitment to nonviolence, or to any other specific response to abuse
beyond that dictated by the natural desire to be accepted by,
and to conform to the code of, the militants whom they join in
action. Obviously, the urge to conformity is not enough, in and
of itself, to maintain nonviolence through the stresses of a mass
direct action movement. And that, precisely, is the chief tactical
dilemma of today's Freedom Movement.

The nonviolent militants, seeking to mount a revolutionary
force capable of toppling manifest racism, need those folk who
are not yet wedded to nonviolence, who are wedded, indeed,
only to their own fierce indignation. They need them from the
pool halls and taverns as well as from the churches, from the
unemployed and the alienated and the rootless. The entire Negro
community wants now, more than ever before, to become directly
involved in the "revolution." Either they will be involved or they
will, by their separation from it, brand the movement as counter-
feit and ultimately destroy it.

The problem, of course, is to see that they do not destroy
it by their involvement. Small, disciplined groups are easy to
control. Untrained masses are more difficult. Violence used
against us by our opponents is a problem only in so far as it may
provoke counterviolence from our ranks. Thus far, sporadic
incidents of violence, where they have occurred in the movement,
have been contained and have not become a contagion. We have
been lucky, but we cannot afford any longer to leave such a vital
matter to chance. Widespread violence by the freedom fighters
would sever from the struggle all but a few of our allies. It
would also provoke and, to many, justify, such repressive measures as would stymie the movement. More than that, many of
our own nonviolent activists would be shorn away by disen-
chantment. None would profit from such developments except
the defenders of segregation and perhaps the more bellicose of
the black nationalist groups.

Recognition of the problem is half the solution. The other
half lies not in stopping demonstrations, as is often counseled
by those of faint heart or less than whole commitment. To give

ear to such counsel would be, in a real sense, to betray the movement. Cessation of direct action is neither desirable nor possible.

What is possible, as well as desirable, is an expeditious and thorough program of discipline—both internal and external. Internally, the need is for rapid expansion of training for nonviolence in the ranks—classes, institutes, workshops—in every city where the struggle is in process or in preparation. The external requirement calls for a specially trained cadre of monitors for every mass demonstration, to spot trouble before it occurs and either resolve it or isolate it. With a sensitivity to any potential break in the ranks, the monitors must have specialized skills in dealing with the untrained who may join the ranks during action.

Herein, then, lies the answer to the danger of the movement's degeneration into mass violence: tighter discipline within the ranks and trained monitors to police the lines. Needless to say, these new demands upon the movement will be met with dispatch.

Need for Coordination

The second problem in the new militants' struggle for full emancipation is more functional than tactical. There has occurred in the past few years a proliferation, though not a splintering, of direct action organizations of a nonviolent character. In addition to CORE, there is the Southern Christian Leadership Conference of Dr. King, the Student Nonviolent Coordinating Committee, and various unaffiliated local groups, jealous of their autonomy. Such established organizations as the NAACP are also engaging increasingly in direct action. Church groups, too, and professional associations which previously had confined their action to pronouncements, are now "taking to the streets."

All of this strengthens the movement immeasurably. But it also poses a problem. What coordination exists between the groups is largely accidental rather than the product of systematic planning. Nor is there sufficient coordination of program within each organization.

What we have, in essence, is a series of guerrilla strikes, generally unrelated to any totally conceived plan. An effective war cannot be waged in such a manner, nor can a revolution likely be won thus. Guerrilla warfare must have its place, but as part of an over-all plan.

An urgent need at this stage of the struggle, therefore, is for coordinated planning for full-scale nonviolent war against color caste. A revolution which, like Topsy, "just grew," must now submit itself to the rigors of systematization. Spontaneity, the trademark of the 1960 sit-ins, has served its purpose; a thrust in one sector must no longer be unrelated to a push in another. Comprehensive actions need to be fashioned now to fit an over-all conceptualization of the problem. And the only realistic concept of segregation is as a total unity, national rather than sectional, with all aspects being interrelated.

What we do in the South and in the North, for example, should be part of a whole, for though its dimensions and contours may vary from place to place, the institution of segregation has no separate existence anywhere. Without subsidies from both the federal government and northern capital, it could not persist in the South. And were the South not an open sore, pouring northward its stream of deprived human beings, the North could never rationalize and maintain its fool's defense—the *de facto* pattern of segregation. The tentacles of the beast are everywhere, but none of them should be mistaken for the octopus itself.

This essential unity of the problem is beginning to take form in action with a growing clarity. If a lunch counter segregates in Atlanta or a retail store in Oklahoma City fails to hire Negroes in nontraditional jobs, while heretofore they were attacked in isolation, they are now coming to be dealt with in more realistic terms: as parts of chains if such they are. The economic boycott is a far more potent weapon when regional or national leverage can be used.

Action on any incident of discrimination should take its shape from the shape of the power structure or the machinery which controls, influences, or sustains the objectionable practice. Maximum effectiveness cannot be achieved otherwise. When, for instance, southern school bonds are floated to build and maintain segregated schools, they are marketed not in the South, but by brokers in New York, New Jersey, Massachusetts, Pennsylvania, Illinois, and California. Wittingly or unwittingly, northern investors thus provide the fuel to keep southern segregation going. Income from such investments is tax exempt. So, despite the Supreme Court's 1954 decision, the Federal government is providing in this manner a subsidy just as supportive of caste as are its outright grants to schools, hospitals, and services which are segregated. No campaign against segregation which fails to confront the source of funds can even approach adequacy. CORE's current campaign in the North against the sale of southern school bonds is an expression of this broadening perspective of the revolution.

What the New Jacobins demand today is total war to achieve total rights. If there is any word more hated in the struggle than "moderation," it is "tokenism." This revolution exacts from its revolutionists, and requires of its friends and allies, a staunch and thoroughgoing commitment in both motivations and concrete actions. Nothing short of that is acceptable any more. If anyone who fancies himself a supporter or an ally or even a leader does not, in the opinion of the revolutionists, "feel" the movement, does not, in the vernacular, "dig" the struggle in the streets, no amount of words or even good deeds will fully qualify him for the Jacobin's trust. If, on the other hand, he appears to "dig" the movement, but falters before the totality of its demands, then to the people in the streets he is, at best, friction within the revolution's machinery, and at worst a betrayer.

The apparently sudden emergence of the Negro's revolutionary mood has caught many of his erstwhile friends—particularly among labor unionists and liberals—unaware. Conditioned to the easy acceptance under the fluid ground rules of an evolutionary phase, they have not yet adapted to, or fully comprehended, the hard requirements of the new revolutionary stage of the struggle. This is the albatross which folk of good, but incomplete, will now bear. This is the towering human tragedy of the movement.

If the New Jacobins judge their friends harshly, they are even more rigorous in their demands upon themselves and each other. The risks, the dangers, the interminable suffering are commonplace. To face brutality is routine; to court death, prosaic. All of the revolutionists, being human, experience fear to some extent and from time to time, but to yield to human frailty under stress is the supreme disgrace.

These exacting criteria and fearsome demands are not new in human experience. They are new, however, in the Negro's struggle for equality in America. Every war and every revolution asks of its participants similar superhuman qualities of character and nerve and will. But the civil rights revolution here has just got under way. The tough discipline which a few starry-eyed youths imposed upon themselves when CORE was begun in 1942 has now spread and encompasses hundreds of thousands.

The masses of Negroes who are thus involved have thereby achieved a measure of spiritual emancipation with which Lincoln's Proclamation could not possibly have endowed them. The segregation barriers erected in America have, for them, ceased to be an extension of their minds. They are no longer chained to the ancient stereotypes. They do not feel inferior and do not believe that they are, and are no longer comfortable in the confines of the caste. In a word, they have found an imposing dignity.

This new dignity has many manifestations, not the least significant of which is a great and burgeoning sense of individual worth, released, ironically, through a mass movement. In a way it is a rediscovery of the individual in American society. The average American, or for that matter, the average man in any industrial society, feels submerged, powerless, helpless, of no real value, a cog in giant machinery. But in his revolution, the individual Negro has found a new meaning for himself. Formerly little and insignificant persons now, in their own eyes, stand ten feet tall. As one student in Atlanta put it: "I, myself, desegregated that lunch counter on Peachtree Street. Nobody else. Little me. I did it by sitting-in, by walking the picket line, by marching. I didn't have to wait for any big shots to do it for me. I did it myself!" Never will that youth and the many like him see themselves as unimportant again.

Yet, spiritual emancipation, important as it is, is only one small step. Economic, social, political emancipation are the longer steps to come. Jobs, housing, schools, and enfranchisement have largely replaced public places as the main focus of the struggle. A man may feel equal and free within the private chamber of his own heart, but if his job is limited by color instead of ability, if he is not free to live where he chooses, if his children cannot be equally educated, then his freedom is a myth and his equality an illusion.

The Jacobins' activities are opening up jobs previously closed to Negroes. They are cracking barriers in northern housing in a neck and neck race against spreading residential segregation. The mask of hypocrisy has been ripped off northern school segregation, leaving exposed a largely semantic difference between *de facto* and *de jure*. Yet, the realization is growing among the new militants that even when the walls are down, and segregation is ended, the task of full emancipation will not be finished. Because of a hundred years of discrimination, the Negro is a built-in "low man on the totem pole." Even after job discrimination is gone, under normally accepted employment procedures the Negro will most often be starting at the bottom while others are already at the middle or the top. And, due to past educational inequities, even after school segregation is over, he cannot compete on an equal footing in this generation or the next.

What is needed, therefore, is compensatory action to wipe out the deprivations of the past. The rear wheels of an automobile cannot catch up with the front wheels while they are traveling at the same speed.

The responsibility of accelerating the Negro's march to equality does not rest with the Negro alone. This cannot be a sheer bootstrap operation. When a society has crippled some of its people, it has an obligation to provide requisite crutches. Industry has an obligation not merely to employ the best qualified person who *happens* to apply, but to seek qualified Negroes for nontraditional jobs, and if none can be found, to help train them. If two or more applicants with substantially equal qualifications should present themselves, and one of them is a Negro, then he should be given a measure of preference to compensate for the discrimination of centuries.

Beyond that, a remedial education and training program of massive proportions needs to be launched. To accomplish more than a gesture, such a program will require billions of dollars— perhaps three billion a year for a five-year period. Anything less will be tokenism. The only source for funds in such amount is the Federal government.

Perhaps a portion of the money saved by virtue of the

nuclear test ban should thus be used to reclaim a people and a nation. But whether or not the Federal government acts, the New Jacobins will continue their revolutionary thrust. To paraphrase a beaten white Freedom Rider: "We'll take beating. We'll take kicking. We'll take even death. And we'll keep coming till we can ride, work, live, study, and play anywhere in this country —without anyone saying anything, but just as American citizens."

●

VIEW FROM A SOUTHERN EXPOSURE

Lincoln's Preliminary Emancipation Proclamation, put forward on September 22, 1862, was followed by an interim period known simply as the "hundred days." Thereafter, all persons held as slaves in certain designated territories were to be "thenceforward, and forever free."

It is a melancholy exercise to leap forward a full century from that hopeful time, and to inquire what the American Negro, thus symbolically unshackled, has done with his freedom. Where does he stand, a hundred years after the hundred days? The disquieting answer is that he stands where his race has always stood, on a lower rung of a society in which he cannot seem to catch up. I am minded to ask the sobering question: Why?

I

The centennial of Lincoln's hundred days, in the fall of 1962, saw a great many events in the field of American race relations that might be singled out for comment in an anniversary essay. In Prince Edward County, Virginia, the public schools failed to open for the fourth consecutive year. In Georgia, three white men, convicted of burning a Negro church, were sentenced to seven years in prison. At Oxford, Mississippi, 22,000 troops and upwards of 500 Federal deputies put down a riot provoked by the admission of a Negro student to the University of Mississippi. In Greensboro, North Carolina, Gadsden, Alabama, and Baton Rouge, Louisiana, Negroes demonstrated at department stores and lunch counters. In Norfolk, Virginia, a Negro was named an Assistant United States Attorney. In Lumberton, Mississippi, whites and Negroes worked cheerfully side by side to build a new home for an aged Negro couple whose house had burned down. Leontyne Price, the Negro opera singer, came home to Laurel, Mississippi, to a loving reunion with the white friends who had sponsored her career in New York. And in Washington, D.C., on the morning of Thanksgiving Day, 50,000 persons turned out to watch the scholastic championship football game between Eastern High School, a predominantly Negro institution, and St. John's, predominantly white; they came to see a football game, but at the final whistle they saw the ugliest race riot in a generation, as hundreds of Negroes gave vent to emotions that the chairman of an official investigating committee was to sum up in a single shocking word: *savagery*.

Any one of these events in the centennial period might provide a topic for rumination. I write from Virginia; the human and legalistic problems of Prince Edward County are very close to me, but this dismal and keenly regrettable situation offers little that is directly relevant to the subject here at hand. I was in Oxford as a newspaperman, and formed my own conclusions there. The riot could have been avoided by the right kind of planning, and patience, and firmness; and James Meredith's right to admission could have been made peacefully secure.

I should rather begin on that Thanksgiving day in Washington, and work forward and backward from the riot. I pick this starting point, in part at least, because relatively few Americans outside the Washington area seem to have heard much about the riot. The *Saturday Evening Post* carried a full account of the affair some months later, but the story was hushed up at the time; the account that went out on press association wires was progressively condensed as the dispatches were relayed across the country. In Chicago, I am told, some persons read an abbreviated account, and judged that white persons, "as usual," were assaulting defenseless Negroes. *The New York Times,* which regularly gives whole pages to its own correspondents reporting upon racial tensions in the South, primly decided to print from Washington only the news that it saw fit; the *Times* of Friday, November 23, gave the story ten inches on page 25 ("34 Hurt in Riot at the Capital"). The determined reader who got as far as the seventh paragraph might have learned that "witnesses said there was evidence of drinking among the spectators and some indication of racial conflict." The *Times* Index does not list the story under "Negro" or "Washington" or "District of Columbia," but inters it under "Football."

A few days after the riot, Washington's Superintendent of Schools, Dr. Carl F. Hansen, created an *ad hoc* investigating committee with a typically euphemistic title: The Special Committee on Group Activities. As chairman, he named the respected Dr. Shane MacCarthy, a former White House aide (under President Eisenhower) who directed the President's Council on Youth Fitness. Dr. MacCarthy in turn named a ten-member, biracial group that spent five weeks interviewing witnesses, taking testimony, and evaluating the causes.[1]

The game began at eleven o'clock in the morning. For the first three quarters, it appeared to be a clean and hard-fought contest, though a number of fights were reported in the stands and several witnesses agreed that an "air of tension" began to build up as the game went on and Eastern's defeat became evident. In the final quarter, fighting broke out on the playing field when Negro players from Eastern attacked white players from St. John's. Fighting increased in the stands. The MacCarthy Commission reported:

> Immediately after the game was over there was a rush of several thousands of persons from the Eastern stands toward the St. John's stands. Officers reported it was physically impossible to stem the rush. Police officers were ordered to escort the St. John's team and band off the field. Other officers proceeded to exits and ramps where numerous attacks were taking place.
>
> Many officers reported attacks on white persons by Negroes in and out of the stadium and seeing a number of white persons injured. . . . The crowd was yelling, cursing, and generally in wild disorder. Three priests, as yet unidentified, were assaulted by a group of Negroes. One priest was bleeding about the face or head. There were reports of unprovoked attacks on white persons by Negroes. . . .
>
> The disorder and assaults spread northward. The worst of these were at 18th and D Streets, N.E., and 21st Street and Benning Road, N.E. . . . It was re-

[1] The text of the Committee's Report, dated January 8, 1963, may be found in the *Congressional Record* of January 23, 1963, pp. 778–84.

ported that Negro residents of the neighborhood viewed the occurrences as disgraceful. Some of these Negro families opened their homes to white persons to protect them from the mob. . . .

One officer was spit upon. Four were struck by thrown bottles. One was struck on the head by some object.

* * *

Eye Witness Accounts from Letters:

A father wrote:

"During the half, in the men's room, a white boy, about 6 ft., 16 years of age, was slugged about the head by about eight colored youths, about 15–17.

"After the game, coming down the upper ramp, [I saw] a white youth, about 15–16, struck to the ground, and while lying doubled up, kicked many times in the back by a group of colored youths. The boy was crying all the while, and the kicking stopped only when some white people reached that place. The boy had a red St. John's jacket on.

"In the parking lot area, a six-foot St. John's boy, about 160 pounds, wearing a grayish jacket, was getting ready to open his car door. I had two of my children by the hands, and my wife had the other two, and was about 20 yards from the happening. Suddenly, a group of about 10–12 colored youths, about 15 to 20 years of age, apparently spotted this St. John's boy and ran around the particular car and struck the boy in the face. The third or fourth blow struck the boy's jaw on the left side. . . . Many other raining blows followed in quick succession. The boy somehow retained his feet, and then escaped to the area of another car about 20 yards away, all the time holding his jaw. The group of colored youths then took off like a pack of wolves, seeking more prey. . . .

There are twenty-seven closely written pages of such testimony. Before the rioting tapered off an hour later, *upwards of five hundred* persons had been injured. The Committee's report methodically documents the casualties in terms of broken jaws, broken noses, knife and razor cuts, teeth knocked out. All but a handful of the victims were white. "It was a nightmare to decent citizens."

Dr. MacCarthy sent his committee's report to Superintendent Hansen with a covering letter. He spoke of the Negroes' "brutal display of irresponsibility and lack of self-discipline," but commented that "not a single teacher to whom I have spoken in the past few weeks was surprised that the outbreak took place. Uniformly came the response, 'Why should we be? We live with this brand of conduct every day in the schools.'"

All this was written of events in the capital of the United States during the hundredth anniversary of Lincoln's "hundred days" before Emancipation. And both before and after the period, a continuing series of ugly incidents in Washington told the somber story of a great and beautiful city blighted by Negro crime and violence and arrogance.[2] All this, let it be noted, has occurred in a city in which the Negro is petted and pampered, cuddled and coddled, coaxed and encouraged to an extent not witnessed elsewhere in the country. For obvious political reasons, the Negro in Washington has job preference with the Federal government. He enjoys totally integrated public facilities. Millions of dollars are lavished on his public schools, specially staffed to cope with his educational and psychological problems.[3] Every conceivable amenity that might contribute to his good citizenship and well-being is conveniently available to him. Where does the Negro stand a hundred years after Lincoln? There he stood at high noon at D.C. Stadium on Thanksgiving Day, razor in one hand, bicycle chain in the other. *Free!*

II

Is it my purpose to shock? Of course it is. But if I do not dwell fairly at the outset upon some of the constructive accomplishments of individual Negroes—if I tend to overstate a critical view —it is because it seems to me imperative to thrust aside the pretty pastel veils that have been draped over the image of the

[2] For typical accounts, see "The Blight in the Nation's Capital," *U.S. News & World Report*, February 18, 1963, pp. 37–39; a column by Arthur Krock, *The New York Times*, West Coast edition, March 18, 1963; an article by Fletcher Knebel, "Washington, D.C.: Portrait of a Sick City," *Look*, June 4, 1963; and a two-part article by Bill Davidson, "Washington: A City in Trouble," *The Saturday Evening Post*, July 13–20, 1963.

[3] See Hearings Before a Sub-committee of the Committee on Appropriations, House of Representatives, 87th Congress, 2d Session, District of Columbia Appropriations, 1963, pp. 655ff.

American Negro, 1963. Through a combination of pragmatic politics and misplaced humanitarianism, especially in the years since the Supreme Court's decision in the school cases, the Negro has been burdened with more good will than he can comfortably carry. In a sense, this is nothing new:

"I'm not so much throubled about th' naygur whin he lives among his opprissors," said Mr. Dooley, "as I am whin he falls into th' hands of his liberators."

In this same essay from *Mr. Dooley's Philosophy* (1900), the sage of Archer Avenue tells the story of a talented Negro youth who tried to be a lawyer and then a businessman, but wound up by opening a gambling house. Mr. Dooley, brooding about the boy, is troubled by his own conscience and by the attitudes of society toward the Negro generally. He asks himself reflectively what it all will come to.

> "Well, they got to take their chances," said Mr. Hennessy. "Ye can't do anythin' more f'r thim than make thim free."
> "Ye can't," said Mr. Dooley; "on'y whin ye tell thim they're free they know we're on'y sthringin' thim."

When Peter Finley Dunne wrote that ephemeral vignette, Emancipation was only thirty-odd years in the past. To read Mr. Dooley's philosophy in 1963 is to reflect wryly upon the aptness of the adage that the more things change, the more they stay the same. In the hands of his Northern liberators, the Negro all too frequently has been ballooned into a caricature of himself. Outside the South, he is still like Mr. Dooley's talented Andrew Jackson George Washington, etc., Hicks, who could find no place to fit in.

Where has the American Negro come in this hundred years of freedom? That is the purpose of our inquiry here. Plainly he has come a long way; just as plainly, he has not come very far.

Certain gains of the American Negro can be chronicled on every hand; and significantly, many of these are gains of the spirit: The almost inarticulate Negro of 1863 now makes himself heard, politically and economically, in ways he could not have been heard in Lincoln's day. The oppressed and bewildered black man who was the object of this strategic "emancipation" is today a decisive political force. A roster of distinguished Negro

View from a Southern Exposure

writers, lawyers, educators, historians, increases steadily. In one area after another, the Negro, having won rights denied him in the past, now can exercise the privilege of being indifferent to them. In my own city of Richmond, Negroes waged a dramatic fight in 1959 for the privilege of eating at a certain department store lunch counter. After a year of bitterness and boycott, they won. Now they do not eat there. Curious, I asked a Richmond Negro leader why not. "We didn't really want to eat there in the first place," he said. "You can have it." He grinned; and I grinned; and we let the matter slide. The telephone rings at my office. It is a leading Negro real estate broker, calling to discuss the assembling of some property in Richmond's Civic Center area. We chat amiably about what might be done to push a zoning amendment through the Council. So far as I can detect, he is not conscious of the slightest constraint, nor am I. There have been for the Negro, gains of the spirit; gains inside.

Manifestly, the century since Emancipation has brought the American Negro material gains also. Late in 1961, a count found at least twenty-five Negro millionaires.[4] Not merely in the North, but in the poorer South as well, the Negro increasingly is college student, homeowner, automobile owner, conspicuous buyer of "big ticket" items. If Negro income, per capita, still lags behind white medians, it gains; it gains.[5] In the whole world, no people of African descent have matched the material wealth and the economic opportunity of the American branch of the family.

And yet . . . and yet. . . . The pathetic, sobering truth is that by any yardsticks used by Western man for the measurement of a society's advancement, the total of Negro accomplishments is not large. Not in the past hundred years; not in the past ten thousand years. And the way things move these days, even a hundred years is a significantly long time. Forget, temporarily,

---

[4] *The Saturday Evening Post,* January 13, 1962.

[5] In my own city of Richmond, for example, fewer than 7 per cent of the city's Negro families in 1949 had incomes of more than $4,000. By 1959, 40 per cent of them had incomes of more than $4,000. The median income of a Richmond Negro family increased in this decade from $1,565 to $3,387. The picture is substantially the same across the South. A study in *U.S. News & World Report,* July 22, 1963, found that the per capita income of the American Negro is exceeded by per capita incomes in only five countries in the world.

the segregated South, where racial separation existed so long under constitutional sanction. What of the Negro in the North? Why his continuing failure there? Is this to be accounted for solely in terms of an instinctive prejudice—even in areas with an abolitionist tradition of great sympathy toward the Negro?—a prejudice based *entirely* on the color of the Negro's skin? I find this hard to believe.

"Oh, well," said Mr. Hennessy, "we are as th' Lord made us."

"No," said Mr. Dooley, "lave us be fair. Lave us take some iv th' blame oursilves."

The image of the American Negro, a hundred years after Emancipation, seems to me a mixed image, subject to distortions that pull against each other. The unreasoning hostility of some Southern whites, and the indifference or paternalism of others, pull the picture in one direction. And both in the South and outside it, elementary political considerations, augmented by a knee-jerk liberalism that does a terrible disservice to the Negro, combine to twist the image another way. As a consequence, it is all but impossible to stand back and take a fairly critical and dispassionate view of the Negro people of America in the mid–1960's.

Of any other group or class, it may be said, reasonably, that the group or class includes the good, the bad, the indifferent. But the centrifugal force of this controversy has sent us all swirling to the outer edges. A racism in reverse sets in: The television variety show must have a Negro entertainer, not especially because he is a good entertainer, but because he is a good *Negro* entertainer; and the audience must applaud him madly, not because the performance is outstanding, but because a failure to applaud him madly might be interpreted as a manifestation of anti-Negro bigotry. In Washington, racial edicts stream from the White House: Greater efforts must be made to place Negroes in higher clerical and supervisory positions. A number of genuinely qualified Negroes are moved up, but that is not the point. Hundreds of other Negro civil servants, lacking in ability or experience, also are promoted, and the government service suffers. In the course of my work as a newspaperman, I am in and out of Federal offices constantly, and I do not know of a case in which agency heads have not complained of this situation. But they complain of it privately; that is to say, they complain of it behind tightly closed doors; publicly, they profess good cheer.

I wonder about this reverse racism. I wonder what it does to the Negro entertainer, the actor, the writer, the office worker. It may be that after generations of being rejected by reason of race, they find it far better now to be promoted by reason of race. And doubtless the Negroes regard it as better, too, that opportunities for success should now be open, even if the opportunities may be exploited by persons not yet prepared for them. But deep in their hearts, how is this fulsome adulation understood? I wonder, too, what this deception does to the critics, the masters of ceremonies, the employers. What does the book or drama critic think of himself, when he has written six hundred words of rapturous praise for a Negro's work that he knows to be second-rate? Who gains from this?

I no longer wonder greatly about the reaction of the public to this delicate national exercise in self-contempt. I think the public is fed up with it. Unless I am greatly mistaken, there is more race feeling in the United States today—more consciousness of race—than there has been for several generations. And remarkably, the white Southerner, long regarded as the most race-conscious of all Americans, seems to be slipping into new patterns of an old unawareness. (The Oxford riot of September 30, 1962, tends to contradict this impression, but Mississippi remains a world all its own.) The South of course is concerned about the Negro—we ought to be; we live with him more closely, in greater numbers, than most white Americans in the rest of the country—but the joint appraisal of white and Negro, viewing each other, impresses me as a little more honest below the Potomac. When I lecture at Northern universities, the first barb thrown in the bear-baiting period ordinarily goes like this: "Why do you treat the Negro as a second-class citizen?" Sometimes I have responded with parry and riposte: "Because all too often, that is what he is." This sort of gladiatorial exchange does not explain or excuse the South's continuing, and keenly regrettable, and not yet correctable tendency to hold back the Negroes who are first-class men, but the response has the merit of candor.

It is the absence of this candor that, unless I err, is contributing to a growing racial consciousness, or downright racial antagonism, in parts of the United States that had been pre-conditioned in the postwar period to a warm acceptance of the Negro moving North. Beyond the South, the notion had been carefully cultivated that the arriving Negro was just as good, just as talented, just as law-abiding, as anyone else. He might seem a little backward at first, perhaps, by reason of the cruel oppression he had suffered in the segregated South, but these shortcomings were not to be regarded as anything very serious. Nothing, in any event, that the good schools of the North, and the tolerant atmosphere encouraged by a liberal press, could not shortly put to rights.

It has not worked out quite that way. A process of disillusion has set in. It is like the tale of the emperor's clothes: Seen in a sudden, limpid clarity, the Negro comedian simply is not funny; the Negro singer is palpably off key; the Negro clerk has botched up the files; the schools of Washington are a national scandal; young women, working at the Supreme Court and the House Office Buildings, ask for police escorts to their cars by night. And why is all this covered up, condoned, minimized? Why is the appalling crime rate among Negroes rationalized away? Why are the facts on illegitimacy obscured in a smoke screen of fog words? Why are the progress records of Negro students, as a group, varnished over in glossy explanations that records no longer can be kept by race? Who is fooling whom? When Dr. MacCarthy brought in his verdict of "savagery," the *Washington Post* was aghast; but its readers knew a moment of blinding truth. And some months later, when a Washington policeman shot and killed a fleeing Negro hoodlum who had just robbed and mugged a pregnant young woman, the *Post* wept for the poor dear boy: He was only "the product of this city's slums, the victim of community neglect."[6] But a substantial segment of public opinion was ready to award a medal to the cop.[7]

III

Again I raise the question: Why? Why is the Negro where he is? I am not so presumptuous as to attempt a positive answer to

[6] *The Washington Post,* March 14, 1963.
[7] Editorial, the *Washington Daily News,* March 15, 1963.

View from a Southern Exposure

the question, which is more than one can say for the didactic anthropologists of the Boas-Montagu school; I simply raise the question. Why? Why is it, as Toynbee has said, that alone among the primary races of mankind, the Negro has not made a creative contribution to any one of our twenty-one civilizations?[8] Why was it that the Negro lived a thousand years beside the sea and never conceived the sail? Who can explain the echoing, echoing absence of invention, writing, computation, among the Negro tribes?

The rationalizations that ordinarily are advanced by way of explanation would be brushed aside as ludicrous in any other field of academic inquiry. It is said that the Negro tribes of sub-Saharan Africa were isolated for centuries from contact with contemporaneous civilization. The evidence on this point is not convincing or persuasive. Assuredly they were not as isolated as the Mayan and Incan tribes, whose achievements may be seen to this day. It is said that the early Negroes suffered from geographical disadvantages—desert, and terrible heat, and plagues of insects; and this explanation has an equally hollow ring. Other peoples, at other times, suffered as fearsomely; and adapted, and improved; and moved upward. Other peoples were enslaved, defeated in war, held in captivity. But the Negroid culture signally failed to rise out of indolence and ignorance and poverty of circumstance, and to build a civilization to command the respect and admiration of mankind.

It is said—and this is the feeblest rationalization of them all —that it is unfair to judge Negro achievements by our own yardsticks. The phallic sculptures, we are told winningly, are truly very fine phallic sculptures. Doubtless they are. The mud huts were the strongest mud huts ever contrived. The point may be conceded. The barter system of sub-Saharan Africa really was a flourishing commerce—after its primitive fashion.[9] All this is interesting, if true; but if true, what then? Is a mud hut a Monticello, a carved root a bust by Rodin? Are jungle drums seriously to be equated with Beethoven's Third? What alien

[8] Quoted by Nathaniel Weyl, in *The Negro in American Civilization* (Washington: Public Affairs Press, 1960), and by Carleton Putnam in *Race and Reason, A Yankee View* (Washington: Public Affairs Press, 1961).

[9] For an especially gushing account, see Ruth Benedict, *Race: Science and Politics* (New York: Viking Press, 1950).

113

values are we asked to accept in the name of a Negrophile cause?

Is it not time—I ask it as gently as possible, but as urgently —is it not time that the West faced this question of "why"? Is it not time for the social anthropologists at least to permit responsible discussion of the racial differences that cannot be concealed from the common observation of mankind? I am puzzled by the deliberate suppression of inquiry, by the unanimity of scholars to whom unanimity on *anything* ought always to be shunned; I do not understand it. We live in an age when freedom of inquiry is defended on every side—on every side, that is, save inquiry into the possibility of some innate inferiority in the Negro race. A few courageous men excepted, at this point the anthropologists say tabu. They are like the cartographers of Spain, these docile pedagogues, who mapped the globe as a cube; they are descended from the obliging burghers of the Kipling story, who firmly voted the world was flat.[10]

Why? In any other area of genetics, the scholars speak a common-sensical tongue. A horse bred for racing, by easy agreement is acknowleged to be swifter than a horse bred for pulling wagons. A cow bred for milking admittedly is unsuited for beef. No one denies that in a field of corn stubble, searching for upland game, a Pekinese is inferior to a pointer. When it comes to carrying heavy loads in tropical climes, a white man typically is inferior to the Negro. I am told by competent students of the art that when it comes to playing jazz, the Negro almost always is superior to the white. And these musicologists mean *innately* superior to the white; inherently superior; they are saying that a gift for jazz is something in the gene string. But at about this point, concessions stop abruptly. With an infuriating blandness, contemporary social anthropologists demand that laymen accept simply on their say-so, without that strict proof demanded in other disciplines, that the Negro race, as a race, is in fact equal to the white race, as a race, in all the aptitudes and capabilities by which Western civilization may be judged. In their obsessive urge to condone, to justify, to rationalize, to cover up, the very word "race" must be obliterated.[11] There are only "ethnic

[10] "The *fact* is, *of course*," said a statement from the Group for the Advancement of Psychiatry in May, 1957, "that the Negro possesses the same capacities and potentialities as does the white." The emphasis is my own.
[11] See any book by Ashley Montagu or Otto Klineberg.

groups," and all ethnic groups have equal capacities for achievement. And with that, the stupid layman is told to shut up.

Not all students of the subject have been browbeaten into
silence. In May of 1962, Dr. Carleton Stevens Coon, a former
president of the American Association of Physical Anthropologists, published a second edition of *The Story of Man;* he followed this in the fall with *The Origin of Races.*[12] Dr. Coon is
one of the most respected scholars in the field; he served from
1948 until his retirement in 1963 as curator of ethnology and
professor of anthropology at the University Museum in Philadelphia. In these authoritative works, Dr. Coon discusses the
slow transition of primitive man from *Homo erectus* to *Homo
sapiens;* he distinguishes the successive skulls of evolving man;
and his conclusion, honestly stated, is that Caucasoid man took
the prodigious step from *erectus* to *sapiens* at least 200,000 years
before the Negroid man of Africa took the same vital step.[13] The
expression of these conclusions on Dr. Coon's part has created
consternation among liberal anthropologists; to judge from the
reviews I have seen of Dr. Coon's works, his critics turn away
from the implications with a moan that Southern segregationists
will read all the wrong things into his disclosures.[14] It is as may be.

A few other anthropologists, geneticists, anatomists, and
archaeologists have dared to stand against the conformist tide.
The venerable Dr. Wesley Critz George, for many years professor
(now emeritus) of histology and embryology at the University
of North Carolina Medical School, bravely published a monograph in 1962, in which he examined some of these questions in
scholarly, temperate fashion.[15] As if lecturing to freshmen, Dr.
George takes his readers through an elementary course in
genetics. Then he faces the question without flinching: Are
there fundamental differences between the white and Negro
races? Many persons, he acknowledges, have advocated persist-

[12] Both books were published by Alfred P. Knopf, New York.
[13] Coon, *The Story of Man,* pp. 28–38, 60–62.
[14] For example, see *The New York Herald Tribune Book Review,* December 9, 1962.
[15] Dr. George's monograph, "The Biology of the Race Problem," may be
obtained through the National Putnam Letters Committee, P. O. Box 3518,
Grand Central Station, New York. I am indebted to him for the quotations
and citations that follow.

ently the dogma that no significant differences exist. A famous UNESCO pamphlet advances the view that "such biological differences as exist between members of different ethnic groups have no relevance to problems of social and political organizations, moral life, and communication between human beings."[16] Dr. George draws a long breath:

"That statement is unproven and almost certainly untrue. The thesis is supported mostly by tricks of writing, not by scientific investigation and orderly presentation of established facts."[17]

As far back as 1871, Dr. George observes, Darwin commented in *The Descent of Man* that races differ in constitution, in acclimation, and in liability to certain diseases. "Their mental characteristics," said Darwin, "are also very distinct." George C. Carter, professor of geography at Johns Hopkins, wrote in 1961 that factors of climate and geography had sculptured man into biologically divergent races, and these factors "molded his mind, too."[18] Dr. George quotes Professor Raymond Hall, in a 1946 article in the *Journal of Mammalogy:* "The subspecies of man are distinguished one from the other by the same sorts of differences—characters, in zoological parlance—as are subspecies of almost every other kind of mammal. . . . Not only do subspecies of man differ in shape of parts of the skeleton, color of skin, and shape of the hair, as do subspecies of other kinds of mammals, but they differ in psychological characteristics. . . ."[19]

Why do we pretend these cultural and intellectual differences do not exist? Who gains by the sham? At regular intervals, over a period of more than fifty years, some of the ablest psychologists and educators in the country have tested earnestly to see what might be learned of comparative white and Negro intelligence. In every possible way, they have sought to eliminate from their investigations the distorting effect produced by the advantages a white child might derive from circumstances of environment. Time after time, almost without exception, the studies have produced substantially the same conclusions: On the

[16] UNESCO, "The Race Question in Modern Science," 1950. Ashley Montagu was the principal author.
[17] George, *op. cit.,* p. 13.
[18] George F. Carter, "The Earth," *Johns Hopkins Magazine,* XII (May-June, 1961), 24–29.
[19] XXVII (1946), 358–64.

average, the I.Q.'s of American Negroes are between 15 and 20 points below those of American whites at the same age level. About six times as many whites, proportionately, as Negroes fall in the "gifted child" category. About six times as many Negroes as whites fall below 70 I.Q.—that is, in the feeble-minded group. These findings have been attested by such scholars as Dr. Frank C. J. McGurk, of Villanova; Dr. Audrey M. Shuey, of Randolph-Macon Woman's College, and Dr. Henry E. Garrett, professor emeritus of psychology at Columbia University and now professor of education at the University of Virginia.[20] In two world wars, army intelligence tests repeatedly have confirmed the disparity.[21] What advantage is gained by pretending the disparity does not exist?

In his treatise, Dr. George remarks that members of all races commit crimes. No one questions that. But there is no blinking the undeniable fact that in the United States, crime among Negroes is proportionately far higher than crime among whites. The felony rate among Negroes regularly runs almost three times the national average. Though Negroes constitute only 11 per cent of total population, in a typical year they will be charged with 30 per cent of the major crimes. In 1960, for example, the FBI's *Uniform Crime Reports* found that Negroes made up 61 per cent of those charged with murder, 56 per cent of those charged with robbery, 43 per cent of those charged with aggravated assault.

The same bleak picture obtains in the area of illegitimacy. Year after year, in the South and outside the South, illegitimate births among Negro women run nearly *ten times* the rate among whites. A quarter-century of better housing, better incomes, better education, decreased segregation, have not affected this condition in the slightest. Indeed, in my own Virginia, the rate of Negro illegitimacy goes up, little by little, year after year. In 1962, the centennial of Emancipation, it reached a record of 25.3 per cent. To the acute anguish of *The Washington Post,* the District of Columbia now holds a shameful title: It is the world

---

[20] The most comprehensive work on the subject is Dr. Shuey's *The Testing of Negro Intelligence* (Lynchburg, Va.: The J. P. Bell Company, 1958).

[21] *Ibid.,* pp. 179–219.

capital of illegitimacy.[22] And this is overwhelmingly Negro illegitimacy, not white.

Negro leaders do not like to be reminded of these unpleasant facts. Roy Wilkins, of the National Association for the Advancement of Colored People, brushes aside such figures as mere "statistics." Their easy explanations pour over one another: This massive immorality is the fault of segregation; it is the fault of poor housing; it is the fault of job scarcities; it is the fault of inadequate education; it is the fault of the white plantation slaveowners of 1855; it is everybody's fault but the Negro's. The reports on illegitimacy are explained away in a dozen ingenious fashions: White girls are better able to afford abortions; the reporting is faulty in centers of vital statistics; it is all a conspiracy to make the Negro race look bad. Administrators of public welfare are not deceived. Their records abound with case histories of second- and third-generation illegitimacy in the pampered public housing projects of a well-fed welfare state. Doubtless the frustrations of segregation play a part, but other races, in other times, have overcome frustrations and restrained their carnal passions. What is wrong with the Negro race?

IV

The Southerner does not really expect to be listened to when he says these distasteful things. He is viewed these days, *a priori*, as a bigot. As a consequence, the Southerner who counts himself a conservative, or retains some respect for the traditions and wisdom of his ancestors, has just about subsided. He has lived with the Negro people a long time, and as the Negro migration from the South continues apace, the South's difficulties grow less as the rest of the country's problems of adjustment grow more severe. But it is not only the population ratios of the South that change. The white Southerner himself, unless I am sorely mistaken, also is going through a significant change. He remains adamantly, unyieldingly opposed to any true "integration" of the races. His knowledge of genetics is instinctive, not academic, but it leads him unerringly to the conclusion that miscegenation

[22] In 1961, Washington reported 4,251 illegitimate births, of which 3,893 were to Negro mothers. In 1962, 265 illegitimate babies were born to girls in Washington public schools; 250 of these were Negro.

is a bad thing. This he will not condone or promote. But certain white attitudes are shifting nonetheless, in ways that seem to me sound and hopeful, and I should like to speak to the point for a moment or two.

The Southerner has done a lot of thinking these past few years, especially since the hurricane winds of *Brown* v. *Board of Education* swept over the South and threatened to blow the house of his fathers clean away. Most storms seem to be worse, in the midst of them, than they are seen to be when the flood waters ebb. This is true, I think, of the *Brown* decision. I am still convinced that Warren's opinion in *Brown* was very bad law, a perversion of the Constitution, a gross invasion of long-established State powers—in effect, an amendment to the Constitution ratified not by thirty-six States but by nine men on a Monday. If the Supreme Court is capable of committing an unconstitutional act—and I believe it is—this repudiation of the plain intention of the framers of the Fourteenth Amendment was an unconstitutional act.

But I am not arguing law here. I am brooding about things in general. The opinion of 1954 flashed like a lightning bolt; there was a whole year's ominous silence; and with the follow-up opinion of 1955 the downpour came. Our house rocked and the timbers shook; the winds of social change howled in the gables. We of the South were mad clean through at the Court, and we were filled with terrible forebodings. Not long ago, I had occasion to reread some of the hundreds of letters to the editor *The Richmond News Leader* carried in this period. We did not print the really violent letters—and there were plenty of them—but the letters that did appear in the Forum were as passionate as the cries of the Southern press against Emancipation a hundred years ago. These letters of 1955, most of them, read now as if they had been written then. And a good many of my own editorials read the same way. This was a bad time.

The storm in the South is not over yet. It will not be over in my lifetime. But it subsides; it subsides. In the spring of 1963, before violence broke upon Birmingham, *The New Leader*'s Forum was receiving not more than three or four letters a month from avowed Southern segregationists. Southern Governors, in their inaugural addresses—save in Alabama and Mississippi—no longer harp on old wounds; they harp on new industry. Georgia has a Negro State Senator. The storm subsides. If I could predict its course hereafter, I would venture a forecast that the thunderheads will move north and west. In any event, from Richmond to New Orleans, we emerge, blinking, and do not find nearly the devastation we had feared. The house, it is the old house yet. Some rotten boards—bus segregation, for example—have been swept almost clean away; some tattered fences have come down, and we see no need to put them back again. There is a good deal of remodeling to be done, but at least in some quarters of the old conservative South, a feeling grows that in some ways the storm was not so great a calamity after all; this is remodeling that needed to be done.

To put the metaphor aside, I have a feeling that many Southerners who share my own tastes, convictions, prejudices, upbringing, and conservative traditions have been reflecting long and powerfully about where we have been, and whither we are going. Some of my staunch friends in Mississippi and Alabama will deny it, but there is a thoughtful sense of repentance here and there. Not just on Sunday mornings, but off and on through the week, we are beginning to think about some of the things we have left undone which we ought to have done, and some of the things we have done which we ought not to have done. We are not to the point of saying there is no health in us—nobody really believes that pious protestation—but out in the yard a few trees are down, and we are looking at things a bit differently.

Let me try not to be misunderstood. The Southerner I am talking about, the Southerner who has steadfastly opposed race-mixing even if he hasn't joined the Citizens Council or written his congressman about it, still believes basically in separation of the races. He remains determined to resist the massive desegregation of his public schools in every way his ingenious mind can contrive, because racially separate schools are of paramount importance to him. (Louis Lomax says school desegregation is not of paramount importance to the Negro,[23] which is interesting, and indeed amazing, but the schools rank ahead of all else to the Southern white.) When "integration" is defined as a complete, color-blind mixing of the races as social equals, in schools,

[23] *The Negro Revolt* (New York: Harper & Row, 1962), pp. 113–15.

homes, churches, beaches, country clubs, this Southerner is steadfastly opposed to integration. The house, it is the old house yet.

But with those several caveats stated, the prospect remains, or so it seems to me, that a condition is emerging in which the American Negro is likely to find more peace of mind, more dignity, more sense of security and tolerance and acceptance, in a South inherited from Lee than in a North inherited from Lincoln. The Southerner who once looked on certain practices of segregation unthinkingly now looks on some of them a bit uncomfortably. In time, I believe, he will acquiesce as they quietly disappear. Segregation of public libraries is an example of what I have in mind; prior to World War II, there wasn't a public library in Virginia that was open to Negro users; now there isn't one that is closed to them. Areas of public and private employment offer another example. At present, no Negro doctor, no matter how well qualified, can become a member of the Medical Society of Virginia, and because he is barred from the State society, he cannot belong to the American Medical Association either. This is preposterous; but this too will pass.

Many of these changes, I would concede readily, have been accelerated by outside pressures—by actions of the Federal government, by litigation brought by Negro organizations, by the amorphous weight of Northern public opinion. But I believe there has been insufficient acknowledgement of the immense strides that have been taken voluntarily by the South; and I make the point that these changes, because they have come voluntarily and with total community acceptance, are likely to count for the most. It is evident, on the record, that some of the more militant techniques of the Negro leadership can be effective, especially when these techniques have a clear local identification; but it seems to me equally clear that trumped-up agitation by outside meddlers accomplishes little or nothing of lasting value. The "Freedom Riders," for example, did much more harm than good. Like strange birds of passage, this exotic flock descended upon the South in bedraggled flights of white-collared loonybirds and ruffle-throated gabblers. They were not impressive; they were absurd. And so far as the affected Southerners were concerned, the result was not to get their barriers down, but their backs up. This is not the way that lasting change is achieved.

I cannot predict the speed or course of Southern change. In some areas, it will come smoothly, as it came to Clemson University early in 1963; elsewhere it will continue to come slowly, painfully, or, as at Oxford, bloodily, or not at all. Candor compels the statement that in many counties of the Deep South, members of the white power-structure will continue to refuse wholesale voting rights to the Negro. They cannot possibly yield on this, short of bayonets or drastic citations for contempt, for reasons that might be quoted from Lomax. He speaks of Harlem as the New World's Congo, a land occupied by black people but run by white people. "If the white people left tomorrow morning, the Negroes could not run their own town. It is not that the Negroes don't have the talent and ability [the Southerner might file a demurrer on that], but that they have not been allowed to gain the technical and business experience necessary to keep a modern community going."[24] Even so in Sunflower County, Mississippi. The county may not be a large community,[25] but there are those who love it. They surmise that the Negroes, given the vote, would vote as a bloc; they know that such a bloc is now incapable of governing; and they will bitterly resist any step that might lead to surrender of local control to a manipulable Negro mass whose investment in local values is small. My guess is that in the long haul, the problems of Negro voting in the Deep South will be resolved by a combination of factors—property qualifications in wholly local elections, literacy tests, gerrymandering, and to some extent by Negro out-migration and by the Negro's own apathy. But the white Southerner knows that in denying the vote to genuinely qualified Negroes, he does not have a constitutional leg to stand on; and he is not immune to the argument that if the South expects the rest of the country to respect the Tenth Amendment, the South cannot trifle with the Fifteenth. This picture will improve.

I ask myself: Why am I optimistic, in view of the past, about the future of white and Negro relationships in the South? The answer may be, Because of the past. James Baldwin makes a great point in his books of the Negro's intimate knowledge of the white man, whose blood-stained sheets he has washed, whose

[24] *Ibid.*, p. 213.
[25] The 1960 population of Sunflower County, Miss.: White, 14,730; Negro, 45,750.

children he has tended. The same point, to be sure, would be as valid of the Swedish washerwoman and the Irish cook as it is of the Negro mammy—valid, indeed, of the servant-master relationship anywhere. *Il n'y a point de héros pour son valet de chambre.* Still, Baldwin's point is valid.

But the past that has revealed a good deal of the Southern white to the Southern Negro also has revealed a good deal of the Negro to the white. The races have lived together a long time in the South; they have lived through hard times together, often holding each other up. Something has been gained from this sharing, something Mr. Baldwin will never understand or acknowledge. Neither race cherishes many illusions about the other. If we meet on many plains as good friends, it is just that: Good friendship. And if we meet in other quarters as antagonists, this is honest, too: Honest antagonism. After all these years, the Southern Negro does not expect anything very good from the Southern white; and the Southern white does not expect anything very good from the Southern Negro. We start every day from scratch, each disillusioned with the other. Our hopes are separate, but our fears are equal. There is no place to go but up.

Almost every white Southerner, at some point along the way, has had some experience with Negroes who were inept, or unreliable, or simply "shif'less." The Southerner also has known, of course, pleasantly and affectionately, faithful and competent Negroes for whom he cherishes a warm regard. He sees them as human beings who are dear to him, and if he sees them through Will Percy's "barrier of glass," it may be said that glass is not necessarily an impermeable wall. The spirit filters through. Love filters through. Respect filters through. Today, the white Southerner is seeing a changing image beyond that wall of glass. He is seeing Negro educators, doctors, lawyers, businessmen. The old master-servant relationship dissolves, and something else takes its place that I cannot precisely define—a neutrality, a reserve, a separateness that places us farther apart and yet not so far. White and black alike, we move away from the old paternalism, from the old sense of the white man's personal responsibility for the Negro, and into a new relationship of cautious independence. It is better all around.

Over much of the country, however, generations have grown

up that have known almost no Negroes at all. The out-migration of the Negro from the American South is still a fairly recent phenomenon. In the North, Midwest, and West, many persons, with the best will in the world, are discovering for the first time that close co-existence with massive numbers of Negroes takes a little getting used to. And the increasingly self-evident fact is that even in these liberal and more progressive climes, sometimes the best will in the world is not altogether evident.

To these signs of friction, the Northern power-structure sometimes appears to respond with such floods of oil that the machinery of human relationships drowns in a greasy hypocrisy. Some of this is politics. Some of it is a gushing liberalism that for all I know may have some Freudian base. Part of it is hard economics: The Negro is a market, ripe for exploitation. And while many of these public professions of praise and friendship doubtless are sincere, many of them, at bottom, are sham; and I suspect the Northern Negro knows it. Something more substantial is required. I don't know; I am merely speculating here; but it may be that some period of spiritual apartness is necessary before there can be a spiritual coming together. The North hasn't known the apartness yet.

The very tentative and uncertain development of interracial social relationships at some of the higher levels of education, business, and the arts, is only one aspect of the Northern Negro's position, a hundred years after Emancipation. The Northern press is finding a great deal more than social relationships to worry about. The grand plan had called for assimilation of the Negro into the white community, but the Negro is not assimilating by the plan. It was a shock to many good-hearted white persons to be told bluntly by Mr. Baldwin, in *The Fire Next Time,* that the Negro is not interested in adopting the white man's cultural, social, religious, or moral values—that the Negro wants nothing from the white man but his power.[26] But the white man surely is not interested in adopting the Negro's cultural, social, religious, or moral values—not as he sees them interpreted in Baldwin's Harlem jungle—and he does not propose to give up his power simply on demand. Where do we go from here?

[26] James Baldwin, *The Fire Next Time* (New York: Dial, 1963), pp. 61, 108–10.

View from a Southern Exposure

V

It was early on a Sunday morning in April of 1963 when I finished the first draft of this essay. There was a spring breeze, soft as sleeping, slipping through the garden. The camellias had stopped blooming, but the azaleas were out; my thought was to work for an hour or two, and then go fishing. At the time, race relations were remote from my mind. I remember thinking that race relations, as such, probably were equally remote from the minds of most of the hundred thousand Negroes of Richmond. It was a relatively peaceful spring.

Then, in May, came Birmingham, and the summer of violence was swiftly upon us. The next four months provided a shocking chronicle of riot, civil disobedience, and wild disorder. From Alabama to New York, to the dismay of responsible whites and Negroes alike, we witnessed sit-ins, stand-ins, lie-ins, chain-ins, kneel-ins, wade-ins, and all the rest. Often it seemed there was nothing else in the papers but race news. Public opinion polls disclosed that white Americans, outside the South, were not sympathetic. They were appalled.

Now it is the end of August. The great "March on Washington" is behind us, and the summer nightmare hopefully is dissolving into a much less violent fall. I do not believe these arrogant "demonstrations" have brought white and Negro closer together; I suspect they have driven the races still farther apart.

I have been reading James Baldwin's books lately, and I have been reading Louis Lomax's *The Negro Revolt*. I have been sifting out my own thoughts for this paper, and asking myself how, or whether, and when, if ever, the formidable gulf between the races might be bridged. In my own judgment, much less hatred and much more affection and kindness flow between the races, at least in the South, than these two Negro writers perceive, but I venture no very positive assertions on the point. Evidently Baldwin sees little or none of this feeling. His characters in *Another Country* direct toward the white man a current of pure loathing, now hotly passionate, now coldly contemptuous. "I know what the [white] world has done to my brother," Baldwin writes to his nephew, "and this is the crime . . . for which neither I nor time nor history will ever forgive them, that they have destroyed and are destroying hundreds of thousands of lives and do not know it and do not want to know it."[27] So purulent a hatred would indicate an inoperable cancer of the soul; it makes rational discourse impossible. Lomax, a more temperate and perhaps more careful observer, does not see the future so bleakly, but he makes the flat statement: "American Negroes are becoming increasingly anti-white."[28]

It may be so. It may also be so, or so it seems to me, that outside the South, American whites are becoming increasingly anti-Negro. In many of the urban centers of the North, if I am not mistaken, the turbulent summer of 1963 has seen the Negro drawing down his reservoirs of good will more rapidly than he is filling them up. It seems a doubtful way to launch a second century of freedom.

I am wondering if this second century might not better begin with a candid look by the Negro at the Negro. Granted that some brilliant members of his race have emerged. Granted that there have been gains of the spirit. Granted that his political future is brighter and that certain economic opportunities are developing more rapidly than Negroes can fill them. Things still are dreadfully wrong. What might be done to improve them?

If the answers to such an inquiry trail off into self-pitying justifications based on "the slums," or "the ghettoes," or "the man," or "slavery," or "Southern segregation," nothing much will have been gained. The Negro has been blaming everybody else for a hundred years; the phonograph record begins to wear thin. What does the Negro want to be? Does he want to be like the white man? Baldwin says not.[29] So does Malcolm X. Do they truly speak for the great body of American Negroes? If so, there's an end to it. The white race has plenty of sins on its head, from the Crusades to slavery to the H-bomb. Maybe Baldwin is right; maybe the white race is so steeped in greed, rapacity, and bloody war that Negroes properly should reject any thought of emulating its historic record.

But when we talk of the values of a contemporary American civilization in ordinary, everyday terms, we are not talking of

[27] *Ibid.*, p. 19.
[28] Lomax, *op. cit.*, p. 181.
[29] Baldwin, *op. cit.*, pp. 22, 36, 66, 108.

the burning of Troy or the sacking of Carthage, nor yet of Buchenwald or Hiroshima. We are talking of competence on a job, of obedience in a classroom, of a law-abiding citizen's safety as he walks in Washington by night. We are talking of chastity, if you please; it is an old commandment, and God knows the white man has dishonored it—but the rate of illegitimacy among American Negroes creeps steadily toward the point at which one of every four Negro babies will be born in bastardy. We are talking of manners, of civility, of sobriety, of restraints upon carnality. No, the white man is no paragon of virtue! He often falls dismally short of the values he professes. Much of his music is banal; his prevailing tastes in art have yet to rise above Whistler's Mother; his suburban split-level often is occupied by dull people who lead dull lives. But on the record of achievement as the West measures achievement, the white man has come a long way. His values may be a little tarnished now and then, but they still shine. His organized religion may exhibit a sort of Rotarianism remote from Galilee. True, true! But to the typical middle-class white American, his own social, moral, cultural, religious, political, ethical, and economic way of life still seems to him the best in the world. The American Negro occupies a small place in this world now. It is a larger place, to be sure, than he occupied a hundred years ago; but it is still a small place.

"If the American Negro is going to realize his full role in the American experiment," writes Louis Lomax, "he must become a much more responsible fellow than he now is. For a long time we could justly blame the white man for our weaknesses and shortcomings; this day is about over."[30]

Dr. MacCarthy, in his Washington report, commented simply that "for the colored as well as the white, it must be acknowledged that lawbreaking anywhere—at school, in the street, or in a stadium—is not the result of being underprivileged. Breaking the law results from a fundamental lack of self-discipline. Social background unquestionably affords some of the reasons for malcontent, but persons, if they are to be contributive citizens, must learn to rise above their environment."

I do not know if the American Negro, a century after Lin-

[30] Lomax, *op. cit.*, p. 181.

coln, will find total freedom any time soon. He has the opportunity. He has powerful political pressures working in his behalf. Through individuals of conspicuous attainment, the race moves forward; but in the behavior patterns of Washington schools, and in a Thanksgiving riot, he sometimes moves backward, too. And this he can ill afford. Lomax is right: If the Negro people of America are going to realize their full role in the American experiment, they must somehow face up to the reality of Frederick Douglass' advice a century ago.

"What would happen to the Negroes once they were freed?" Lincoln asked the famed former slave. "Who would take care of them?"

"Let them take care of themselves," Douglass replied, "as others do."[31]

[31] John Hope Franklin, *The Emancipation Proclamation* (New York: Doubleday, 1962), p. 32.

ABRAM L. HARRIS

●

EDUCATION AND THE ECONOMIC STATUS OF NEGROES IN THE UNITED STATES

An educated colored man, in the United States, unless he has within him the heart of a hero, and is willing to engage in a lifelong battle for his rights, as a man, finds few inducements to remain in this country. He is isolated in the land of his birth—debarred by his color from congenial association with whites; he is equally cast out by the ignorance of the *blacks*. The remedy for this must comprehend the elevation of the masses; and this can only be done by putting the mechanic arts within the reach of colored men.[1]

—Frederick Douglass (1853).

The diffusion of education in the two meanings of formal knowledge and technical training among the masses of people has a twofold significance in the theory and practice of democracy. The significance is political and economic. From the political standpoint the accepted objective of education is the development of the individual's capacity for intelligently exercising the rights of citizenship and executing the obligations that this involves. In the broadest political or social perspective the purpose of education is to make man a better moral agent by the cultivation not only of his intellect but of his feelings, imagination, and aspirations, and by inculcating a critical appreciation of the values that make civilized society possible. As stated by one writer there "are certain primary elements and means of knowledge which it is in the highest degree desirable that all human beings born into the community should acquire

[1] Carter G. Woodson, *The Education of the Negro Prior to 1861* (New York: G. P. Putnam's Sons, 1915), p. 390. Copyright 1915 by C. P. Putnam's Sons.

during childhood." If their parents, or those on whom they depend fail to obtain this instruction for them, "they commit a double breach of duty, towards the children themselves and towards the members of the community, generally, who are . . . liable to suffer . . . from the consequences of ignorance and want of education in their fellow-citizens."[2]

The economic importance of education is inseparable from its political significance. It is a commonplace observation that one's standard of living and also his value to society depend upon his contribution to the production of goods and services. Economists, as far back as Adam Smith, have taken cognizance of the fact that man's productive capacity and, hence, his income are improved by means of education. And the idea that education is a form of capital investment is a recurrent theme in economic literature. But it is only very recently that economists have sought to establish analytically a specific relationship between levels of education as a form of "investment in human capital" and its costs, and returns. The investigations are guided by the idea that "the economic capabilities of man are predominantly a *produced* means of *production* and . . . except for some pure rent (in earnings) for differences in inherited ability most differences in earnings are a consequence of differences in the amounts that have been invested in people. Here, then, the hypothesis is that the structure of wages and salaries is primarily determined by investment in schooling, health, on-the-job training, searching for information about job opportunities and by investment in migration."[3] The contribution of education to earning and producing capacity is only a part of the picture. Earnings "are an incomplete measure of the productivity of education to the extent that production occurs outside the market. In addition, emphasis on incremental earnings attributable to education disregards external effects. Schooling benefits many persons other than the student. It benefits the student's future children, who will receive informal education in the home; and it benefits neighbors, who may be affected

[2] John Stuart Mill, *Principles of Political Economy*, ed. W. J. Ashley (New York: Dutton, 1929), p. 954.
[3] Theodore W. Schultz, "Reflections on Investment in Man," *Journal of Political Economy*, Supplement, LXX, No. 5, Part 2 (October, 1962), 1–2.

favorably by the social values developed in children by the schools and even by the quietness of the neighborhood while the schools are in session. Schooling benefits employers seeking a trained labor force; and it benefits the society at large by developing the basis for an informed electorate."[4]

Long ago the leaders in the movement for Negro freedom and citizenship recognized the economic and social effects of education and sought to impress the importance of their insight upon the mind of the free Negro community. In 1830, one of these leaders, William Lloyd Garrison, addressed a Convention of Free People of Color with these words:

> An ignorant people can never occupy any other than a degraded place in society; they can never be truly free until they are intelligent. It is an old maxim that knowledge is power; and . . . rank, wealth, dignity, and protection. That capital brings highest return to a city, state, or nation . . . which is invested in schools, academies, and colleges. If I had children, rather than that they should grow up in ignorance, I would feed them upon bread and water: I would sell my teeth, or extract the blood from my veins.[5]

Whether the status of the Negro since his emancipation is considered politically or economically, the limiting and the accelerating factor in his advancement has been education in the broad sense of instruction in formal knowledge, technical or vocational training, and informal instruction in the family. The masses of Negroes at or below the level of poverty are the uneducated; and there is no doubt a positive correlation between Negro crime and illiteracy. The Negroes who have acquired property, who have the higher incomes, and who have benefited most from the newly acquired political power of urban Negroes, are the educated.

It is a mistake to assume that the education of Negroes began after the Civil War with the establishment of schools and colleges by the Freedmen's Bureau and later by Northern philanthropy. Much of the Negro's education between the American

---

[4] Burton A. Weisbrod, "Education and Investment in Human Capital," *Journal of Political Economy*, Supplement, LXX, No. 5, Part 2 (October, 1962), 106–7.

[5] Woodson, *op. cit.*, p. 256.

Revolution and the Civil War was obtained, informally, by contact with the white man. The contact was more intimate and frequent for the house servant (frequently a blood relative of the master class), than for the field worker, and in the more or less patriarchal slave system of the Old South—Virginia, Maryland and North Carolina—than in the cotton plantations of the Deep South. Furthermore, opportunities for observing and assimilating the ways of the white man were greater in the cities and towns than in rural areas. The process of the early informal education of Negroes is described by Carter G. Woodson as follows:

> The rise of the American city made possible the contact of the colored people with the world, affording them a chance to observe what the white man was doing, and to develop the power to care for themselves. The Negroes who had this opportunity to take over the western civilization were servants belonging to the families for which they worked; slaves hired out by their owners to wait upon persons; and watermen, embracing fishermen, boatmen, and sailors. Not a few slaves in cities were mechanics, clerks, and overseers. In most of these employments the rudiments of an education were necessary, and what the master did not seem disposed to teach the slaves so situated, they usually learned by contact with their fellowmen who were better informed. Such persons were mulattoes resulting from miscegenation, and therefore protected from the rigors of the slave code; house servants, rewarded with unusual privileges for fidelity . . .; and slaves who were purchasing their freedom.[6]

The formal education of Negroes before 1861 falls into two periods. The first begins with the introduction of slavery and ends with Negro insurrectionary movements around 1835. The second period was ushered in by the rise of the Cotton Kingdom in the black belt of the South. The early advocates of the education of Negroes were: (1) masters who wished to increase the efficiency of their labor force and (2) humanitarians. The last comprised two main groups: religious leaders who taught the slaves the English language in order that they might learn the principles of the Christian religion and those

[6] *Ibid.*, p. 123.

who wished to educate the slaves for freedom by enlightening them according to Western ideals. The last group was rather mixed as it included those who advocated emancipation on the condition of African colonization of the freedmen, as well as the early abolitionists who wished to educate the Negroes for citizenship in this country. John Wolman and John Jay, who assisted in the promotion of several colored schools in New York City, belonged to the last of this group. Jefferson belonged to the first. Alexander Hamilton assisted the New York African Free Schools, although he "said and did little to promote the actual education of the colored people."[7] Both Madison and Jefferson, who entertained misgivings concerning the Negro's intellectual capacity, endeavored to train their slaves in the practical arts. Both were influenced by the Polish general Thaddeus Kosciuszko, who authorized Jefferson, his executor, to use the whole of his property in the purchase of Negroes for liberation and in educating them in trades or otherwise, and "in having them instructed for their new condition in the duties of morality."[8] Anthony Benezet, a Quaker, not only taught Negroes but left a considerable sum which helped to construct a schoolhouse for them in Philadelphia in 1787. Benjamin Franklin was a supporter of Benezet and was president of the Abolition Society of Philadelphia which founded a colored school in 1774.[9] This school continued about a hundred years.

The private instruction of Negroes and the founding of schools for their benefit by individual whites were supplemented and, in numerous instances, supported by religious bodies and other voluntary associations—the Quakers, who organized the Society For the Free Instruction of the Orderly Blacks and People of Color in 1789, the African Colonization Society, and organizations by Negroes who had acquired freedom. Until the restrictive laws of the late 1830's, the majority of Negroes who had been able to purchase their freedom or had had it bestowed by benevolent masters lived in the cities and towns of the South. In these urban centers they established organizations for self-help, particularly for the promotion of education. For example,

[7] *Ibid.*, p. 58.
[8] *Ibid.*, p. 79.
[9] *Ibid.*, p. 78.

in Charleston, South Carolina, the Brown Fellowship Society organized by the free colored people maintained several schools for Negro children. The "Minor Society" was organized in the same city in 1810 for the education of orphan children.[10] According to Woodson:

> Enjoying . . . unusual advantages the Negroes of Charleston were early in the nineteenth century ranked as economically and intellectually superior to any other such persons in the United States. A large portion of the leading mechanics, fashionable tailors, shoe manufacturers, and mantua-workers were free blacks who enjoyed a consideration in the community far more than that enjoyed by any of the colored population in the Northern cities.[11]

In other Southern cities, notably Baltimore, Fredericksburg, Virginia, and Washington, D.C., schools maintained and supported by the free Negroes themselves were organized as early as 1807.[12] In 1850 in 16 Southern and Northern cities, the number of adults in the free Negro population who could not read or write was almost negligible.[13] By the 1850's the Negro's educational opportunities had greatly improved in the North, where the free Negro population had greatly increased. In New England an "epoch in the history of Negro education . . . was marked in 1820, when the city of Boston opened its first primary school for the education of colored children." In New York the African Free Schools were fused with the New Public School Society in 1834, but the schools for Negro and white children were operated separately, and the quality of the schooling for Negroes was quite inferior to that for whites. The separate but equal provision for the education of Negro and white children became New York law in 1864 and was not abolished until 1900 in the administration of Governor Theodore Roosevelt. The story of the efforts of Negroes to gain admission to the emerging free public schools and the colleges and universities of the North in the 1830's and 1840's is too long and complex to recite in

---

[10] E. Franklin Frazier, *The Free Negro Family* (Nashville, Tenn.: Fisk University Press, 1932), p. 15.

[11] Woodson, *op. cit.*, p. 129.

[12] Frazier, *op. cit.*, p. 15.

[13] *Ibid.*, p. 24.

this place.[14] It is interestingly told by Woodson, to whom the reader is referred.

On Free Soil the education of Negroes in antebellum days was frequently as strongly opposed as it came to be in the South toward the middle of the nineteenth century. Negro schools were often burned and white and Negro teachers forced to leave town by riotous mobs. But the movement was not halted by this opposition even when it took the form of mob violence. In the South, the legal restrictions on the education of Negroes enacted after the 1830's were so laxly enforced that the educational opportunities of the free Negro were not greatly limited. Moreover Negro slaves continued to be taught the three R's, clandestinely, by members of the white master class. Furthermore, despite frequent protests by the nonslaveholding poor whites and the restrictive legislative measures, the diversification of industry in the states of the Old South caused the training of a considerable part of the black labor force in the mechanical arts.

With the declining profitability of tobacco cultivation, the white masters found in the training and contracting out of Negro mechanics a good source of revenue. Many masters permitted their slave mechanics to hire out on their own time in return for a fixed return or for a certain percentage of the slave's earnings. In some instances, the enterprising slave mechanics were subcontractors in the black labor market.[15] Advertisements of the following kind were not infrequent in newspapers of the antebellum South:

> Wanted immediately, an apprentice to the blacksmith's business a smart, active boy, from 12 to 15 years of age, who can come well recommended. A black boy of this description will be taken. Wanted also a journeyman who understands his business, and has good recommendations for honesty, industry and sobriety. A black man would not be rejected.[16]

[14] In the higher education field, no Negro had graduated from college before 1828. In that year John B. Russworm, the first Negro to receive a college degree in this country, was graduated from Bowdoin College.

[15] Sterling D. Spero and Abram L. Harris, *The Black Worker* (New York: Columbia University Press, 1931), p. 6. Also, Ulrich B. Phillips, *American Negro Slavery* (New York: Appleton, 1918), Chapter XX.

[16] Spero and Harris, *op. cit.*, p. 6.

The sale value of a slave mechanic, estimated at $2,000 to $3,000, was considerably higher than that of the black field hand. By years of saving, thrifty mechanics were able to purchase at such prices the freedom of themselves and their families.

In Virginia the Tredegar Iron Company furnishes a striking example of the use of slave labor in the budding manufacturing establishments of the South in the early nineteenth century. The Company began to train and employ Negroes under white supervision around 1842. In 1850 Tredegar's manager described 35 slaves that he owned as "a picked lot of men and boys whom he had brought up to be puddlers, heaters, and rollers—as a choice set equal to any white hands who had ever worked for him."[17] In 1863, Tredegar was employing about 750 Negroes in all its operations. Some of these were expert rollers and squeezers. The few whites employed were "Boss men" who presided over the rolls and furnaces. "At the puddling furnaces . . . in 1848, were seven or eight white men; as many negro foremen; and . . . fifteen or sixteen negro 'helpers' . . . learning to be puddlers."[18] Farther South, in North Carolina, South Carolina, and Georgia, slaves were being similarly trained and utilized, especially as skilled craftsmen in the building trades.

In the North, the position of the free Negroes in industry was less fortunate than that of the Southern slave artisans. In Philadelphia, which had always had a large free Negro population, it is probable, according to W. E. B. Du Bois, that up to about 1820, a large proportion, if not a decided majority of the artisans of the city were colored. After that the influx of foreign immigrants and "the demand for new sorts of skilled labor of which the Negro was ignorant, and not allowed to learn, pushed the black artisans more and more to the wall."[19] As a result only about 350 out of the 10,500 Negroes in the city were engaged in skilled trades in 1837. Throughout the North, white mechanics refused to work with Negroes, and white master

[17] Kathleen Bruce, *Virginia Iron Manufacture in the Slave Era* (New York: Century, 1931), p. 239.

[18] *Ibid.*, p. 249.

[19] W. E. B. Du Bois, *The Philadelphia Negro* (Publications in Political Economy and Public Law, No. 25; Philadelphia: University of Pennsylvania Press, 1896), p. 33.

mechanics, generally, refused to accept Negroes as apprentices. The free Negro Martin A. Delaney in 1848, advised, "Let our young men and women . . . prepare themselves for usefulness, trading and other things of importance. . . . Educate them for the store and the Counting House . . . to do everyday practical business."[20] Delaney's admonition was probably influenced by the narrowing employment opportunities of free Negroes in the mechanical trades. His advice was by no means unrealistic inasmuch as a number of Negroes like Paul Cuffee, shipbuilder and overseas trader, had had successful careers in commerce and trade since the early 1800's.[21] But Frederick Douglass, the leading Negro abolitionist of the time and, himself, a runaway slave, thought that the only way to reverse the trend of increasing economic insecurity and poverty in the Northern Negro communities was by learning the mechanical trades.

Exclaiming in 1853, "Learn Trades or Starve,"[22] Douglass did not attribute the disadvantages of Negroes in the Northern labor market simply to the opposition of white mechanics and employers. He attached great importance to the fact that with the loss of their monopoly in domestic and personal service occupations, resulting from white immigrant competition, the Negroes had failed to acquire knowledge of the new emerging industrial skills. "At present," he stated, "we are, in the Northern States, unknown as mechanics. We give no proof of genius or skill at the county, State or National fairs. We are unknown at any of the great exhibitions of the industry of our fellow-citizens, and being unknown, we are unconsidered."[23] Douglass was not only an orator and journalist but a very hard-headed reformer. Invited by Harriet Beecher Stowe to her home to consider plans for the elevation of the colored people in the North, Douglass proposed the establishment of an industrial college. The institution was to comprise "a series of workshops, where colored people could learn some of the handicrafts, . . .

[20] Martin A. Delaney, *The Condition, Elevation, Emigration, and Destiny of the Colored People in the United States* (Philadelphia, 1852), pp. 42–45.
[21] Abram L. Harris, *The Negro as Capitalist* (Philadelphia: American Academy of Political and Social Science, 1936), pp. 18–20.
[22] Woodson, *op. cit.*, p. 390.
[23] Frederick Douglass, *Life and Times of Frederick Douglass* (Boston: DeWolfe, Fiske & Co., 1895), p. 356.

to work in iron, wood and leather, and where a plain English education could also be taught."[24] Nothing came of the project as Mrs. Stowe was unable, as she had hoped, to secure the necessary financial support.

When the Civil War ended, 4,000,000 Negroes had achieved freedom by the Emancipation Proclamation and the subsequent collapse of the slave system. There were then about 500,000 Negroes already free, of whom about 260,000 were in the South. In spite of the deterioration in their economic position that apears to have set in by the 1840's, the total real and personal property of free Negroes on the eve of the war has been estimated at $50 million. Of the 500,000 free Negroes in 1860, some had been born free, others were fugitive slaves, and still others had been liberated by their masters or had purchased their freedom. The number who had purchased their freedom is hard to determine; but it seems fair to assume that at least one-fifth were in this class. Assuming that on the average $200 per person was paid in the purchase of freedom, the amount of investment by Negroes in themselves amounted to about $20 million. The amount invested in education and in maintaining fraternal-insurance societies throughout the country cannot be determined.[25]

The early nineteenth-century efforts to advance the education of Negroes were expanded and accelerated after 1865. During and after the Civil War, elementary and industrial schools were set up by the Freedmen's Bureau; and the much maligned black and tan Reconstruction Governments gave the South its first free public school system. White men and women, educated in the best Northern colleges, went South to teach the Negroes. Supported by Northern philanthropy, they established between 1865 and 1868, such institutions as Howard University, Atlanta, Fisk, Morehouse College, and Virginia Union University at Richmond. Lincoln University had been founded in Pennsylvania in 1854, and Wilberforce in Ohio in 1856. The primary purpose of these institutions was to give Negroes the opportunity for a college education and, in the case of Howard University and Meharry Medical School (1876), to provide training

[24] *Ibid.*, p. 352.
[25] Harris, *op. cit.*, p. 9.

in the legal and medical professions. But nearly all of them were forced to maintain high schools or academies, as they were called, because of the inadequate secondary education provided in the Southern States. By present-day standards the education provided by the academies was of high quality; but the colleges, even in the case of Howard, advertised as the capstone of Negro education, would have to be ranked at the junior level. Hampton Institute, founded by General S. C. Armstrong in 1868, and Tuskegee, founded in 1881 by Booker T. Washington, the illustrious product of Hampton, were designed to provide industrial and vocational training. With the progressive isolation of Negro life by legal segregation and disfranchisement between 1880 and 1900, these institutions and their graduates became an assimilating force in the black community and the means of connecting it with the social values and outlook of the surrounding white culture.

In the urban centers to which the Negroes as well as the whites moved in increasing numbers between 1870 and 1900, a more or less separate social and economic Negro community emerged, due partly to the refusal of whites to render certain services to Negroes and partly to an urge for self-help. A group economy, as Du Bois called it, was established on the basis of Negro banks, the Negro educational institutions, real estate concerns, the undertaking business, insurance and fraternal societies, amusement concerns, retail trade, restaurants and hotels, and the Negro church. There was thus an increasing number of Negroes in the legal, medical, teaching and religious professions, and in other self-employed occupations like barbering, that serviced an exclusively Negro market. This development, accounted as evidence of the ability of the race to stand on its own feet, strengthened the middle-class Negro's optimism concerning the possible achievements of his people in the face of racial discrimination and the political disfranchisement that had followed the Reconstruction. But disquieting clouds were already gathering on the horizon.

Between 1890 and 1900, the decline in Negro farm ownership, which was to continue in the succeeding decades, had become evident. Southern Negro farm laborers migrated in increasing numbers to the cities and found employment in the heavy unskilled occupations. The Negro skilled artisans, who at the end of the Civil War were five times the number of whites, had begun to lose ground. It is true that in 1900 there were 215,369 Negroes in skilled trades, mainly in the South, or twice as many as in 1865; but they were a rapidly decreasing proportion of the skilled labor force. Southern white workers were crowding into the cities, competing with Negroes in the traditional skilled trades; and they were also finding employment on the railroads, where the emerging trade unions restricted and, eventually, prevented the employment of Negroes in the transportation service, in the new mills, and in construction, where new techniques were being introduced. Thus in 1900 the largest proportion of the Negro skilled artisans was in carpentry, bricklaying, and blacksmithing, where handicraft methods continued to prevail. Racial discrimination was undoubtedly a major factor in the decline and eclipse of the Negro skilled worker. But it was not responsible for the failure of the Negro's schools to furnish him adequate industrial training. Du Bois noted in 1910 that the more than one hundred schools offering industrial training were simply not preparing Negro youth for modern industry. He stated:

> In nearly all these schools "carpentry" is confined to hand tools and bench work. Blacksmithing and forging are taught by the simplest tools and not by modern power methods. Tailoring is not taught as modern garment making but as individual cutting and mending. Shoe repairing is taught but there is but little or no use made of shoe making machinery which is universally in vogue. Wheels and wagons are made chiefly by hand and at a cost which would make competition with machine made wagons impossible. *Negro youth are being taught the technique of a rapidly disappearing age of hand work.* The training has undoubtedly good physical and mental results but if used as a means of livelihood it will command the poor and decreasing wages of tinkers and repairers; and those who follow these methods will be completely shut out of modern machine industry.[26]

Until World War I, the migrations of Negroes from the

[26] W. E. B. Du Bois and Augustus Granville Dill, eds., *The Negro American Artisan* (The Atlanta University Publications, No. 17; Atlanta, Ga.: Atlanta University Press, 1912), p. 121.

farms to the cities, mainly Southern, though steady had not been on a mass scale. During and after the war migrations began occurring in massive waves and became primarily a movement to the large industrial centers in the North. But tight labor markets in the heavy industries caused a rapid absorption of the newcomers, and the gradual upgrading of many of them into skilled jobs. A report of the Department of Labor concerning the increase of skilled Negro workers in Northern industry during 1922–23 seems to indicate that many of the migrants formerly resided in Southern cities, where they learned some trade or followed semi-skilled occupations. By the late twenties and into the forties, the northward migrations assumed gigantic proportions. It is probable that most of these later migrants had come directly from the cotton patches of the South. They were for the greater part illiterate and lacked training in the elementary skills. Some absorption took place in menial jobs and in occupations requiring little skill, in meat packing and other industries. Although the advancement of Negroes in Northern industry had been steady between 1915 and 1930, as latecomers they had acquired less "seniority" on the average than white workers; and the overwhelming majority of the latest migrants were unfitted for anything but the lowest-paying unskilled jobs. Even before the depression of the 1930's there was, therefore, a considerable number of Negroes chronically unemployed or working part-time. At the height of the depression in the mid-thirties, unemployment and underemployment of Negroes was probably four to five times greater than that of white workers. This high volume of unemployment of the Negro industrial worker precipitated the collapse of Negro business enterprises and produced economic havoc among the professional and self-employed classes. The Negro community was rocked to its very foundation; and became enshrouded with a gloom of despair which has been made more ominous in its demoralizing effects upon the Negro family and the youth by the subsequent mass unemployment and unemployableness among the migrating hordes of the forties and fifties.

The role of education as a limiting and as an accelerating factor in the economic progress of Negroes is as important today as it ever was; perhaps, more important. Since 1940, improvement of the occupational status, incomes, and employment of Negroes has been due mainly to better educational preparation and technical training in schools and on the job, while high rates of unemployment and low incomes have tended to be positively correlated with low levels of knowledge, skill, ambition, and incentive. Although occupational and income differences between Negroes and whites in the civilian labor force remain large, the gains achieved by Negroes have in some respects been more rapid.

For example, the percentage of Negroes working as skilled craftsmen or foremen more than doubled between 1940 and 1962 while that of the whites increased by about 5 per cent. The magnitude of the change was of the same order in professional and technical operations, and among nonfarm managers and officials. However, in 1962, only 8 per cent of the Negro males as compared with about 25 per cent of the whites were in professional or managerial occupations. Approximately 20 per cent of the whites were skilled craftsmen or foremen but only 9 per cent of the Negroes were in this category. Over 15 per cent of the Negro males were in service occupations and an equal percentage in farm work, as compared with 6 and 9 per cent, respectively, for the whites. Negro women are still mainly employed in domestic service work, although between 1940 and 1962 the percentage fell from 58 to 37. The number of Negro women in clerical work had increased by 1962; but it was a small fraction of the percentage of the white women in clerical work. In 1940, approximately 214,000 Negroes were working in Federal, state, and local governments. The number had increased to over one million in 1962, the proportion to all government employees thus increasing from 5.6 to 12.1 per cent.

A major factor of improvement has been the considerable shift of Negroes from part-time to full-time employment. Along with this increase in the number of Negroes to full-time, there has been an increase in the number of Negroes remaining in school. It is highly probable that with expanded and more certain income the savings of the family formerly held against contingencies incidental to part-time employment have been used to prolong the education of their children.

Education and the Economic Status of Negroes

TABLE 1

DISTRIBUTION OF EMPLOYED PERSONS BY MAJOR OCCUPATION GROUP, COLOR, AND SEX, APRIL 1940 AND APRIL 1962

Major Occupation Group and Sex	Number (thousands)		Percent			
	White	Nonwhite	White		Nonwhite	
	1962	1962	1940	1962	1940	1962
Males						
Total	40,104	4,079	100.0	100.0	100.0	100.0
Professional, technical, and kindred workers	4,924	181	5.9	12.3	1.9	4.4
Managers, officials, and proprietors, except farm	6,119	157	10.6	15.3	1.6	3.8
Clerical and kindred workers	2,891	255	7.1	7.2	1.2	6.2
Sales workers	2,576	65	6.7	6.4	.9	1.6
Craftsmen, foremen, and kindred workers	7,982	367	15.5	19.9	4.4	9.0
Operatives and kindred workers	7,497	968	18.8	18.7	12.2	23.7
Laborers, except farm and mine	2,352	895	7.5	5.9	20.5	21.9
Service workers, except private household	2,305	600	5.8	5.7	12.4	14.7
Private household workers	27	22	.2	.1	2.9	.5
Farmers and farm managers	2,379	221	14.0	5.9	21.3	5.4
Farm laborers and foremen	1,052	349	6.8	2.6	19.9	8.6
Occupation not reported	—	—	1.0	—	.7	—
Females						
Total	19,914	2,727	100.0	100.0	100.0	100.0
Professional, technical, and kindred workers	2,740	201	14.3	13.8	4.3	7.4
Managers, officials, and proprietors, except farm	1,103	45	4.3	5.5	.8	1.7
Clerical and kindred workers	6,669	279	24.6	33.5	1.0	10.2
Sales workers	1,625	61	8.0	8.2	.6	2.2
Craftsmen, foremen, and kindred workers	220	18	1.2	1.1	.2	.7
Operatives and kindred workers	2,891	397	20.2	14.5	6.6	14.6
Laborers, except farm and mine	90	22	.9	.5	.9	.8
Service workers, except private household	2,752	613	11.3	13.8	10.5	22.5
Private household workers	1,259	1,016	10.8	6.3	58.0	37.3
Farmers and farm managers	130	7	1.2	.7	3.2	.3
Farm laborers and foremen	437	66	1.2	2.2	12.8	2.4
Occupation not reported	—	—	2.0	—	1.1	—

NOTE.—1962 estimates are not completely comparable with 1940.

Source: U.S. Department of Commerce, Bureau of the Census, and U.S. Department of Labor, Bureau of Labor Statistics. Taken from U.S. Department of Labor, *The Economic Situation of Negroes in the United States*, Bulletin S–3, Revised 1962, p. 7.

As should be expected, the improvements in occupational status are reflected in the higher earnings of Negroes. In 21 metropolitan areas, it is reported that the number of non-whites earning $4,000 a year increased from 59,000 in 1949 to 740,000 in 1959. The number earning over $6,000 increased from 12,000 to 210,000 in the same period. The differential between the earnings of whites and Negroes is still wide but it has been progressively narrowed in the last twenty-five years. In 1939, the earnings of Negro male workers averaged about 41 per cent of those of white workers; but by 1960, about 60 per cent. This comparison includes earnings in part-time or part-year employment. When full-year, full-time work is made the basis of comparison, Negro males averaged $3,789 in 1960, or about 67 per cent of the rate for white males.

TABLE 2

MEDIAN WAGE AND SALARY INCOMES OF WHITE AND NONWHITE PERSONS, 1939–1960

Year	Male		Female		Nonwhite as Percent of White	
	White	Non-white	White	Non-white	Male	Female
All persons with wage or salary income:						
1939	$1,112	$460	$676	$246	41.4	36.4
1947	2,357	1,279	1,269	432	54.3	34.0
1957	4,396	2,436	2,240	1,019	55.4	45.5
1958	4,569	2,652	2,364	1,055	58.0	44.6
1959	4,902	2,844	2,422	1,289	58.0	53.2
1960	5,137	3,075	2,537	1,276	59.9	50.3
Year-round full-time workers with wage or salary income:						
1939	1,419	639	863	327	45.0	37.9
1957	4,950	3,137	3,107	1,866	63.4	60.1
1958	5,186	3,368	3,225	1,988	64.9	61.6
1959	5,456	3,339	3,306	2,196	61.2	66.4
1960	5,662	3,789	3,410	2,372	66.9	69.6

Source: U.S. Department of Commerce, Bureau of the Census. Taken from U.S. Department of Labor, *The Economic Situation of Negroes*, p. 9.

No impartial consideration of the facts would lead one to conclude that the discrepancies between the educational opportunities of Negroes and whites have disappeared. And, yet it is certain that in the last twenty years, expenditures for the

Education and the Economic Status of Negroes

education of Negroes have increased more rapidly than for whites in Southern states. In the North, where *de facto* segregation of schools is fairly general, the education available to Negroes is undoubtedly superior to what they can obtain in the South. In the 1960–61 school term, approximately 7 per cent of the Negro children in Washington and 17 Southern and border states were in public schools with whites. Integration in the public schools will be slow for reasons that are to be

TABLE 3
PERCENT OF WHITES AND NONWHITES ENROLLED IN SCHOOL, BY AGE, 1940, 1956, AND 1960

Age	*April* 1940		*October* 1956		*October* 1960	
	White	Non-white	White	Non-white	White	Non-white
Total, 7–24	59.7	55.3	73.8	69.9	75.1	72.8
7–13	95.5	91.2	99.4	98.4	99.6	99.1
14–17	80.7	68.2	89.2	81.2	90.8	86.8
18–24	13.8	9.1	20.1	15.8	21.8	15.9
18–19	29.8	21.1	35.9	31.8	38.9	34.6
20–24	6.9	3.8	13.4	8.7	13.9	7.5

Source: U.S. Department of Commerce, Bureau of the Census. Taken from U.S. Department of Labor, *The Economic Situation of Negroes*, p. 27.

TABLE 4
MEDIAN YEARS OF SCHOOL COMPLETED BY PERSONS 25 YEARS OLD AND OVER, AND 25 TO 29 YEARS OLD, BY COLOR AND SEX, 1940 TO 1959

Date and Age	Male		Female	
	White	Non-white	White	Non-white
25 years and over				
April 1940	8.7	5.4	8.l	6.1
April 1947	9.0	6.6	9.7	7.2
October 1952	10.1	6.8	10.8	7.4
March 1957	10.7	7.3	11.3	8.1
March 1959	11.1	7.6	11.6	8.4
Increase, 1940 to 1959, in years completed	2.4	2.2	2.8	2.3
25 to 29 years				
April 1940	10.5	6.5	10.9	7.5
March 1957	12.3	9.4	12.3	10.3
March 1959	12.5	10.9	12.4	11.0
Increase, 1940 to 1959, in years completed	2.0	4.4	1.5	3.5

Source: U.S. Department of Commerce, Bureau of the Census. Taken from U.S. Department of Labor, *The Economic Situation of Negroes*, p. 28.

indicated later. Nevertheless, the number of Negroes who continue school has increased. In 1940, 91 per cent of Negro children aged seven to thirteen and 96 per cent of the whites in this age group were in school. In 1960, the percentages for the two races were about equal. Furthermore, in 1959 Negro males aged twenty-five to twenty-nine had 4.4 years more schooling than in 1940.

We have referred to the relative rise of the occupational levels of Negroes and the reflection of it in higher earnings in the last two or three decades. Whether better educational preparation is considered as cause or effect of this improvement, the level of income and the level of educational attainment are definitely interrelated. Table 5 indicates that the Negroes with the greater amounts of education tended to have the higher incomes.

TABLE 5

MEAN INCOMES OF NONWHITE MALES.
BY AGE AND EDUCATIONAL LEVEL.
UNITED STATES 1950.
(In Dollars)

	Education			
Age	*No Schooling*	*Elementary Schooling*	*High School*	*College or More*
18–19	570	809	809	—
20–21	808	1,177	1,349	—
22–24	997	1,520	1,783	1,555
25–29	1,109	1,747	2,137	2,121
30–34	1,187	1,916	2,374	2,950
35–44	1,300	2,008	2,453	3,437
45–54	1,254	2,068	2,419	3,639
55–64	1,108	1,921	2,238	3,246

Taken from Jacob Mincer, "On-the-Job Training; Costs, Returns, and Some Implications," *The Journal of Political Economy*, Supplement, LXX, No. 5, Part 2 (October, 1962), 79.

Although the amount of education of Negroes has significantly increased, the quality has hardly improved to the same degree. It is only the exceptional Negro youth whose elementary and secondary schooling was not in an effectively segregated school. Either because of low family income, or timidity and fear of competing for scholarships in Northern colleges and universities, most Negro high-school graduates who continue to college go to all-Negro institutions. A study of management practices with respect to Negro employment points out that "Negroes who have undertaken advanced study in all-Negro educational institutions emerge less well equipped than white students with an equivalent period of college training."[27] The curriculum of the Negro institutions of higher learning is geared to preparation for careers in the professions of teaching, law, medicine, dentistry, and religion. Thus, in spite of the shortage of scientific and engineering personnel in recent years, few Negroes had been prepared for these professions. In 1957, less than 200 Negro students graduated as engineers from colleges and universities throughout the country, although in 1956, approximately 26,000 students graduated with engineering degrees in the country as a whole.[28] The few all-Negro institutions that have engineering courses are not only limited in size but also, with one possible exception, deficient in standards. In its emphasis upon preparation for the teaching, legal, and medical professions, the all-Negro university reflects the prestige value traditionally attached to these professions by the Negro community and the fact that the Negro community affords a sheltered market for services of the graduates. Today the employment of Negroes in the scientific and engineering fields is limited *not by racial barriers* but by the number who have the requisite professional training.

Leaders in the integrationist movement would admit that the relatively poor educational preparation of Negroes and their inferior income-employment status are causally linked. They would insist, however, that both phenomena are caused primarily by racial discrimination. The contention cannot be dismissed out of hand, as there is much to be said in support of it. The strongest support is found in the racial pattern of employment prevailing in Southern industry.

In the view of one authority there are certain "uniformities," virtually "laws" of labor, used in the economy of the

[27] Paul H. Norgren, Albert N. Webster, Roger D. Borgeson and Maud B. Patten, *Employing the Negro in American Industry* (Industrial Relations Monograph, No. 17; New York: Industrial Relations Counselors, Inc., 1959), p. 24.
[28] *Ibid.*

South. They are: (1) "Negro workers seldom hold jobs which require them to give orders to white workers," and (2) Negro and white workers do not ordinarily work side by side on the same job. The first "law" is unexceptional, more or less. Exceptions to the second are numerically important only in "dirty, low-wage and, generally low 'net advantage' employment."[29] Because of these two rules, Negroes and whites do not compete "as individual workers on their respective merits" but as "in bloc" work groups. An employer may choose between using white or Negro workers in a given set of jobs; but "he seldom has the third option of using a mixed work group."[30] Given this employment pattern, the upgrading of Negroes is difficult. "Since most skills are developed by on-the-job experience which Negro workers perforce cannot acquire the decision to introduce a Negro work group usually means the willingness to train it from scratch—without even a cadre of experienced workers to build upon. . . ."[31] Thus, as "the quality of male white labor available at a given wage rate declines, a southern employer reacts by exploring the possibility of upgrading white women, since they can be fitted into his labor force far more easily than Negro men."[32] A reasonable but not greatly optimistic prediction of the future seems to be this: when the migration of rural white Southerners diminishes, an impressive number of Negro workers may gain employment in jobs requiring skills that can be obtained by formal schooling, e.g., typing, bookkeeping, and nursing, even though the general pattern of employment remains unchanged. "Color lines will show their greatest tenacity in the skilled trades and organized factory employment. . . . No aspect of race relations in the South makes the mass upgrading of Negro workers 'inevitable' in the short run; that is, neither the removal of discriminations enforced by law nor the spread of Negro voting will automatically undermine the color bars in industry."[33]

An indirect support for the view that racial discrimination

[29] Donald Dewey, "Negro Employment in Southern Industry," *Journal of Political Economy*, LX, No. 4 (August, 1952), 281.
[30] *Ibid.*, p. 283.
[31] *Ibid.*, p. 286.
[32] *Ibid.*, p. 287.
[33] *Ibid.*, p. 291.

is the main deterrent in the industrial advancement of Negroes is to be found in the changes effected in the Armed Forces since the President's Executive Order 9981, July 26, 1948. Prior to this time the overwhelming majority of Negro servicemen were assigned to segregated units with specialized tasks, especially those of a housekeeping character. The acceptance of Negroes in the three branches, Army, Air Force, and Navy, was limited by the number of men needed to maintain the strength of these separate units. Today in each service in all branches of the Armed Forces, the number employed is limited only by the number of Negroes qualified for the service. In the National Guard, and the Reserve Components the color bar remains, but this appears to be due to state laws. Some idea of the result of the change in the policies in the regular Armed Forces is gained from Table 6. With the removal of the color

TABLE 6

NEGRO PERSONNEL AS PERCENTAGE OF TOTAL PERSONNEL
IN MILITARY SERVICES.

	1949	1954	1956
Army officers	1.8	2.9	2.9
Army enlisted men	12.4	13.7	12.8
Navy officers	—	.1	.1
Navy enlisted men	4.7	3.6	6.3
Air Force Officers	.6	1.1	1.1
Air Force enlisted men	5.1	8.6	10.4
Marine Corps Officers	—	.1	.1
Marine Corps enlisted men	2.1	6.5	6.5

Taken from United States Commission on Civil Rights Report, *Employment*, Book 3, 1961, p. 47.

bar, enlistment in the Armed Forces has become particularly attractive to Negro youth. Many have elected to become military career men. Others have been enabled by the training programs of the military services to secure civilian jobs requiring technical skill. Within the brief span of a decade or more, progress in the utilization of Negro manpower in the Armed Forces has been phenomenal. Today the main deterrent to a greater utilization is caused not by the color bar but by the Negro's deficient education and training. For instance, in the General Classification Test given by the Army from March 1941 through

May 1946, 67.8 per cent of the 8,720,764 enlisted white males scored 90 and above; but of the 1,036,819 enlisted Negro males, only 16.6 per cent scored 90 and above. Only 14.4 of the whites tested were below 70, while 51.6 per cent of the Negroes were below 70. The results of later mental tests did not differ greatly. The percentage distribution among mental groups of men examined for military service in December 1951 was as follows for the country as a whole:

Mental Groups	White	Negro[34]
I	6.3	0.4
II	24.0	3.5
III	34.3	14.1
IV	31.3	52.3
V	4.1	29.7

In brief, 65 per cent of the whites scored in the upper three of the five groups and 35 per cent in the two lowest groups. Only 18 per cent of the Negroes scored in the upper groups while 82 per cent fell in the lowest groups.[35]

When the difference in the educational levels of Negroes and whites, and the high degree of functional illiteracy among Negroes (i.e., inability to read and write as well as the average fifth-grade student) are considered, racial discrimination becomes less significant as a handicap to Negro employment and earning opportunities in the North. In Chicago, an operator of a personnel service for Negroes observed, "Anybody who comes in here with technical skill, we can place him, just like that."[36] He then referred to employment forms showing that 62 Negro girl high-school graduates failed to get office jobs because they could not pass vocabulary and arithmetic tests of sixth to seventh grade difficulty. A Chicago firm without a color bar canvassed 250 Negro men and women during a three-month period. Only *one* was hired. The others were not hired because of (1) low intelligence quotients; (2) unstable job records; and (3) "personality characteristics that indicated poor reliability, from operating machines to showing up for work."[37] The newspaper

[34] Eli Ginzberg, *et al.*, *The Negro Potential* (New York: Columbia University Press, 1956), p. 103.

[35] *Ibid.*, p. 102.

[36] *Chicago Sun Times*, Jan. 7, 1962.

[37] *Ibid.*, Feb. 10, 1962.

that reported this incident observed editorially that "in view of the prevalence of free day, night, and trade schools, there is no excuse for it, and no future for the incompetent and unreliable except on relief."[38] But this is not a uniquely Chicago story. It is repeated many times in the urban centers of the North. The aforementioned study of management practices states that "even if Negroes comprised a substantial proportion of the population in areas of plentiful employment, and if they had complete equality of opportunity in the competition for more skilled and better paid jobs, only a small number would be able to qualify."[39]

It is a fact, of course, that racial discrimination is most significant among the historical and sociological circumstances that have determined the character of the existing Negro occupational structure. However, an employer with no taste for discrimination will not hire, even for break-in jobs, a man who lacks the elementary skills and the level of ability to deal with words and figures. Thus, in the North, at least, the relatively higher volume of Negroes unemployed and on relief rolls is not immediately caused by discrimination but by deficient educational preparation and a lack of elementary skills. In the business downturn of 1958, unemployment rose among both Negroes and whites. At that time about 14 per cent of nonwhite male workers, mainly in the unskilled and semiskilled occupations, were unemployed, as compared with 6 per cent of whites. The rates were lower for both groups in 1961, but nearly 13 per cent of nonwhites even then were still unemployed in comparison with 5.7 per cent of whites. Unemployment by annual average and by race for 1961 is given in Table 7.

Preparation for the world of work does not begin with formal school training. It begins informally in the home. It is here that the habits and aptitudes in speech and in the handling of figures are developed in the early formative years of childhood. It is, also, here that the basic values of the community, including those connected with work, are first taught, and ambition and incentive first inspired. In the discharge of these normal functions, the homes of Negro children in low-income and migrant families are grievously deficient. As a re-

[38] *Ibid.*
[39] Norgren, *et al., op. cit.,* p. 23.

TABLE 7

UNEMPLOYED AS PERCENT OF CIVILIAN LABOR FORCE, BY AGE,
ANNUAL AVERAGE, 1961

Age	Male		Female	
	White	Non-white	White	Non-white
Total, 14 years and over	5.7	12.9	6.5	11.9
14–17 years	13.3	25.5	13.3	24.6
18 and 19 years	15.2	23.8	13.6	28.1
20–24 years	10.1	15.3	8.4	19.6
25–34 years	4.9	12.9	6.6	11.1
35–44 years	4.0	10.7	5.6	10.7
45–54 years	4.4	10.2	4.8	7.4
55–64 years	5.3	10.5	4.3	6.6
65 years and over	5.2	9.2	3.8	6.5

Source: U.S. Department of Labor, Bureau of Labor Statistics. Taken from U.S. Department of Labor, *The Economic Situation of Negroes*, p. 3.

sult, Negro children in these families are handicapped long before they begin school.

The problem of the Negro family arises from three inter-related conditions: (1) parental relationships, (2) the large number of Negro mothers who must work outside the home, and (3) excessively large families that reflect a constantly high natural increase of population. A "disproportionately large number of young Negroes are brought up in homes in which the father has deserted or in other situations where major responsibility for the continuance of the family unit centers around the mother and her relatives."[40] At the 1950 Census, "over one-third of the Negro women who had ever been married were no longer married or no longer living with their husbands. This was true of only one-fifth of the white women. The absence of the father, or the fact that he often plays a secondary role when present, makes it difficult for the young Negro male to develop strong motivation for work."[41] The role of the father in the disorganization of the Negro family has been described by E. Franklin Frazier in this manner:

> The incidence of desertion on the part of the male . . . is much greater among Negroes than among other

[40] Ginzberg, *op. cit.*, p. 98.
[41] *Ibid.*

racial or ethnic elements in the population. . . . Since
family disorganization is so widespread, the family
environment of a large number of Negro children is
precarious and fragmentary. . . . Because of the lack
of discipline, the children in such homes never acquire
the most elementary habits in regard to cleanliness or
even as to eating. . . . They do not even acquire the
domestic work skills necessary to make a living. . . .

Negro children from disorganized families often exhibit little interest in the knowledge and the skills provided by the public schools because it has little or no
meaning for them in terms of their family background.
. . . The lack of family discipline and a failure of the
disorganized family to provide models . . . of the values
of the community are partly responsible at least for the
irregular work habits and lack of ambition among
many Negro youths. . . . The mitigation of this problem must await those changes in the Negro and American society which will enable the Negro father to play
the role required of him.[42]

The irresponsibility of the father, and where this is not the
case, his low level of employment and income, forces the mother
into part-time or full-time employment outside the home. Accordingly, the proportion of Negro women in the civilian labor force
exceeds that of white women. In 1961, there were approximately
13 million Negroes in the civilian population fourteen years of
age and over. The number of Negro women in the civilian labor
force was 46 per cent of the Negro civilian population. The
white civilian population fourteen years of age and over was
about 112 million. White women in the labor force were a little
over 21 million, slightly less than 36 per cent of the white civilian
population.

The inability of the Negro mother to give her children
proper care and upbringing, because she must work either as
the breadwinner or to supplement the husband's income, is augmented by the large number of children in the family. The
Negro birth rate and also the death rate were for some time
higher than the white. In 1920 the Negro birth rate was around
35 per 1,000 population while the death rate was 25, giving an
increase of 10. The white birth rate was approximately 27 and

[42] *Ibid.*, p. 99.

the death rate about 13, giving an increase of 14. With the better medical care available to Negroes in the North, and with improvement in their knowledge of sanitation and the conditions of health, the Negro death rate has steadily decreased and now closely approximates that of the white. The Negro birth rate remains higher than the white. The situation in Chicago is probably typical of all Northern cities with heavily concentrated Negro populations. In 1940, the white birth rate was 15 and the death rate was 11, while the Negro birth rate was 18 and the death rate 15. But in 1955, the white birth rate was 20 and the death rate 11, while the Negro birth rate was approximately 37 and the death rate 10. For the white population in Chicago, the excess of births over deaths was 9, and for the Negro 27. For the country as a whole in 1940, the white birth rate was 18.6, the death rate 10.4, and the natural increase 8.2. The Negro birth rate was 26.7, the death rate 13.8, and the natural increase 12.9. But in 1950 the white birth rate was 23.8, the death rate 9.2, and the natural increase 14.6. But the Negro birth rate in 1950 was about 34.7, while the death rate was 10, an increase of 24.7. The death and birth rates for nonwhites and whites from 1900 to 1960 for the country as a whole are given in Table 8.

TABLE 8

BIRTH AND DEATH RATES, WHITE AND NONWHITE, 1900–60
(Number per 1,000 population)

Year	Birth rate			Death rate		
	Total	White	Non-white	Total	White	Non-white
1900	(¹)	(¹)	(¹)	17.2	17.0	25.0
1920	27.7	26.9	35.0	13.0	12.6	17.7
1930	21.3	20.6	27.5	11.3	10.8	16.3
1940	19.4	18.6	26.7	10.8	10.4	13.8
1950	24.1	23.0	33.3	9.6	9.5	11.2
1958	24.6	23.4	34.2	9.5	9.4	10.2
1959	24.3	23.1	34.0	9.4	9.4	9.9
1960	23.7	22.7	32.1	9.5	9.4	10.0

(¹) Not available.

NOTE.—Birth rates, except 1960, have been adjusted for underregistration.

Source: U.S. Department of Health, Education, and Welfare, Public Health Service. Taken from U.S. Department of Labor, *The Economic Situation of Negroes*, p. 1.

The increase of the number of children since 1940 has been at least twice as great in Negro as in white families. This production of excessive offspring in the Negro family results, partly, from ignorance, and, partly from the persistence of habits fostered by the Negro's rural conditioning, whereby the child is considered as an income-producing asset rather than as a consumer of expenditures that are made, in the main, for no other purpose than the child's own cultivation. If the habit of producing large families could be changed by the education of the parents, economic distress would be considerably lessened among Negroes of low incomes and the assimilation of their offspring to urban ways and manners immensely facilitated. But if in the next decade the present rate of natural increase continues, the problem of slums and family demoralization will hardly lessen even if the incomes of these families rise.

The gap between the economic status of the Negroes and whites is cause and effect of cultural and educational differences. The success of integration in the schools will depend not only upon the public's compliance with the Supreme Court's decision of 1954, voluntarily or by legal coercion, but upon narrowing the cultural and economic gap between the two races. Until this gap is greatly narrowed, integration will of necessity be "token." If the gap is to be eventually closed, the Negro mass must be taught to understand and brought to accept certain characteristics of our society. The first of these is that notwithstanding the increasing assistance of the state to the unfortunate, our society in its economic relations is still one that rests upon individual responsibility and the value of one's performance to other people. This is the logic of the competitive market place; and able-bodied adults who do not order their lives according to this logic must expect to be the wards of the welfare state. The second fact is that although racial discrimination may be a potent cause of the economic disabilities of Negroes as a group, with the availability of free public instruction, technical and academic, in day and night schools, Negro youths who are unable to secure good jobs because of educational deficiencies cannot legitimately attribute their misfortune to the white employer's prejudice. The displacement of labor by automation is now a cause of great alarm. In the twenties it was the technological revolution. In the eighteenth century it was the Industrial Revolution. But in all three of these phases of economic progress the machines not only displaced old skills, but created newer ones and increased the demand for a better-trained work force. The age of automation differs only in that jobs at the break-in level will require a much higher educational preparation than twenty years ago. Thus the third fact that has to be impressed upon Negro youth is that a high school diploma has a decreasing employment value and that the drop-outs will be forced to compete for unskilled jobs where competition becomes fiercer every day. The situation is described by a white employer in these words:

> In our plant we employ skilled tool and die makers (educated in trade schools and experienced by years of shop work), and individuals for a specialized hand operation requiring no education, but training for two years before workers begin to earn even a small wage. This is an expensive investment.
> For both jobs—or either—by what indicators are we to know how ambitious a boy is? One who hasn't the backbone or old-fashioned gumption to stick to school probably will not stick on the job. . . .
> A high school education is barely enough. Two years of trade school, such as electronics, tool and die, machine shop, bookkeeping, or other specialized courses, will barely be enough for last year's and this year's graduates.
> Competition for unskilled jobs this year is fantastic. One of our trainees even asked for a pay cut because he is not doing too well, and he feared being fired.
> In industry we need young people who can think, reason, and be responsible.
> Even the high school graduates who apply for jobs as trainees do not impress us much. What kind of an impression do you think a dropout makes?[43]

These facts of our social life will impress Negro youth to the extent that they can be fired with ambition and hope in the

[43] Lawrence N. Gabriel, Vice President, Acme Scientific Company, "High School Barely Enough; Job Competition 'Fantastic,'" *Chicago Daily News*, Feb. 13, 1963.

face of great obstacles, and the fire must be started initially in the family. The legal movement for equal rights of citizenship will and should continue. But the chief beneficiaries of the removal of discriminations by law (and this includes fair employment practice laws) and the spread of Negro voting will be the educated, talented, and politically astute Negroes. The advancement of the masses of Negroes will depend upon improving their productive capacity as industrial workers; raising the morale of the family and assimilating it to urban life; increasing the concern for family planning; and finally—the basis of the three preceding conditions—improving their education, formal and informal, and their technical training.

Louis H. Pollak

•

EMANCIPATION AND LAW: A CENTURY OF PROCESS

> . . . It is a fact that every American Negro bears a name that
> originally belonged to the white man whose chattel he was. I
> am called Baldwin because I was either sold by my African tribe
> or kidnapped out of it into the hands of a white Christian
> named Baldwin, who forced me to kneel at the foot of the cross.
> I am, then, both visibly and legally the descendant of slaves in a
> white, Protestant country, and this is what it means to be an
> American Negro, this is who he is—a kidnapped pagan, who was
> sold like an animal and treated like one, who was once defined
> by the American Constitution as "three-fifths" of a man, and
> who, according to the Dred Scott decision, had no rights that a
> white man was bound to respect. And today, a hundred years
> after his technical emancipation, he remains—with the possible
> exception of the American Indian—the most despised creature
> in his country.

These prefatory sentences are, of course, written by James Baldwin. They are taken from his overwhelming "Letter from a
Region in My Mind."[1] There, at pitiless length, he itemizes and
analyzes the ingredients of "technical emancipation." It is a
status which most American Negroes probably know all too well
without Mr. Baldwin's assistance. And, by the same token, it is
questionable whether even Mr. Baldwin's "Letter" can commu-
nicate more than a smattering of the grotesque reality to most
American whites. But possibly there are ways in which whites
can supplement Mr. Baldwin's text, and thereby sense a little
more of what he means. It might be fruitful, for example, to
think about what our society is doing for and to James Mere-

---

[1] *Down at the Cross*, reprinted from *The Fire Next Time* by James
Baldwin, and used by permission of the publishers, The Dial Press. Originally published in *The New Yorker*, Nov. 17, 1962, p. 128, as "Letter
from a Region in My Mind."

dith, who was constantly in danger of being harassed out of "Ole Miss," the state university he survived a civil war to enroll in, until his graduation eight months later. Or one might ponder the fate of the late Clyde Kennard, a young man who made so bold as to apply for admission to Mississippi Southern, and who paid for his arrogance by doing time in a Mississippi prison, until released to undergo treatment for a fatal stomach cancer. Perhaps, too, a walk through Harlem would sufficiently indicate that Mr. Baldwin has real cities in mind.

The essay which follows does not purport to evaluate the totality of Mr. Baldwin's "Letter." It seeks only to explore the implication, evident in the quoted prefatory sentences, that, in the century which has elapsed since the Emancipation Proclamation, American legal institutions have not contrived to add one cubit to the stature of the American Negro—that he is still no more than "three-fifths" of a man. The ensuing pages venture a different conclusion: In the first half-century the law was not merely impotent, but largely retrograde. In the second half-century the law—slowly, as is its way—regained its integrity and momentum, and is today a forceful instrument for fashioning a democratic America.

THE EMANCIPATION PROCLAMATION

By midsummer of 1862, Lincoln was in a quandary. In the preceding months, Congress had passed laws abolishing slavery in the territories and the District of Columbia, and providing for the confiscation of the slaves of those persons in the rebellious states who persisted in supporting the Confederate cause. These laws of course harmonized with Lincoln's individual predilections—it was, as he assured Horace Greeley, his *"personal* wish that all men everywhere could be free."[2] But there was the troublesome question of whether the federal government had power to end slavery, particularly within the states—a question which doubtless contributed to Lincoln's reluctance to enforce the confiscation statute with any vigor. Doubts as to the extent of federal power to halt slavery stemmed chiefly from Chief Justice Taney's opinion in the *Dred Scott* case,[3] which Lincoln had

[2] Letter to Greeley, Aug. 22, 1862.
[3] *Scott* v. *Sandford,* 19 How. 393 (1857).

publicly denounced as mischievous and wrongheaded in the extreme; but the opinion was still the law of the land—and Taney was still Chief Justice.[4] And overarching all these considerations was Lincoln's sense of his official responsibility, which he also communicated to Greeley: "My paramount object is to save the Union, and is *not* either to save or to destroy slavery."

So the issue of emancipation was, in the last analysis, a practical one: Would it advance the Union cause? Lincoln knew that his military efforts would get great moral impetus from a declaration linking the advance of his armies to the freeing of slaves: this would be so throughout the North, and, perhaps even more important, among the great European powers which must at all costs be kept isolated from the Confederacy. Yet timing was obviously vital: a declaration launched from a position of military weakness could be counterproductive. And the news from the battlefronts—Richmond and Bull Run—was inauspicious. But then, on September 17, came Antietam, and five days later Lincoln announced that one hundred days thereafter, "on the 1st day of January, A.D. 1863, all persons held as slaves within any State or designated part of a State the people whereof shall then be in rebellion against the United States shall be then, thenceforward, and forever free. . . ."

One hundred days came and went, and on New Year's Day, 1863, "Abraham Lincoln, President of the United States, by virtue of the power in [him] vested as Commander in Chief of the Army and Navy of the United States in time of actual armed rebellion . . . and as a fit and necessary war measure for repressing said rebellion," issued the promised Proclamation.

> This was no ringing call to freedom. It sounded like a legal document; it was about as emotional as a bill of sale. Its terms . . . did not assert that all slaves, everywhere, "are, and henceforward shall be, free," but only those slaves in areas still actively rebellious. . . . Contemporaries commented, both at home and abroad, that Lincoln was declaring the slaves free only in the places where, at the moment, he had no real power to free them. . . . After two years, when the war was drawing

[4] As Lincoln knew full well from the Chief Justice's stirring protest against Lincoln's suspension of *habeas corpus*. See Ex parte *Merryman*, Fed. Cas. No. 9, 487 (C.C.D. Md., 1861).

to a close, Lincoln estimated that some 200,000 slaves had gained their freedom in consequence of his proclamation. That was only about one in twenty of all the slaves, who at the start of the war had numbered nearly four million. And even those 200,000 could not be sure that their freedom would be permanent. Lincoln himself doubted the constitutionality of his edict, except as a temporary war measure.[5]

If the Emancipation Proclamation was, in its inception, an ambivalent document, the ambivalence evaporated as the fighting went on. By the winter of 1865, as the war entered its last months, history had merged the moral and the merely instrumental. Lincoln, in his Second Inaugural, acknowledged not only that both sides had always known slavery "was somehow the cause of the war," but also that the war to save the Union was indissolubly a war to end slavery:

> Fondly do we hope, fervently do we pray, that this mighty scourge of war may speedily pass away. Yet, if God wills that it continue until all the wealth piled by the bondsman's two hundred and fifty years of unrequited toil shall be sunk, and every drop of blood drawn with the lash shall be paid by another drawn with the sword, as was said three thousand years ago, so still it must be said, "the judgments of the Lord are true and righteous altogether."

THE THIRTEENTH, FOURTEENTH, AND FIFTEENTH AMENDMENTS

Within weeks, the fighting was over and Lincoln was dead. Within months, the Thirteenth Amendment announced that slavery was at an end, forever, throughout the American domain. But the freed Negro had, for a time, good reason to doubt that the face of the law had really changed. For the directives closest at hand were not the lordly imperatives of the Constitution. They were local Black Codes which, while conferring certain limited civil rights to own property and to sue, typically "required [the freedman] to have some steady occupation, and subjected [him] to special penalties for violation of labor contracts. Vagrancy and apprenticeship laws were especially harsh, and lent themselves readily to the establishment of a system of peon-

[5] Richard N. Current, "Lincoln and the Proclamation," *The Progressive,* XXVI (Dec., 1962), 11.

age."[6] But federal power was not wholly quiescent: the Radical Republican Congress produced a series of Federal Civil Rights Laws (including a law making peonage a federal crime) ; sponsored federal military rule in wide areas of the South; and submitted to the states two proposed changes in the Constitution. In 1868 and 1870, respectively, these changes were ratified by the states as the Fourteenth and Fifteenth Amendments.

The Fourteenth Amendment is complex and diffuse. Looked at in retrospect, two of its major purposes overshadow the others. The first of these was to establish—in repudiation of the holding in *Dred Scott* that neither slaves, nor former slaves, nor the issue of slaves, could become citizens of the United States—that "all persons born or naturalized in the United States . . . are citizens of the United States and of the State wherein they reside." The second was to protect all persons (whether or not citizens) from being victimized, *at the hands of their state governments,* by arbitrary procedures or discriminatory policies: ". . . nor shall any State deprive any person of life, liberty, or property without due process of law; nor deny to any person within its jurisdiction the equal protection of the laws."[7]

The Fifteenth Amendment sought to insure participation by the freed Negro in the political life of the nation, by proscribing state or federal abridgment of the right to vote "on account of race, color, or previous condition of servitude."[8] The Amendment was the nation's redemption of a moral commitment Lincoln himself had acknowledged, not alone Lincoln the Emancipator, but Lincoln the Commander-in-Chief, who knew himself to be "the nation's guardian of these people, who have so heroically vindicated their manhood on the battle-field, where, in assisting to save the life of the Republic, they have demonstrated in blood

[6] S. E. Morison and H. S. Commager, *Growth of the American Republic* (3d ed.; New York: Oxford, 1942) , II, 17.

[7] This summary of Section 1 of the Amendment deliberately omits the privileges and immunities clause and the controversies engendered thereby. Also, again deliberately, no mention is made of the thus-far-moribund Section 2 of the Amendment, or of Sections 3 and 4.

[8] The Fifteenth Amendment re-enforced, in the area of voting rights, the generality of the Fourteenth Amendment's equal protection clause. It also supplemented the mechanism created by Section 2 of the Fourteenth Amendment for reducing the Congressional representation of states which disenfranchised Negro males—a mechanism which has never become operative.

their right to the ballot, which is but the humane protection of the flag they have so fearlessly defended."[9]

The central purposes underlying the Thirteenth, Fourteenth, and Fifteenth Amendments seem plain enough. So plain, indeed, that the Supreme Court had no difficulty in identifying these purposes in the first case it considered in which challenges to state legislation were predicated on the Thirteenth and Fourteenth Amendments. The year was 1873. The challenged legislation was a Louisiana statute, enacted in 1869, which conferred upon one corporation a twenty-five-year monopoly of the slaughtering business in New Orleans, and required that corporation to service all comers at prescribed rates. Independent butchers, barred by the operation of the statute from competing with the monopoly, contended that the state-ordained circumscription of their freedom to engage in their chosen calling transgressed rights embodied in the Thirteenth and Fourteenth Amendments. By a five-to-four margin, the Supreme Court, in the *Slaughter-House Cases,* concluded that the amendments were addressed to a wholly different realm of anticipated governmental preferences:

> We repeat, then, in the light of this recapitulation of events, almost too recent to be called history, but which are familiar to us all; and on the most casual examination of the language of these amendments, no one can fail to be impressed with the one pervading purpose found in them all, lying at the foundation of each, and without which none of them would have been even suggested; we mean the freedom of the slave race, the security and firm establishment of that freedom, and the protection of the newly-made freeman and citizen from the oppressions of those who had formerly exercised unlimited dominion over him. It is true that only the Fifteenth Amendment, in terms, mentions the negro by speaking of his color and his slavery. But it is just as true that each of the other articles was addressed to the grievances of that race, and designed to remedy them as the fifteenth.
>
> We do not say that no one else but the negro can share in this protection. Both the language and the

[9] From a letter written by Lincoln in January, 1864. Two months later Lincoln indicated that as an initial matter he favored extending the franchise to Negroes who were "very intelligent, and especially those who have fought gallantly in our ranks."

spirit of these articles are to have their fair and just
weight in any question of construction. Undoubtedly
while negro slavery alone was in the mind of the Congress which proposed the thirteenth article, it forbids
any other kind of slavery, now or hereafter. If Mexican
peonage or the Chinese coolie labor system shall develop
slavery of the Mexican or Chinese race within our territory, this amendment may safely be trusted to make it
void. And so if other rights are assailed by the States
which properly and necessarily fall within the protection
of these articles, that protection will apply, though the
party interested may not be of African descent. But
what we do say, and what we wish to be understood is,
that in any fair and just construction of any section or
phrase of these amendments, it is necessary to look to
the purpose which we have said was the pervading spirit
of them all, the evil which they were designed to remedy,
and the process of continued addition to the Constitution, until that purpose was supposed to be accomplished, as far as constitutional law can accomplish it.[10]

The Erosion of the Negro's Constitutional Rights

The dissenting Justices in the *Slaughter-House Cases* did not
seriously dispute the majority's assessment of the basic purposes
of the amendments. They saw those amendments—and especially
the Fourteenth—as a hospitable constitutional haven large enough
to embrace those subjected to differential state treatment of an
economic as well as of a racial dimension. And the dissenters thus
set in motion the lines of doctrine which were, in the ensuing
two generations, to spell out a new *substantive* economic freedom—"freedom of contract"—in the theretofore *procedurally*
oriented due process clause of the Fourteenth Amendment.

With the nuances, or even the major mileposts, of that phase
of American constitutional development this essay has no direct
concern. It is enough to remember that from the eighties and
nineties forward (with some backing and filling) to the mid-
1930's, the Supreme Court used the Fourteenth Amendment
against the states (and in due time, against Congress, the due
process language of the Fifth Amendment) as a device for invali-
dating myriad laws regulating business activity—maximum hour
and minimum wage laws, tax laws, laws regulating public utili-

[10] 16 Wall. 36, 71–72.

ties, consumer protection laws, etc. Today, and for the past quarter-century, the Court has recognized that this segment of constitutional history—however congenial to emergent business interests—was a calamitous, indeed a well-nigh ruinous, form of judicial displacement of the majority will. Today it is plain—as Justice Holmes vainly sought to persuade his colleagues back in 1905—that "a Constitution is not intended to embody a particular economic theory, whether of paternalism and the organic relation of the citizen to the State or of *laissez faire*."[11] But the Supreme Court wandered in the constitutional wilderness for several decades precisely because it routinely failed to examine the endlessly iterated Fourteenth Amendment–*laissez faire* equation in the light of those constitutional purposes spelled out in the *Slaughter-House Cases*. In consequence, as Justice Henry B. Brown, writing for the Court in 1898, acknowledged, "A majority of the cases which have . . . arisen [since *Slaughter-House*] have turned not upon a denial to the colored race of rights therein secured to them, but upon alleged discriminations in matters entirely outside. . . ."[12]

And, as Justice Brown well knew, not only were a minority of the Fourteenth Amendment cases ones involving Negro rights, but those which did arise tended to be decided adversely to those rights. To be sure, this was not invariably the case. In 1880, the Court invalidated a state law barring Negroes from jury service. The Court rested its decision in *Strauder* v. *West Virginia* on the ground that the equal protection clause of the Fourteenth Amendment meant precisely "that the law in the States shall be the same for the black as for the white," and that a law making Negroes ineligible "because of their color, though they are citizens, and may be in other respects fully qualified, is practically a brand upon them, affixed by the law, an assertion of their inferiority, and a stimulant to that race prejudice which is an impediment to securing to individuals of the race that equal justice which the law aims to secure to all others."[13]

But *Strauder*, though not the only such decision, was unrepresentative. Over-all, the Court lent itself readily to the new

---

[11] *Lochner* v. *New York*, 198 U.S. 45, 75–76 (dissenting opinion).
[12] *Holden* v. *Hardy*, 169 U.S. 366, 382–83 (1898).
[13] 100 U.S. 303, 307, 308.

spirit of accommodation—the spirit of let-the-South-work-out-its-own-problems—which was a central feature of the "Compromise of 1877," substituting the gentle ministrations of President Hayes for the Radical Republicanism of the previous decade. Good evidence of the prevailing judicial attitude is found in two cases which, chronologically, bracketed *Strauder*.

The first was *Hall* v. *De Cuir*.[14] There (as in the *Slaughter-House Cases*) the question was the validity of a law enacted in 1869, in the flood tide of Reconstruction, by the Louisiana Legislature. The statute involved in *Hall* v. *De Cuir* forbade racial segregation on common carriers operating within Louisiana. Relying on the statute, the courts of Louisiana had awarded Mrs. De Cuir, a Negro, a money judgment of $1,000 in a law suit against one Captain Benson. Benson was the master of a Mississippi river boat on which Mrs. De Cuir journeyed from New Orleans upstream to the little Louisiana town of Hermitage; during the journey, Benson had excluded Mrs. De Cuir from the "white" passenger cabin. The Supreme Court reversed the judgment, holding the Louisiana law unconstitutional. The Court did not, it should be said at once, do itself the abject indignity of finding the state integration statute inconsistent with the Fourteenth Amendment. Rather, the Court held that the Louisiana statute was a forbidden local interference with Congress' authority to regulate interstate travel. Although Mrs. De Cuir's own trip was wholly within Louisiana, Captain Benson's craft was engaged in interstate commerce, since its ultimate destination was Vicksburg. Since Congress had not itself legislated as to the treatment to be accorded passengers of different races on interstate river boats, Congress plainly intended—so the Court found—to let the master of each boat manage such things as he saw fit. Hence, Louisiana's attempt to instruct the master to maintain an integrated river boat within Louisiana ran afoul the paramount, albeit unarticulated, congressional command. "If the public good requires such legislation," said the Court, "it must come from Congress and not from the States."[15]

One of the oddities of *Hall* v. *De Cuir* was the Supreme Court's confidence that congressional silence reflected congres-

[14] 95 U.S. 485 (1878).
[15] *Ibid.* at 490.

sional acquiescence in the master's racially discriminatory business practices. Offhand it does not seem self-evident that Congress, because it had said nothing, should be understood to have condoned, as to interstate commerce, policies plainly at odds with the national policy of hostility to racial discrimination written into the Fourteenth Amendment. But a greater oddity was why the Court supposed Congress had been "silent." The fact is that in 1875 (which was three years after Mrs. De Cuir's trip, but three years *before* the Supreme Court's decision), Congress had passed the last of the post–Civil War federal civil-rights acts. And Section 1 of the 1875 law provided as follows:

> . . . [A]ll persons within the jurisdiction of the United States shall be entitled to the full and equal enjoyment of the accommodations, advantages, facilities and privileges of inns, public conveyances on land or water, theaters, and other places of amusement; subject only to the conditions and limitations established by law, and applicable alike to citizens of every race and color, regardless of any previous condition of servitude.[16]

The federal statute the Court ignored in 1878 it invalidated five years later. The occasion was the litigation quaintly captioned the *Civil Rights Cases*.[17] There the Court concluded, over the lonely dissent of the elder Justice Harlan, that neither the Thirteenth nor the Fourteenth Amendment authorized Congress to enact what was in effect a national "public accommodations law." As to the Thirteenth Amendment, racial discrimination in public places, however stigmatizing, was thought by the Court not to be an aspect or incident of "slavery." As to the Fourteenth Amendment, the Court felt that discriminations practiced by an individual entrepreneur—the owner of the restaurant, or theater, or public conveyance—were matters of private, not state, policy. This does not mean that the discriminations were not obnoxious ones, but rather that they were discriminations which

[16] 18 *Stat.* 335 (1875). If the Court felt that prior to 1875 Congress had been hospitable to private discriminations impinging on interstate commerce, the Court could then have concluded that the 1875 act did not aid Mrs. De Cuir—but such a course of reasoning ought to have been explicitly advanced.

[17] 109 U.S. 3 (1883).

fell outside the ambit of the amendment, inasmuch as "the prohibitions of the amendment are against State laws and acts done
under State authority." Since the states did not support the
discriminations (indeed, the Court made the curious assumption
that exclusion from places of public accommodation would be
"an ordinary civil injury, properly cognizable by the laws of the
State, and presumably subject to redress by those laws"), the
federal statute reached beyond the umbrella of the Fourteenth
Amendment and could not be sustained.[18]

A third case involving a Louisiana statute gave the Supreme
Court the opportunity to complete the undermining of the
Negro's constitutional rights. The case, decided in 1896, was
Plessy v. *Ferguson*.[19] This Louisiana statute, enacted in 1890, required passenger trains to provide "equal but separate accommodations for the white and colored races." The statute was one
of the Jim Crow laws which multiplied throughout the South
in the closing years of the century. For this was the era when
Southern whites—theretofore politically divided, Populist against
conservative—came together under the one-party banner of "white
supremacy," united in a new resolve to use the law as a weapon
against the Negro, making him an official outcast. As Professor
C. Vann Woodward has observed,

> [T]he Jim Crow laws applied to *all* Negroes—not
> merely to the rowdy, or drunken, or surly, or ignorant
> ones. The new laws did not countenance the old con-
> servative tendency to distinguish between classes of the
> race, to encourage the "better" element, and to draw it
> into a white alliance. Those laws backed up the Ala-
> bamian who told the disfranchising convention of his
> state that no Negro in the world was the equal of "the
> least, poorest, lowest-down white man I ever knew." . . .
> The Jim Crow laws put the authority of the state or
> city in the voice of the street-car conductor, the railway
> brakeman, the bus driver, the theater usher, and also
> into the voice of the hoodlum of the public parks and
> playgrounds. They gave free rein and the majesty of the
> law to mass aggressions that might otherwise have been
> curbed, blunted, or deflected.

[18] *Ibid.* at 13, 24.
[19] 163 U.S. 537.

> The Jim Crow laws, unlike feudal laws, did not
> assign the subordinate group a fixed status in society.
> They were constantly pushing the Negro farther down.[20]

Nevertheless, in *Plessy* v. *Ferguson,* the Supreme Court (except for Justice Harlan, who dissented, and Justice Brewer, who did not participate in the decision) found that Louisiana's requirement of "equal but separate" facilities was in no sense incompatible with the mandate of the equal protection clause. "We consider," wrote Justice Brown for the seven-man majority, "the underlying fallacy of the plaintiff's argument to consist in the assumption that the enforced separation of the races stamps the colored race with a badge of inferiority."[21] Evidently a long sixteen years had passed since the Court in *Strauder,* had described a statutory exclusion of Negroes from jury service as "practically a brand upon them, affixed by the law, an assertion of their inferiority, and a stimulant to . . . race prejudice. . . ."

In a scant three decades, the Supreme Court had worked its magic on the Fourteenth Amendment. In its infancy the Amendment had been a "protection of the newly-made freeman and citizen from the oppressions of those who had formerly exercised unlimited dominion over him."[22] But with the years had come sophistication: in adolescence the Amendment was working overtime at a new role—baby-sitting for American business. This was a comfortable arrangement for all concerned—except "the newly-

[20] *The Strange Career of Jim Crow* (Fair Lawn, N.J.: Oxford University Press, 1957), p. 93. Recently, Professor Woodward has restated his characterization of "the Jim Crow system" in "The South in Perspective," *The Progressive,* XXVI (Dec., 1962), 12:
Far more explicitly than the surreptitious and extra-legal discrimination, such as the stuffed ballot box, the doctored jurors list, or the sly literacy test, the Jim Crow system openly proclaimed the white man's determination to keep the Negro "in his place." This intention could be read not only in the Jim Crow statutes; it glared out from thousands of conspicuously posted signs—*"White"* and *"Colored"*—that marked off the color line. Schools, hospitals, prisons, parks, welfare establishments, every public institution proclaimed the rigid rule of separation. Just as conspicuous and harsh was the enforcement of segregation in private business establishments, in trains, busses, streetcars, hotels, theaters, and playing fields. There it was, for all the world to see.
[21] 163 U.S. at 551.
[22] *Slaughter-House Cases,* 16 Wall. 36, 71.

made freeman and citizen." But he didn't seem to count for much any more.

THE LAW'S ROAD BACK

"Technical emancipation" sufficiently describes the status of the Southern Negro at the turn of the century and for some three decades thereafter. In every significant, openly visible aspect of his life, he was segregated by the law from—which is to say, ostracized by—his white fellow citizens. Most public or quasi-public facilities were either wholly closed to him or open only on the most inadequate and degrading terms—libraries, museums, hospitals, churches, theaters, stadia, restaurants, hotels, parks, beaches; even government offices and the National Guard. Negro children attended "separate" but never "equal" schools—schools which at least made little pretense of preparation for the white skilled trades and the white white-collar jobs which were forbidden territory. The poll tax, the manipulated literacy test, the white primary, and straight-out intimidation all conspired to accomplish the Negro's disenfranchisement. If the white police felt he had transgressed the white law, the Negro was defended by a white lawyer or none, and tried, in a segregated courtroom, by a white judge and jury. If convicted of an offense against a white man (or woman!), he was likely to be punished with a severity seldom visited on a white defendant guilty of the same crime. On the other hand, if his offense was against another Negro, he might well be treated with a lenity comparable with the official indifference which commonly exculpated the white charged with an offense against a Negro. When war came, he was entitled, indeed required, to play his part—in a colored unit, and assigned to dirty and dangerous duty—in defending a "New Freedom" that knew the Negro not. If he survived, he could, if he wished, return home—that is, return to "his place," living out his physical life in Catfish Row and his fantasy life in Green Pastures.

The peculiar viciousness of it all was, of course, that the mortar which held the structure together was law—local segregation statutes, backed up by local criminal codes. And to this local law the "higher law" of the Constitution seemed to provide no antidote. Quite the contrary: *Plessy* v. *Ferguson* had bathed the structure in a sort of constitutional pseudo-legitimacy.

Emancipation and Law: A Century of Process

The first major crack in the smooth supporting wall appeared in 1915, when the Fourteenth Amendment was just short of fifty years old. The case was *Buchanan* v. *Warley*.[23] The plaintiff, a white landowner, sued to compel the Negro defendant to live up to his agreement to purchase land located in a white neighborhood. The defense was that the agreement was illegal, by virtue of a city ordinance barring Negroes from occupying homes in predominantly white blocks, and vice versa. The defense was insufficient, said the Supreme Court, because the ordinance contravened the Fourteenth Amendment. The trouble with the ordinance was not, however, that the racial division of the city contravened the equal protection clause. The trouble with the ordinance was that it unduly interfered with the white seller's "liberty" to sell to whom he chose—a substantive economic "liberty" protected by the due process clause under the latitudinarian, business-oriented reading of the clause which was then fashionable.

However quixotic the rationale, the result was of first importance: legislative racial zoning was unconstitutional. A new technique for keeping neighborhoods "pure" had to be relied on. And for the next three decades the job of keeping Negroes (and Jews and Italians and Poles and other "undesirables") out of white Protestant neighborhoods, in the North and West as well as in the South, fell to the courts, through the enforcement of racially restrictive covenants. But at last, in 1948, the Supreme Court, in *Shelley* v. *Kraemer*,[24] held that, although private individuals were free to indulge their bigotry by agreeing with one another to "protect" their neighborhood by not selling their homes to those they disapproved of, judicial enforcement of such private agreements implicated the state in racial or religious discrimination. And when the state let its judicial machinery be used in this way, the Fourteenth Amendment—the *equal protection* clause thereof, to be precise—was violated.

The unanimous decision in the *Shelley* case appears to have vast, and thus far largely uncharted, potential significance. For it seems to mean that when state and local judges, police, and administrators enforce private preferences, those preferences tend

[23] 245 U.S. 60.
[24] 334 U.S. 1.

to become—within limits not yet judicially declared—policies for which the state must be held constitutionally accountable. This new doctrinal development may, for example, turn out to have formidable implications for the law of wills, since testamentary dispositions, enforced by probate courts, are a happy hunting ground of bigoted whimsy. And it may in the near future substantially qualify hitherto accepted notions that a property owner can invoke police assistance to keep out anyone he chooses, no matter how invidious or arbitrary his standard of selection. Thus, in the several "sit-in" cases now pending in the Supreme Court, a major question is whether *Shelley* does not bar a state from enforcing, through arrest and criminal prosecution for trespass, the policy of a lunch-counter proprietor not to serve Negroes. And one of the elements that makes the question difficult is whether, if the answer is in the affirmative, the same logic leads to the same answer in the context of a private home. It may be safely surmised, however, that the Court will not supply fully dispositive answers to the major questions in the near future: One of the Court's great strengths is its aptitude for prefacing broadly generative pronouncements with a patiently harvested accumulation of limited, perhaps tentative, assessments. But if years go by before the Court defines the limits of *Shelley*'s logic, commentators will have more than filled the void.

Whatever *Shelley* may come to mean in other realms, it certainly means that in the field of residential housing the machinery of the law may no longer be utilized to maintain racial separation. Promoters of bigotry in housing must operate without the law's aid. Unfortunately, builders, realtors, and lending institutions—and, until quite recently, the federal government's own housing agencies—have conducted their business operations on the premise that segregation is the policy which (to use the trade euphemism) best comports with the maintenance of "stable" communities in which homes retain their maximum money value. Although the premise is fallacious, the housing market continues to be shaped by the fallacy—and by the bigotry which has engendered it. And this means that housing is, as the United States Civil Rights Commission has found, "the one commodity in the American market . . . not freely available on equal terms to everyone who can afford to pay."[25]

[25] *1961 U.S. Commission on Civil Rights Report on Housing*, p. 140.

There is an answer to these private conspiracies in aid of racial separation. The answer is to be found in the positive use of the law. Existing antitrust statutes, both federal and state, may prove useful. But even more to the point are fair housing laws prohibiting racial discrimination in both public and private housing.[26] Of course, Southern states and cities will not adopt such legislation. But even Southern communities would be affected by the enormous leverage, in the housing field, of the federal government, if that leverage is effectively utilized. And this is now one of the current items of urgent national business. For in 1962, the late President Kennedy issued his long-awaited housing order, which bars racial discrimination in all housing built hereafter with federal subsidies or insurance. Vigorous enforcement of this new legal mechanism could mean significant progress toward an era of genuinely open occupancy throughout the nation.

VOTING

Three decades ago, in 1932, Negroes in the twelve Southern states "were so effectively disfranchised, regardless of the 14th and 15th amendments to the Constitution, that considerably fewer than a hundred thousand were able to vote in general election[s], and virtually none was permitted to vote in the primary election[s]."[27] But in fifteen years, by 1947, the number of registered Negroes had jumped to 645,000 (out of a voting-age Negro population of some 5,000,000). And by 1961, with the total Negro population in the twelve states remaining approximately constant, the number of registered Negroes had again risen dramatically, to 1,361,944.[28]

The chief operative factor in this process of enfranchisement has been the law. First came a series of Supreme Court decisions which, cumulatively, spelled the constitutional demise of the white primary, the instrument on which the Democratic Party principally relied to foreclose Negro participation in Southern

---

[26] Seventeen states and fifty-five cities had adopted one or another form of fair housing legislation by the end of 1962.

[27] U.S. Department of Justice, *Protection of the Rights of Individuals* (1952), p. 4.

[28] *1961 U.S. Commission of Civil Rights Report on Voting*, p. 22.

political processes.[29] Second, there has been a substantial mitigation—except in the Deep South—of that amalgam of discriminatory administration and outright intimidation which has for so long kept Negroes from becoming registered voters (and hence eligible to participate in the decisive primary elections). Third, in 1957 and 1960, Congress passed the first federal civil-rights legislation since 1875. These new laws created the United States Civil Rights Commission, and assigned to that Commission the authority to inquire into denials of equal protection of the laws, with particular emphasis on voting rights. And the new laws gave to the Department of Justice enlarged powers to initiate law suits to curtail racial disenfranchisement. Moreover, there is good reason to expect that, when Congress completes action on the 1964 Civil Rights Act (pending in the Senate as this essay goes to press), the Department of Justice's authority to deal with racial restrictions on voting will have been further strengthened. Finally, at the outset of 1964, the requisite thirty-eighth state ratified a new constitutional amendment—the Twenty-fourth—abolishing the poll tax throughout the United States.

As of 1961, the Commission on Civil Rights found "reasonable grounds to believe that substantial numbers of Negro citizens are, or recently have been, denied the right to vote on grounds of race or color in about one hundred counties in eight Southern states: Alabama, Florida, Georgia, Louisiana, Mississippi, North Carolina, South Carolina, and Tennessee. Some denials of the right to vote occur by reason of discriminatory application of laws setting qualifications for voters. Other denials result from arbitrary and discriminatory procedures for the registration of voters; still others occur by reason of threats and intimidation, or the fear of retaliation."[30] But the recalcitrant counties are plainly on the defensive. Scores of dedicated young men and women, working under the auspices of the Student Nonviolent Coordinating Committee and similar groups, are, at great personal hazard, conducting voter registration campaigns throughout the Deep South. And backing up these efforts is a comprehensive, patient, well-organized litigation program under-

[29] *Nixon* v. *Herndon*, 273 U.S. 536 (1927); *Nixon* v. *Condon*, 286 U.S. 73 (1932); *Grovey* v. *Townsend*, 295 U.S. 45 (1935); *United States* v. *Classic*, 313 U.S. 299 (1941); *Smith* v. *Allwright*, 321 U.S. 649 (1944) (overruling *Grovey* v. *Townsend*, *supra*); *Terry* v. *Adams*, 345 U.S. 461 (1953).

[30] *1961 Report on Voting*, pp. 135–36.

taken by the Civil Rights Division of the Department of Justice. Moreover, it is not unlikely that impending changes in state legislative apportionment, following the Supreme Court's 1962 decision in *Baker* v. *Carr*,[31] will weaken that rural grip on Southern legislatures which has been particularly repressive of legitimate Negro aspirations.

FAIR TRIALS IN STATE COURTS

"Far too many cases come from the states to the Supreme Court presenting dismal pictures of official lawlessness, of illegal searches and seizures, illegal detentions attended by prolonged interrogation and coerced admissions of guilt, of the denial of counsel, and downright brutality." So wrote Justice Brennan in 1961.[32]

What Justice Brennan did not add is that an inordinate number of the State criminal convictions presenting denials of due process of law are cases in which the accused is a Negro. But the Justice and his brethren know this full well. They know that one of the incidents of being a Negro in the United States— and, most particularly, of being a Southern Negro—is that police and prosecutors frequently are quite indifferent to the preservation of his procedural rights, and sometimes have no real concern for his guilt or innocence.

The Court's awareness of this evil dates back almost forty years. *Moore* v. *Dempsey*,[33] in 1923, and the *Scottsboro Cases*,[34] in the early thirties, exposed in ample measure the depths to which criminal justice, corruptly administered, can descend. From *Scottsboro* onward, the Court has militantly overturned conviction after conviction where the record discloses a prejudicial lack of counsel, a coerced confession, or some other flaw fatally undermining the judgment.[35] And at the same time the

---

[31] 369 U.S. 186.

[32] William J. Brennan, Jr., "The Bill of Rights and the States," 36 *N.Y.U.L. Rev.* 761, 778 (1960).

[33] 261 U.S. 86.

[34] *Powell* v. *Alabama*, 287 U.S. 45 (1932); *Norris* v. *Alabama*, 294 U.S. 587 (1935); *Patterson* v. *Alabama*, 294 U.S. 600 (1935).

[35] See *Harris* v. *South Carolina*, 338 U.S. 68 (1949), which is representative of a substantial number of Supreme Court cases in which there is a coalescence of the twin due-process issues of lack of access to a lawyer and a coerced confession. See also *Rogers* v. *Richmond*, 365 U.S. 534 (1961), indicating that the South has no monopoly on such practices.

In twenty-five years, from February, 1936 (when *Brown* v. *Mississippi*,

Court has expanded its traditional insistence that juries be selected without respect to race.

In setting aside the grossest state criminal convictions which come before it, the Court is acting with fidelity to the core concept of the Fourteenth Amendment—protecting with a federal shield those on whom the state's legal processes are unfairly or brutally brought to bear. What the Court has not managed to do—and apparently cannot do without affirmative Congressional assistance—is to go beyond the reversal of convictions which violate the Amendment and take an effective offensive against the miscreant law-enforcement officials. One of the pressing legal tasks of the future is to develop new federal criminal and civil sanctions which might genuinely deter those tempted to abuse their official power over their fellow Americans.[36]

THE DEMISE OF PLESSY

Four score and six years after the adoption of the Fourteenth Amendment, the Supreme Court announced that public schools, separated on race lines by state directive, were "inherently unequal." The 1954 opinion in *Brown* v. *Board of Education*[37] was certainly the most important judicial pronouncement since *Dred Scott,* and very likely the most important single governmental action in America's domestic history since the Civil War.

Technically speaking, *Brown,* a school case, did not overrule *Plessy,* a transportation case. But subsequent *per curiam* de-

---

297 U.S. 278, the path-breaking coerced-confession case, was decided) to June, 1961, the Supreme Court set aside state court convictions on coerced-confession grounds on twenty-two occasions. Of the twenty-seven defendants involved in these cases, nineteen were Negroes and six were whites; the race of the other two is not disclosed by the records. Sixteen of the nineteen identifiable Negroes were tried in Southern courts. Only one of the six identifiable whites, and neither of the two racially unidentified defendants, was tried in a Southern court. These figures are based on the data contained in the table of coerced-confession cases which appears in *1961 U.S. Commission on Civil Rights Report on Justice,* pp. 256–62.

[36] There are some complex constitutional problems involved in determining how far Congress can go, in enforcing the Fourteenth Amendment, (1) to penalize persons abusing their official authority, and/or (2) to impose compensatory money judgments on the states or municipalities whose officials have misbehaved. There is also the very real practical difficulty that the defendant in a federal criminal or civil case is generally entitled to a jury, and most Southern juries do not take kindly to law suits designed to vindicate Negro rights against official oppression.

[37] 347 U.S. 483 (1954).

cisions made it plain that segregation by law was unconstitutional in transportation and in every other phase of American public life. Moreover, *Brown* discredited the underlying rationale of *Plessy: Brown* quoted approvingly a district court finding which recited, in tones reminiscent of *Strauder,* that the debilitating impact of racial segregation is even " 'greater when it has the sanction of law; for the policy of separating the races is usually interpreted as denoting the inferiority of the negro group.' "

There was a special fitness in utilizing a public school case as the vehicle for jettisoning the apartheid philosophy of *Plessy.* "Today," as the Court recognized, "education is perhaps the most important function of state and local governments."[38] But underlying that practical observation is an ethical—one might even say a constitutional—dimension. "The public school," as Justice Frankfurter has remarked, "is at once the symbol of our democracy and the most pervasive means for promoting our common destiny."[39]

But the public school is not yet the symbol of the democracy we profess. A year after announcing its repudiation of the principle of segregation, the Court decreed that desegregation of Southern schools should go forward with "all deliberate speed."[40] But seven years thereafter—in 1962—only 7.6 per cent of the 3,240,000 Negro public school children in the seventeen Southern and border states and the District of Columbia were enrolled in desegregated schools.[41] Meanwhile it has been becoming increasingly apparent that many Northern communities have segregated school systems—most often by virtue of residential patterns, but sometimes through discriminatory design.[42]

To all this one can add the Little Rock riots of 1957, the

---

[38] 347 U.S. 483, 493, 494.

[39] *McCollum* v. *Board of Education,* 333 U.S. 203, 231 (1948) (concurring opinion).

[40] *Brown* v. *Board of Education,* 349 U.S. 294, 301 (1955).

[41] "The Federal Courts and Integration of Southern Schools; Troubled Status of the Pupil Placement Acts," 62 *Colum. L. Rev.* 1448, 1453 n. 28 (1962). By the end of 1963 the figure had risen to 9.3 per cent for the region, but in the eleven states of the old Confederacy the proportion was only 1.06 per cent (*Statistical Summary of School Segregation* [Southern Education Reporting Service, 1963–64], p. 2).

[42] See *Civil Rights U.S.A.: Public Schools North and West 1962* (Staff Reports Submitted to and Published by U.S. Commission on Civil Rights).

New Orleans riots of 1960, and the Oxford riots of 1962. And one can conclude that America does not mean to make good on the promise announced by its fundamental law.

But the conclusion is neither the necessary nor, it is submitted, the proper one. For it leaves out of account the fact that no federal court order of desegregation has, thus far, been successfully defied. Slowly—too slowly, to be sure, but none the less ineluctably—the Constitution is being enforced. And it is a Constitution which no longer countenances racial segregation by law.

A Forward Look

THE "SIT-IN" CASES

The paramount issues of racial discrimination confronting the Supreme Court today are, of course, those presented by the pending "sit-in" cases. It is, as has been suggested, entirely possible that the Court will decline the opportunity to reach the ultimate issues in these cases, provided the convictions can be set aside on narrower grounds—e.g., the existence of an unrepealed segregation ordinance, the participation of a deputy sheriff in the operation of an assertedly private enterprise, state court rulings on evidence foreclosing full exploration of the constitutional issues, etc. For it is reasonable to suppose that the Court is in no great hurry to reach the ultimate issues.

But when the Court runs out of detours, what will it decide? It seems fair to suppose that the Court will be largely guided by its own earlier language: "The more an owner, for his advantage, opens up his property for use by the public in general, the more do his rights become circumscribed by the . . . constitutional rights of those who use it."[43] Looking at the cases in this way, the Court will be able to reject the argument that basic interests of privacy would be jeopardized by judicial refusal to sanction a tresspass prosecution in aid of the retail store owner's desire to select his patrons on racial lines. "The State urges in effect that the corporation's right [to exclude persons distributing religious tracts on the streets of a company town] . . . is coextensive with the right of a homeowner to regulate the conduct of his guests. We cannot accept that contention. Ownership does not always mean absolute dominion."[44]

[43] *Marsh* v. *Alabama*, 326 U.S. 501, 506 (1946).
[44] *Ibid.* at 505–6.

Ownership of a store, a factory, or an apartment house does not mean absolute dominion. The public accommodations, fair employment, and fair housing laws, one or another of which is on the statute books of a majority of the states, bear witness to this. (Such laws are themselves unquestionably constitutional. The Supreme Court has rejected the contention that a nondiscrimination statute deprives the affected enterprise of Fourteenth Amendment rights. Adoption of such a contention, the Court said, "would be a distortion of the policy manifested in that amendment which was adopted to prevent state legislation designed to perpetuate discrimination on the basis of race or color.")[45]

But in one's own home, rights of a higher order of dominion come into play. As Professor Louis Henkin has persuasively argued, "For the state . . . to decree that one may not bar Catholics, or red-headed persons, or even Negroes from his home would . . . be a violation of rights of privacy—of free association and nonassociation—under the fourteenth amendment."[46] And if this is so, the state should not be barred by the Amendment from using its criminal processes to protect the homeowner's right to be bigoted in the privacy of his home, even though the state is held to be barred from protecting the same man's bigotry when he seeks to exercise it, in his entrepreneurial capacity, by discriminating against would-be patrons of his store on the basis of race or color.

LAW AND THE COMMUNITY

In all the major constitutional issues surveyed in summary fashion in the preceding pages, principal attention has been given to the shaping of constitutional policy by the Supreme Court. And there is a certain irony about this, since the expectation of the Radical Republicans who formulated, and secured

[45] *Railway Mail Assn.* v. *Corsi*, 326 U.S. 88, 94 (1945). Justice Frankfurter, in a concurring opinion, said that, "To use the Fourteenth Amendment as a sword against such State power would stultify that Amendment." *Ibid.* at 98. The pending 1964 Civil Rights Act will, when Congress has completed action, probably contain a public accommodations section. And that section will almost certainly be regarded by the Supreme Court as a valid exercise of federal legislative power, notwithstanding the Court's pronouncements in the *Civil Rights Cases.*

[46] Henkin, *"Shelley* v. *Kraemer*: Notes for a Revised Opinion," 110 *U. Pa. L. Rev.* 498 (1962).

adoption of, the Fourteenth Amendment seems to have been that Congress would be the principal architect of policy thereunder.

Congress, however, was silent in the field of civil rights from 1875 to 1957. Then and in 1960 Congress acted in the area of voting. As of February, 1964, there is good reason to hope that Congress will, within three month's time, go far beyond voting, since other aspects of racial discrimination beckon insistently for remedial action. As the pending legislation emerges from the House of Representatives, there is good reason to expect that the 1964 Civil Rights Act will strike effectively at discrimination in places of public accommodation. And if, in addition, Congress were to deal with racial discrimination in employment, a national fair employment practice law, based on the commerce power and complementing the many state fair employment practice statutes, could be a major forward step in the utilization of law as an affirmative mechanism for the promotion of human dignity.

Executive power came into play belatedly, but some important steps have at last been forthcoming: There was President Truman's campaign to desegregate the armed forces. There was President Eisenhower's effort, expanded by President Kennedy and now by President Johnson, to increase employment opportunities for Negroes in the gigantic federal civil service and in the vast range of industries which sell to the federal government. There is the 1962 Kennedy housing order. (And more can be done: for example, a prudent exercise of executive power to curtail federal funds in aid of segregated facilities—e.g., hospitals and colleges—might pay substantial dividends.)

Up to now, however, in default of the assumption of responsibility elsewhere, major governmental initiative for vindicating the Fourteenth Amendment's guaranties at the national level has been forthcoming from the judiciary—that feeble third branch of government which has, in Hamilton's words, "neither FORCE nor WILL, but merely judgment."[47] And underlying that judicial initiative has been the courage and persistence of those who have borne the burdens of litigation—people like Oliver Brown and James Meredith; like Walter White and Charles Houston; like Roy Wilkins, William H. Hastie, and Thurgood Marshall.

In the first half-century since the Emancipation Proclama-

---

[47] *The Federalist*, No. 78.

tion the Supreme Court did virtually nothing—indeed, on a net basis, less than nothing—to promote the fundamental democratic values for which the Civil War was won. In the second half-century it has accomplished much. And it is ready to do more. But courts are not all there is to law. It is imprudent—and it is even nondemocratic—to rely solely on judicial mechanisms. The time has come—it is long since overdue—for our other legal institutions, at every level of government, to assume greater and greater responsibility for the affirmative ordering of a democratic community.

But these other legal institutions are precisely those which—unlike the courts—are intended to be directly responsive to popular will. If they fail to assume responsibility, it is because the majority of the people of the United States have not yet come to terms with the national commitments made in their name. Which means, in turn, that those who presently believe in these national commitments must propagate that belief, and its implications, among their fellow citizens. As James Baldwin puts it in the conclusion of his "Letter":

> If we . . . the relatively conscious whites and the relatively conscious blacks . . . do not falter in our duty now, we may be able, handful that we are, to end the racial nightmare and achieve our country, and change the history of the world. If we do not dare everything, the fulfillment of that prophecy, re-created from the Bible in song by a slave, is upon us: *God gave Noah the rainbow sign, No more water, the fire next time!*

WALTER BERNS

•

RACIAL DISCRIMINATION AND THE LIMITS OF JUDICIAL REMEDY

In the *Dred Scott* case of 1857, the Supreme Court held that
Negroes were not and could never become citizens of the United
States, because Negroes were not and could never be included
among those men who were, by the Declaration of Independence,
declared to be equally endowed by their Creator with certain
unalienable rights. As if this were not enough, the Court held
that Congress had no power to forbid slavery in the territories
and, even worse, it provided the basis for a future declaration
that no *state* had power to forbid slavery. Under these circumstances, it is not strange that this infamous decision, embodying
this intention, was followed by Civil War, or that during that
war the President proclaimed the emancipation of those Negroes
held as slaves in the states whose people were in rebellion against
the United States.

Though thus limited in its immediate application, the
Emancipation Proclamation promised much more. Specifically,
it promised Negroes legal membership in that body known, in
the words of the Constitution's Preamble, as "the people of the
United States," with the hope, if not in every case the expectation, that legal membership would be followed by membership
in the ultimate sense, that is, in the hearts and minds of their
white fellow citizens. This has not yet happened. During the last
quarter of the century since the Proclamation, the Negro, thanks
mainly to a host of Supreme Court decisions striking down state
discriminatory laws and practices, has managed to achieve a close
approximation of legal equality, but membership in the ultimate
sense has continued to be denied him. The Court has nullified
verdicts handed down by juries from which Negroes have been

systematically excluded; it has guaranteed them nonsegregated service in the dining cars of interstate trains and in the restaurants in interstate bus terminals; it has promoted Negro voting, even in primary and preprimary elections. It has, furthermore, invalidated racially-segregated schools, criminated the local police brute for his illegal treatment of Negroes, and nullified racially-restrictive real estate contracts. It has done these things and more. But it cannot force, or even goad, cajole, or drive (the terms are Roy Wilkins'), white parents to send their children to those schools; it cannot, in too many places, get a local jury to convict the brutal policeman; and it cannot prevent whites from moving out of the uncovenanted areas when Negroes move in.

Even as President Kennedy called for new legislation and an end to "the cruel disease of discrimination,"[1] the law was demonstrating its inability to overcome this discrimination which, together with the Negro's response to it, constitutes what is surely the most urgent national domestic political problem of our time. The problem derives from private conduct that springs from— from what? a fear of the Negro, a hatred stemming from guilt, a distrust, a dislike, a contempt, or simply a difference?—at any rate, an attitude that apparently cannot be legislated or "decisioned" out of existence. Perhaps we should have known this; perhaps we should have known that, generally speaking, the laws are dependent on the character of the people, not the reverse, and that laws in conflict with this character or with the sentiment that expresses it will not be obeyed. Perhaps we should have known that this anti-Negro sentiment would not yield to moral exhortation or federal troops or judicial decisions. And perhaps we should have known the price of a failure to recognize the limits of law.

This paper is not concerned with the failure of the exhortation—that, at least, is harmless—or with the use of troops; its concern is the unceasing effort to use the agencies of law against this anti-Negro sentiment, in the opinion or hope that the law will solve the problem. More precisely, it is concerned with the Supreme Court's failure to recognize the limits of the law and with the damage done to the law because of this failure. Not

[1] Message to Congress, Feb. 28, 1963.

resting on principles "that satisfy the mind," as one friendly critic has said,[2] some of these decisions may not only fail to achieve their purpose (with what consequences to the morale of those who relied on them?), but they pose a serious threat to certain basic principles of American government, and they threaten to promote a contempt for the Court and for the law in general. In short, in its efforts, unsupported by public sentiment, to make Negroes a part of "the people of the United States" in every sense, the Court is threatening the true character and force of the Constitution ordained and established by "the people of the United States."

UNPRINCIPLED DECISIONS

It is outrageous for a state to take no action against the likes of Claude Screws, the Georgia sheriff who arrested a young Negro for the alleged theft of a tire, handcuffed him, then beat him to death with a "solid-bar blackjack about eight inches long and weighing two pounds."[3] Surely it is frustrating to see the state refuse to act and to see Screws acquitted of the only federal crime for which he could be indicted, that of willfully depriving Hall, the Negro, not of his life, but of his constitutional right not to be deprived of his life without due process of law, that is, without a fair trial. The *Screws* case involved a particularly heinous offense, but there are many injustices, and many of them hiding behind the barriers, or within the interstices, of the federal system. This explains, although it does not justify, the Court's impatience with the various limitations of the federal government's authority, and its willingness sometimes to sacrifice "principled adjudication," to "cut corners," to "take short cuts" —in brief, to be guided primarily, if not wholly, by a determination to redress the imbalance against Negroes, rather than by principles of constitutional law.

Most civil rights cases come to the Supreme Court under the Fourteenth and Fifteenth Amendments, but not all of them. Some have come under the commerce clause,[4] whose principles

[2] Herbert Wechsler, "Toward Neutral Principles of Constitutional Law," 73 *Harvard Law Review* 29 (1959).

[3] *Screws* v. *United States*, 325 U.S. 91, 92 (1945).

[4] "The Congress shall have Power . . . To regulate Commerce with Foreign Nations, and among the several States, and with the Indian Tribes." Article I, Sec. 8, (3).

Thomas Reed Powell, one of the most distinguished of all authorities on the American Constitution, once said he could state in three sentences: "Congress may regulate interstate commerce. The states may also regulate interstate commerce, but not too much. How much is too much is beyond the scope of this statement."[5] The continuing problem in commerce clause cases arises when Congress has not regulated a subject of commerce; and since the first case in 1824, the Court has had the duty of deciding whether, in the absence of federal law, a particular state law, such as a licensing act or a tax, obstructs the free flow of commerce among the states, or constitutes a burden on it. Such cases will come to the Supreme Court so long as the federal system is maintained. One such case, which is also a civil rights case, is *Bob-Lo Excursion Co.* v. *Michigan,* decided in 1948.[6]

Bois Blanc Island (known in Detroit as Bob-Lo Island) lies just above the mouth of the Detroit River, fifteen miles upstream from the city. It is a part of the Province of Ontario, Canada, but almost all of it is owned by the Bob-Lo Excursion Company and is used as an amusement park for Detroiters, who are transported to it on two steamships owned by the company. In 1945, the company refused passage to a Negro girl, a member of a group of school girls on a holiday, on one of its steamships plying between Detroit and the island. For this it was convicted of violating a Michigan civil rights statute, and the Supreme Court of the United States, on appeal, upheld the conviction. The company argued, citing a number of precedents in its favor, that the state law was unconstitutional as applied to its steamship because the steamship was engaged in foreign commerce, which only Congress may regulate. But the Court, not by any means unanimously, said, essentially, that though this was foreign commerce, it was not very foreign, and that therefore the state might regulate at least this aspect of it. One has only to change a couple of the presumably nonmaterial facts in the case to recognize that this case was not decided on the basis of any principle flowing from the commerce clause.

[5] Thomas Reed Powell, *Vagaries and Varieties in Constitutional Interpretation* (New York: Columbia University Press, 1956), p. 14.
[6] 333 U.S. 28 (1948).

Walter Berns

Suppose the action had arisen in Texas, for example, and the steamship carried passengers from Brownsville to some Mexican island, and that the excursion company refused passage to a Negro girl. There is no doubt whatever that if the company acted by virtue of a state segregation law, that law (in 1948) would have been invalidated as an unconstitutional regulation of foreign commerce; and if the company acted without authority from state law but simply on its own, it would have been held to have violated the Interstate Commerce Act. The decisive fact in the *Bob-Lo* case had nothing to do with whether the commerce involved was foreign or intrastate; the decisive fact was that the state law favored the Negro—just as in a case decided two years before, in which the Court had struck down a Virginia statute requiring segregation on buses,[7] including interstate buses, the decisive fact was the discrimination against the Negro. Yet both cases are indexed under commerce, and the opinions of the Court purport to be explications of the law of the commerce clause. True, not much had to be sacrificed in order to reach the decision upholding the right of a Negro girl to make the voyage to Bob-Lo Island with her classmates—the law of the commerce clause has survived decisions as unprincipled as that in the Bob-Lo case—but this one case is by no means unique.

Arkansas public school teachers are hired on a year-to-year basis. In 1958, the state enacted a statute compelling every teacher, as a condition of employment, to submit an affidavit listing all the organizations to which he belonged or to which he had regularly contributed within the preceding five years. B. T. Shelton, a teacher in the Little Rock schools and a member of the National Association for the Advancement of Colored People, suspecting, not without reason, that members of the NAACP were not likely to have their contracts renewed, refused to file the affidavit and petitioned a federal district court to declare the statute unconstitutional. This the district court refused to do, but the Supreme Court reversed. With four justices dissenting, the Court held the statute unconstitutional. On what grounds? Not, quite evidently, on the ostensible grounds.

The Court did not hold that the states have no authority to compel teachers to disclose the names of the associations to

[7] *Morgan* v. *Virginia*, 328 U.S. 373 (1946).

which they belonged; indeed, it said "there can be no question of the relevance of a State's inquiry into the fitness and competence of its teachers," and it conceded implicitly that to judge fitness and competence, the state may inquire into a teacher's associations. "The question to be decided," the Court said, "is not whether the State of Arkansas can ask certain of its teachers about all their organizational relationships," but rather whether it may "ask every one of its teachers to disclose every single organization with which he has been associated over a five-year period."[8] Many associational ties, it went on, "could have no possible bearing upon the teacher's . . . competence or fitness." But if the state may ask "certain of its teachers about all their organizational relationships," then it is not true that many of them "have no possible bearing upon the teacher's . . . competence or fitness"; all of them may have some bearing some time. At any rate, the Court did not attempt to determine which associational ties are related to competence or fitness and which are not. All it said was that the statute was too broad—while conceding that under some circumstances a statute with the broadest possible scope, such as the one involved in this case, would be perfectly valid. The four dissenters expressed their view of all this with less acerbity than is customary in such cases, perhaps because they agreed that it was a nasty thing Arkansas was (probably) trying to do to Negro teachers who belonged to the NAACP.

Nothing Mr. Justice Stewart said in his opinion for the majority can disguise what Alexander Bickel has called the decision's lack of "intellectual coherence."[9] This statute was invalidated, not because it was too broad, but because it was aimed at the NAACP; not because there was no rational connection between it and a state's legitimate interest in the competence or fitness of its teachers, but because five members of the Court, being determined to extend the protection of the Constitution to Negroes whenever they are threatened by a state law, were willing to forget the "restraints that attend constitutional adjudication," as Mr. Justice Harlan put it in dissent. Arkansas lost, not for any reason stated in the Court's opinion, but simply

---

[8] *Shelton* v. *Tucker*, 364 U.S. 479, 485, 487–88 (1960).
[9] Alexander M. Bickel, *The Least Dangerous Branch* (Indianapolis and New York: Bobbs-Merrill Company, 1962), p. 53.

because it was engaged in a reprehensible course of action against its Negro citizens that the Court, with no more than a "thus saith the Lord," called unconstitutional.

To some undefinable extent, however, the Constitution also lost, because the force of its authority depends ultimately on the authority of the force wielded in its name. As two law professors recently had occasion to say about the state action doctrine, "formulas tend to catch up with the Court when they are empty. But more serious are the consequences of such a failing of candor for the rule of law. Law does not rule when the motivations behind judicial decisions are kept hidden. Reasoned opinions announce the law only when the stated reasons truly reflect the real reasons for deciding."[10] Though we may wish it to be otherwise, and though it is frustrating to have to acknowledge helplessness in the face of gross miscarriages of justice, it is entirely possible that there are some unjust acts that are not, by that fact alone, unconstitutional. And it is also possible that, finally, there is no remedy in federal law for these injustices, and that the attempt to provide one will lead to other injustices by damaging the Constitution itself.

Acting under the authority of the cumbersome Civil Rights Act of 1957, the United States Civil Rights Commission received some 67 formal complaints from individual Negroes charging Louisiana voting registrars with having deprived them of their right to vote because of their race or color, contrary to the Fifteenth Amendment. A hearing was scheduled in Shreveport during midsummer, 1959, and subpoenas were served on the registrars ordering them to appear with various voting and registration records. The Commission refused to disclose the identity of the persons making the complaints or the specific charges made; furthermore, it informed the registrars that they would not be permitted to cross-examine any witnesses at the hearing. Under these circumstances, the registrars refused to obey the subpoenas, and filed a complaint in the federal district court alleging that the Commission had not been authorized by the Civil Rights Act to adopt such rules of procedure, and, if it had been so authorized, that the Act was unconstitutional. The

[10] William W. Van Alstyne and Kenneth L. Karst, "State Action," 14 *Stanford Law Review* 58 (Dec., 1961).

district court, agreeing with the registrars that the allegations raised a serious constitutional issue, found that Congress had not specifically authorized such rules. The Civil Rights Commission appealed.

The issues raised were similar to some of those involved in cases concerning congressional investigations. Like them, the proposed civil rights hearing was not an adjudicatory proceeding; like the typical committee of Congress, the Commission does not indict, issue orders, punish, or impose any legal sanction. Both bodies are confined to investigation and finding facts, although this limited function has not permitted congressional committees to escape criticism, a great deal of it from the Supreme Court, and a great deal of that from Chief Justice Warren. Here, however, he wrote the opinion of the Court upholding the Commission, citing the practices of congressional committees as authority! Only Douglas, with Black, dissented: ". . . important as these civil rights are, it will not do to sacrifice other civil rights to protect them."

> We live and work under a Constitution. The temptation of many men of goodwill is to cut corners, take short cuts, and reach the desired end regardless of the means. Worthy as I think the ends are which the Civil Rights Commission advances in these cases, I think the particular means used are unconstitutional.[11]

Douglas went on to point out that if the charges against the registrars were true, and if they had acted willfully, they were criminally responsible under a federal statute. The Commission is an arm of the Executive, and there is, he said, "only one way the Chief Executive may move against a person accused of a crime and deny him the right of confrontation and cross-examination and that is by the grand jury." The grand jury brings "suspects before neighbors, not strangers," and therefore protects him. "The grand jury, adopted as a safeguard against 'hasty, malicious, and oppressive' action by the Federal Government . . . stands as an important safeguard to the citizen against open and public accusations of crime."[12]

A grand jury, made up of "neighbors, not strangers," was

[11] *Hannah* v. *Larche,* 363 U. S. 420, 494 (1960).
[12] *Ibid.* at 497, 498, 499.

impanelled in Bibb County, Georgia, in 1960 and charged by
the judges of the Superior Court of the county with the duty to
investigate the "persistent rumors and accusations" of the illegal
use of money in connection with the solicitation of Negro votes,
and to determine the truth or falsity of them. A man named
Wood was the elected sheriff of the county, and the day following the impanelling of the grand jury, he issued a press release
denouncing the judges and, allegedly, threatening the jurors. " 'It
seems incredible,' he said in one part of this statement, 'that all
three of our Superior Court Judges, who themselves hold high
political office, are so politically naive as to actually believe that
the negro voters in Bibb County sell their votes in any fashion,
either to candidates for office or to some negro leaders.' " As to
the grand jury, he hoped it would " 'not let its high office be a
party to any political attempt to intimidate the negro people in
this community.' " Not content with this, the following day he
delivered to the bailiff stationed at the entrance to the grand
jury room, an open letter to the grand jury in which he asserted
that the judges' charge was false and that the local Democratic
Executive Committee was responsible for the purchasing of votes
and that the grand jury " 'would be well-advised . . . to investigate that organization.' "[13] For these acts he was cited for contempt, given a hearing, and adjudged guilty. This judgment was
affirmed on appeal in the state courts, and he appealed to the
Supreme Court of the United States, alleging that he had been
deprived of his freedom of speech under the First and Fourteenth Amendments.

Anglo-American courts have long taken a serious view of
such publications. In fact, a federal statute provides punishment
up to six months imprisonment or a fine up to $1000 for anyone
who "attempts to influence the action or decision of any grand
or petit juror of any court of the United States [i.e., not a state
court] upon any issue or matter pending before such juror, or
before the jury of which he is a member, or pertaining to his
duties, by writing or sending to him any written communication,
in relation to such issue or matter. . . ."[14] And Justice Holmes
once said that even publications not sent to, but merely likely to

[13] *Wood* v. *Georgia*, 370 U.S. 375, 380 (1962).
[14] 18 USCA 1504.

reach the eyes of a jury "would be none the less a contempt" even if containing nothing but true statements. "The theory of our system," he said, "is that the conclusions to be reached in a case will be induced only by evidence and argument in open court, and not by any outside influence, whether of private talk or public print."[15]

There is no question but that the Supreme Court had, even before *Wood* v. *Georgia,* restricted the freedom of a state judge to punish out-of-court comment on pending cases and had, conversely, enlarged the freedom to comment on such cases.[16] Since 1941, the rule has been that the comment must constitute a "clear and present danger," or an imminent, and not merely a likely, threat to the administration of justice before it can be punished as a contempt. (The rule has led to a reversal of the contempt judgment in every case in which it has been applied.) But here the Court went further. The Georgia judges had determined that Wood's publications "presented a clear and present danger to the proceedings of the court and grand jury"; but Chief Justice Warren, along with Justices Black and Douglas, Brennan and Stewart, held that the findings of clear and present danger were unsupported in the trial record, and Warren went on to say that there was no "showing of an actual interference with the undertakings of the grand jury." Now, whatever might be said about the use of the clear and present danger test as a rule governing the issue, it would seem that the test does not require a showing of actual interference, but only of an imminent danger of such interference. Justice Harlan, in dissent, said that the "Court cannot mean that attempts to influence judicial proceedings are punishable only if they are successful."[17] Yet one cannot be sure that the Court did not mean just that, and if it did, then it will have gone a long way toward eliminating entirely the old rule prohibiting out-of-court comment on matters pending in state courts, for it would seem almost impossible to adduce evidence proving the success of attempts to influence or

[15] *Patterson* v. *Colorado*, 205 U.S. 454, 462 (1907).

[16] The power of a federal judge summarily to punish such comments is governed by a federal statute which has given rise to a distinct body of law. This statute is in addition to the one quoted in the text above regarding communications sent to jurors.

[17] *Wood* v. *Georgia* at 400.

coerce the judgments or decisions of judges or jurors. Would this require a confession from the judge or juror that he had acted out of fear of the likes of Sheriff Wood? Or would a fellow judge be permitted to determine the success of the attempt by evaluating the decision made by the judge or juror?

In its solicitude for Sheriff Wood, who, it must not be forgotten, purported to speak for the Negroes of Bibb County, the Supreme Court extended the rule in still another direction. Prior to this case, the clear and present danger test had not been applied to out-of-court publications addressed to members of *a jury* before their verdict was announced. In each previous case, it was *the judge's* act that was pending. In the 1941 case, for example, the defendants had been found guilty but had not yet been sentenced when the *Los Angeles Times* had editorialized on the case, telling the judge that he ought to send the defendants to the "jute-mill." In the *Wood* case, for the first time, the Court held that attempts to influence a jury are punishable only according to the clear and present danger test. Yet, the distinction drawn, or formerly drawn, between attempts to influence or coerce a judge and attempts to influence or coerce a jury is not fictitious. Justice Harlan spoke to this point in his dissenting opinion in the *Wood* case:

> Of equal if not greater importance is the fact that petitioner's statements were calculated to influence, not a judge chosen because of his independence, integrity, and courage and trained by experience and the discipline of law to deal only with evidence properly before him, but a grand jury of laymen chosen to serve for a limited term from the general population of Bibb County. It cannot be assumed with grand jurors, as it has been with judges . . . that they are all "men of fortitude, able to thrive in a hardy climate." What may not seriously endanger the independent deliberations of a judge may well jeopardize those of a grand or petit jury.[18]

Jeopardizing the "independent deliberations" of a jury is a polite way of saying "intimidating a jury" (and is there no possibility that Sheriff Wood was doing precisely this by issuing his statements?), and an intimidated jury has no place in the

[18] *Ibid. at 401–02.*

fair administration of justice. In fact, the loss of the power to punish out-of-court contempt jeopardizes, under conditions that are by no means rare in this country, the very possibility of a fair trial before an impartial jury; and such a trial before such a jury is a constitutional right.

Almost exactly one year before the *Wood* case, the Supreme Court vacated a death sentence in a murder case coming from Indiana on the ground that the jury was not impartial, and it was not impartial because it was subjected to a tremendous volume of publicity adverse to the accused. As Justice Frankfurter said in his concurring opinion:

> How can fallible men and women reach a disinterested verdict based exclusively on what they heard in the court when, before they entered the jury box, their minds were saturated by press and radio for months preceding by matter designed to establish the guilt of the accused. A conviction so secured obviously constitutes a denial of due process of law in its most rudimentary conception.[19]

More immediately relevant is the problem of "trial by newspaper" in a southern court in which a Negro is on trial, and here the *Wood* decision may have serious and detrimental consequences for the Negro's cause, because it may make it even more difficult for a Negro to obtain a fair trial. In 1949, in Lake County, Florida, a seventeen-year-old white girl reported that she had been raped, at pistol point, by four Negroes. A week later a grand jury indicted Samuel Shepherd and one other Negro for this offense, and a month later they were convicted and sentenced to death. The Supreme Court of the United States reversed without opinion, citing an earlier case holding that the method of jury selection discriminated against Negroes. Justices Jackson and Frankfurter concurred in the result, and they contributed an opinion. The real evil in the case, as they saw it, was the extent to which "prejudicial influences outside the courtroom, becoming all too typical of a highly publicized trial, were brought to bear on this jury with such force that the conclusion is inescapable that these defendants were prejudged as guilty and the trial was but a legal gesture to register a verdict already

[19] *Irvin v. Dowd*, 366 U.S. 717, 729–30 (1961).

dictated by the press and the public opinion . . . generated."[20]
The presence of Negroes on the jury could not have made this
trial a fair one. Mobs had burned the home of Shepherd's
parents, and two other Negro houses; Negroes had to be moved
out of the community to save them from being lynched, and
others fled; the National Guard had to be called out to maintain
order; and the newspapers did their best to fan the flames of
racial hatred. One of them published, during the "deliberations"
of the grand jury, a cartoon "picturing four electric chairs and
headed, 'No Compromise—Supreme Penalty.' " As Jackson said:
"I do not see, as a practical matter, how any Negro on the jury
would have dared to cause a disagreement or acquittal."

> The only chance these Negroes had of acquittal would
> have been in the courage and decency of some sturdy
> and forthright white person of sufficient standing to face
> and live down the odium among his white neighbors
> that such a vote, if required, would have brought. To
> me, the technical question of discrimination in the jury
> selection has only theoretical importance. The case pre-
> sents one of the best examples of one of the worst
> menaces to American justice.[21]

Verdicts of petit juries can be vacated by an appellate court,
but this is by no means a satisfactory solution to the problem.
The indictment of Leslie Irvin, the accused in the Indiana
murder case, was returned on April 21, 1955, more than six years
before the Supreme Court vacated the death sentence and re-
manded the case with instructions permitting a new trial; and
some time in the future the Supreme Court of the United States
will, almost certainly, be asked once again to review the case,
for the press, less restricted now than ever before, will surely
have something to say about a person who is said to have confessed to six murders committed back in 1954 and 1955 and who
has managed for all these years to "cheat the chair." "Trial by
newspaper" is not due process of law, and perhaps the best way
to prevent such trials is to put the press—newspapers, radio, and
television—on notice that they can be punished for contempt.
This was the conclusion in 1961 of two law professors, one from
Yale and the other from New York University:

[20] *Shepherd* v. *Florida*, 341 U.S. 50, 51 (1951).
[21] *Ibid.* at 55.

> Perhaps the most effective way to give real meaning
> to the guarantee of an impartial jury trial in the United
> States is to restore the contempt power to the courts. Is
> it possible [however] to draft a narrow contempt statute
> that would survive American constitutional limitations
> and still be effective?[22]

Since *Wood* v. *Georgia* in 1962, these judge-made constitutional
limitations are more severe than ever.

Since when have Georgia sheriffs enjoyed a reputation that
justifies their being made the beneficiaries of new, and potentially
dangerous, rules of law? Have we reached the point where legal
penalties can be avoided, not only by defending the Negro's
cause—one is entitled to doubt that this is what Sheriff Wood
was really doing—but merely by purporting to defend it? Supposing this had been a federal grand jury, charged with investigating allegations of the use of violence to prevent Negroes from
voting in a federal election; and supposing another Georgia
sheriff—Claude Screws, for example—had issued statements similar
to Wood's. Are we to assume that the Supreme Court's decision
would have been the same? And if the Court is going to assume
grand jurors to be immune to threats of intimidation, why
should it be so eager to protect the anonymity of witnesses in
hearings such as those in Shreveport before the Civil Rights
Commission?

It is right that a Negro girl should be permitted to join
her classmates in an excursion to Bob-Lo Island; but if, as
Justice Stone once wrote, judicial opinions "are not better than
an excursion ticket, good for this day and trip only, they . . .
would be much better left unsaid."[23] The Supreme Court has no
authority to issue "excursion tickets," or to right every wrong
brought to its attention; it is a court of law, deriving its power
from the authority that law has in a law-abiding community. Its
constitutional decisions are supposed to derive from constitutional principles—not from consideration of the immediate consequences to the parties to the case—and its opinions are supposed to elaborate the applicability of the principles to the facts

[22] Richard C. Donnelly and Ronald Goldfarb, "Contempt by Publication
in the United States," 29 *Modern Law Review* 254 (1961).

[23] As quoted in Alpheus Thomas Mason, *The Supreme Court from Taft
to Warren* (Baton Rouge: Louisiana State University Press, 1958), p. 106.

of the cases being decided, and to do so in a convincing manner or not at all. To assume the power of a "kadi under a tree dispensing justice according to considerations of individual expediency,"[24] is to cause its authority to be questioned in a way that is certain to damage the law in general. And with what consequences, finally, for the beneficiaries of its decisions?

This country has had experience with a Court that, in Professor Wechsler's words, "could not articulate an adequate analysis of the restrictions it imposed on Congress,"[25] which is to say, could not support its decisions in favor of its cause—economic freedom—with reasoned constitutional arguments. Justice Day's opinion for a bare majority of the Court in the first child-labor case[26] is absurd, as Holmes and a generation of constitutional lawyers delighted in demonstrating to more than one generation of students; and the child-labor case was not unique. In fact, great judicial reputations were built on dissents in these economic freedom cases. Did these majority justices not damage the cause they sought to uphold by defending it beyond the point where it was defensible? Did they not succeed in bringing judicial review itself into disrepute, not only with a President who would have "packed" the Court, but with many constitutional lawyers, the men whose job it was, and is, to profess the law of the Constitution? A cause cannot long be sustained by judges alone, and if the attempt to do so leads to judicial fiat, the cause is made to appear unworthy.

THE EXTENSION OF "STATE ACTION"

The Fourteenth Amendment provides that all persons "born or naturalized in the United States, and subject to the jurisdiction thereof, are citizens of the United States and of the State wherein they reside." It also provides that no state shall abridge the privileges or immunities of citizens of the United States, or deprive any person of life, liberty or property without due process of law, or—and it is this provision that has proved most effective in the struggle for Negro equality—"deny to any person

[24] Justice Frankfurter dissenting in *Terminiello* v. *Chicago*, 337 U.S. 1, 11 (1949).
[25] Wechsler, *op. cit.*, p. 23.
[26] *Hammer* v. *Dagenhart*, 247 U.S. 251 (1918).

within its jurisdiction the equal protection of the laws." Its concluding section authorizes Congress to legislate in order "to enforce . . . the provisions of this article." Acting primarily under this grant of constitutional authority, Congress enacted the Civil Rights Act of 1875, the purpose of which was to secure to all persons the "full and equal enjoyment of the accomodations, advantages, facilities, and privileges of inns, public conveyances . . . theaters and other places of public amusement." Section 2 of this statute made it a penal offense for *any* person, state official or private citizen, to deny to any citizen, because of his race or color, the privileges secured in the first section of the statute.

In five separate cases, known collectively as the *Civil Rights Cases* of 1883, six persons were indicted for denying Negroes accommodations in inns, theaters, and a railroad car. On appeal, the Supreme Court, with only Justice Harlan dissenting, held that the Fourteenth Amendment prohibits only state or official discrimination, which means that the rights established in that amendment (as well as in the Fifteenth Amendment) can be denied only by states, or by persons acting under color of state law (i.e., in the name of the state). This is known as the "state action" doctrine. By providing for the punishment of private discrimination, Congress had exceeded its authority, the Court held. The statute was declared unconstitutional.[27]

So long as the Supreme Court was dealing with discriminatory state laws, or, so long as it was trying to promote equality in the legal sense, the state action doctrine did not stand in the way of effective judicial action on behalf of the victims of such laws. When West Virginia enacted a statute disqualifying Negroes from jury service, the Supreme Court struck it down as a denial of equal protection of the laws.[28] When, even in the absence of a state law requiring or authorizing his action, a Virginia jury commissioner excluded Negroes from jury service, the Court had no difficulty in finding this too to be state action: "Whoever, by virtue of public position under a state government, deprives another of property, life or liberty without due process of law, or denies or takes away the equal protection of the laws, violates the constitutional inhibition; and as he acts in the name

---

[27] 109 U.S. 3 (1883).
[28] *Strauder* v. *West Virginia,* 100 U.S. 303 (1880).

[of] and for the State, and is clothed with the State's power, his act is that of the State."[29] And even when the states became more subtle, by enacting laws that did not expressly discriminate against Negroes, the Court still did not hesitate to carry out the mandate of the postwar amendments. A case in point is a 1910 amendment to the Oklahoma constitution that exempted from a literacy test, imposed as a condition of voting, those persons who, on January 1, 1866, or earlier, were entitled to vote, and the descendants of such persons. Other persons, which of course meant Negroes, were required to take the literacy test, which was then administered with a rigor sufficient to bar them from the polls. The Court unanimously declared this provision to be a violation of the Fifteenth Amendment.[30] As Justice Frankfurter was to say some twenty years later, the amendment "nullifies sophisticated as well as simple-minded modes of discrimination."[31] The same fate befell a state law forbidding Negroes to vote in primary elections, and a subsequent law that, in effect, authorized the central committees of the political parties to do the same thing was also struck down as a denial of equal protection. But when the parties themselves, acting under no authority from the state, excluded Negroes from the primaries, the Court, in 1935, confronted a form of the issue that characterizes most discrimination cases today: To what extent, if any, is the discriminatory action that of the state? At first, it found no element of state action present: the exclusion of Negroes from the Texas Democratic primary election was held to be the act of a private organization and, according to the state action rule, was not a violation of a constitutional right;[32] but nine years later it overruled this decision by holding that when a state entrusts a political party with the selection of candidates for public office, that party is an agency of the state and its actions are state actions.[33] Whereupon South Carolina, in an effort to show that it did not entrust political parties with any public function, proceeded to repeal all its statutory provisions regulating primary elections and party organizations, claiming that

[29] *Ex parte Virginia*, 100 U.S. 339; 25 L.Ed. 676, 679 (1880).
[30] *Guinn* v. *United States*, 238 U.S. 347 (1915).
[31] *Lane* v. *Wilson*, 307 U.S. 268, 275 (1939).
[32] *Grovey* v. *Townsend*, 295 U.S. 45 (1935).
[33] *Smith* v. *Allwright*, 321 U.S. 649 (1944).

the parties were "private voluntary associations" and entitled to
conduct their affairs, including their elections, as they saw fit.
As might be expected, however, this stratagem did not succeed.[34]

These cases illustrate a few of the variety of ways in which
some states attempted, despite the commands of the post-Civil
War amendments, to continue the exclusion of Negroes from
legal membership in the body known as "the people of the
United States." In disposing of them, the Court was not always
unanimous, but the decisions rested firmly and easily on principles that are embodied, and are readily seen to be embodied,
in the amended Constitution. The same cannot be said of many
of the decisions that followed, for it is not easy to adhere to the
theory of the *Civil Rights Cases,* according to which private conduct is immune to federal law, and simultaneously to find some
principle according to which this conduct is not immune to
federal law. The Jaybird case shows why.

Here the Court was dealing with what can best be described
as a preprimary election. The Jaybird Association was an organization of white voters in Fort Bend County, Texas, that selected
its own candidates to run in the Democratic party primary. The
successful Jaybird candidates were not compelled to run in the
Democratic primary, but they almost always did so and almost
always won, both in the primary and in the subsequent general
election. The Court held that it was unconstitutional for the
Association to exclude Negroes from its elections,[35] even though
it would appear to have been a private organization and its
actions, however benighted, not the actions of the state of Texas
and therefore immune to federal government supervision.[36] Yet
eight members of the Court said it was not really private; that
is to say, they agreed that the exclusion of Negroes from the
Jaybird election was, somehow, the action of the state of Texas,
although they could not agree on why, or in what respect, it
was the action of the state of Texas. In fact, there is no opinion

[34] *Rice* v. *Elmore,* 165 F (2d) 387 (1947); certiorari denied, 333 U.S.
875 (1948).

[35] *Terry* v. *Adams,* 345 U.S. 461 (1953).

[36] The first section of the Fifteenth Amendment reads as follows: "The
right of citizens of the United States to vote shall be not be denied or abridged
by the United States or by any State on account of race, color, or previous
condition of servitude."

of the Court in this case. Black, Douglas, and Burton, who announced the Court's judgment, found state action in the fact
that the state permitted the Jaybird election:

> For a state to permit such a duplication of its elec-
> tion processes is to permit a flagrant abuse of those proc-
> esses to defeat the purposes of the Fifteenth Amendment.
> The use of the county-operated primary to ratify the
> result of the prohibited election merely compounds the
> offense. It violates the Fifteenth Amendment for a state,
> by such circumvention, to permit within its borders the
> use of any device that produces an equivalent of the pro-
> hibited election.[37]

Frankfurter, alone in his concurrence in the judgment, found
the case "by no means free of difficulty," but managed to resolve
his doubts by finding state action in the fact that county election
officials (state officers) voted in the Jaybird preprimary. Unable
to accept either of these rules, Clark, Vinson, Reed, and Jackson
asserted that the Jaybird Association was really the Democratic
party in "disguise," or was an "auxiliary" of the Democratic
party, or an "adjunct" of it. Only Minton could not find state
action anywhere, and he dissented.

It is not easy to see what the Negro beneficiaries of this
dubious reasoning will gain by being permitted to vote in the
Jaybird election. They were legally free to vote in the party
primaries and in the general election, and the local politics of
Fort Bend County will not change if they are legally free to vote
in the Jaybird election. There is no reason to doubt that it was
the only election that "counted in this Texas county," or that the
Jaybirds existed for a reason having something to do with the
desire of the white population to exclude Negroes from a share
in the governing of the county—because, perhaps, this was the
most convenient way of excluding them. It is not, however, the
only way, and since the white population of the county is four
times greater than the Negro population, it is probable that the
vote of a Negro, if the whites are united, is no more "effective"
now than it was before the decision.

On the other hand, it is easy to see why the members of
the Court should have trouble agreeing on the rule of the

[37] *Terry* v. *Adams*, p. 469.

case and why one highly respected constitutional lawyer should look on the decision as a threat to the freedom of association: ". . . the constitutional guarantee against deprivation of the franchise on the ground of race or color has become a prohibition of party organization upon racial lines, at least where the party has achieved political hegemony."[38] Does the decision mean, since the Constitution surely forbids a denial of the franchise on religious grounds, that religious parties are proscribed? Would not such a proscription "infringe rights protected by the first amendment"?

It is also easy to understand why the Court should believe it necessary to "find" state action in what the Jaybirds did. Unless it is somehow extended, the state action rule constitutes a barrier to judicial (and, if Congress were disposed to do something, legislative) action with respect to private discrimination, because it prevents federal law from reaching the source of the discrimination, the private individual or group. When, nevertheless, the Court, believing that its decisions will somehow promote Negro membership in "the people of the United States" in the ultimate sense, began the attempt to reach this private discrimination despite the apparent constitutional barrier, it initiated a threat to more than the freedom of association. It began to threaten privacy itself.

The initial step was taken in 1948 in *Shelley* v. *Kraemer*, a case that opened new vistas in the search for state action. Briefly, the facts are as follows: In 1911, the owners of various pieces of property located in a contiguous area in St. Louis, Missouri, entered into a formally recorded agreement known as a racially restrictive real estate covenant providing that for fifty years from that date the occupancy and use of the property would be restricted to persons "of the Caucasian race." In 1945, a property owner broke the agreement by selling a piece of this property to Shelley and his wife, who were Negroes; a Mr. and Mrs. Kraemer, owners of other property subject to the agreement, brought suit to restrain the Shelleys from taking possession. On appeal, the Supreme Court of the United States acknowledged the legality of the covenant itself, an acknowledgment consistent with the doc-

---

[38] Wechsler, *op. cit.*, p. 29.

trine of state action, but held that judicial enforcement of this legal covenant was state action denying the equal protection of the laws and was therefore contrary to the Fourteenth Amendment.

> State action, as that phrase is understood for the purposes of the Fourteenth Amendment, refers to exertions of state power in all forms. And when the effect of that action is to deny rights subject to the protection of the Fourteenth Amendment, it is the obligation of this Court to enforce the constitutional commands.[39]

The *Shelley* rule, in other words, provides a means whereby the Supreme Court can reach certain kinds of private discrimination, which is the only remaining problem of discrimination today, even while acknowledging the legality (within the terms of the *Civil Rights Cases*) of the private discrimination. It does this by denying the assistance of the courts to private persons who discriminate and, thereby, depriving such persons of any means of effecting their discrimination. This became even more obvious five years later when the Court had a case in which one white covenantor broke the racially restrictive agreement by selling a house to a Negro and was sued for damages by a co-covenantor. The problem in the case was whether the party who had acted "illegally" by breaching a legal agreement could rely on the rights of others in her defense to the breach of contract action. The Supreme Court held that an award of damages by a state court would constitute state action depriving—someone—of the equal protection of the laws. But depriving whom? The Negro purchaser had the house and would not stand to lose it whatever the outcome of the suit; the seller was not being deprived of equal protection—the state had in no way discriminated against her. But an award of damages would affect the ability of other Negroes to persuade other covenantors to breach the "legal" agreements they had entered into. So the Court solved the problem by allowing the seller to rely on the rights of "unidentified but identifiable Negroes." Thus, restrictive covenants are legal, but they cannot be enforced in the courts, either directly or, by permitting collection of damages for their breach, indirectly.[40]

[39] *Shelley* v. *Kraemer*, 334 U.S. 1, 20 (1948).
[40] *Barrows* v. *Jackson*, 346 U.S. 249 (1953).

But what, precisely, is the meaning of *Shelley* v. *Kraemer?* The Court said in that case "that restrictions on the right of occupancy of the sort sought to be created by the private agreements in these cases could not be squared with the requirements of the Fourteenth Amendment if imposed by state statute or local ordinance.[41] If this statement contains the essence of the *Shelley* rule, if, that is, a state may not do judicially what it is forbidden to do legislatively, the decisions in the sit-in cases would have seemed to follow as a matter of course, because it is quite clear that a state may not by law require separation of the races in privately owned lunch counters. Essentially, these cases involved Negroes who, upon being refused service at a lunch counter because of their race or color, refused to leave the premises when asked to do so by the manager, were arrested by the police for trespass, indicted, tried, convicted, and sentenced to jail. As might be expected, the southern state judges, in the course of rejecting the Negroes' constitutional arguments on appeal, discovered a difference of constitutional proportions between state action that enforces a discriminatory real estate covenant and state action that enforces other kinds of private discrimination; but they did not succeed in demonstrating in what this difference is supposed to consist. Such a demonstration would not be easy, for, if it is solely the enforcement of these acts that is illegal, if the private discriminatory acts themselves are not illegal under the Constitution, then there is no principle in the *Shelley* case that permits the drawing of a distinction among the *equally legal* private acts.

In its decisions of May 20, 1963, the Supreme Court did not even essay such a distinction. It avoided the question altogether, by denying that the cases involved private discrimination, and it was able to do this because Greenville, South Carolina, where the leading case originated, had an ordinance requiring separate lunch-counter facilities for Negroes, and the Court held that the decision to refuse service originated in that ordinance, not in a private decision of the store manager.[42] New Orleans did not have such an ordinance, but the Court placed the blame on the city anyway. Shortly before the incident that gave rise

[41] *Shelley* v. *Kraemer,* at 11.
[42] *Peterson* v. *City of Greenville,* 83 S.Ct. 1119 (1963).

to the case, the mayor and the police superintendent had issued statements condemning and urging an end to the sit-in demonstrations taking place in the city, and the Court held that the store's refusal to serve the Negroes had been "coerced" by these statements.[43] Thus, the Court found illegal state action not in police or judicial enforcement of private discrimination—the *Shelley* situation—but in the discriminatory act itself, and it left the grave question first raised in *Shelley* unanswered.

It cannot go unanswered for long. The ordinances will be repealed, the city officials will remain silent, and the Court will then be confronted with a sit-in case in which the basic question, the question of the extent to which private persons are permitted to rely on the law to enforce their "preferences," cannot be avoided; and the Court will have to define the *Shelley* rule.[44] It will not be any easier then than it would have been this year to limit its application to only some private discriminatory acts if, as Professor Frank once said, "logic is to be maintained."[45] But logic, especially very troubling logic, need not be maintained, and there are very good reasons why it should not be maintained in the next round of sit-in cases.

Let us assume that the Court were to apply the *Shelley* rule. This would mean that lunch counters in states that do not have anti-discrimination laws are legally free to discriminate against Negroes, but that the Fourteenth Amendment forbids a state to enforce the discrimination. Thus, just as a person is within his legal rights when he enters into a restrictive real estate contract, he is also within his legal rights when he refuses to serve Negroes at his lunch counter; in neither case, however, may he rely on the law to enforce his discrimination. But there is a difference between these two situations that now becomes visible. In the first case, the white covenantor, for whatever reasons (and this is, after all, a pre-condition of the litigation), ceases

---

[43] *Lombard* v. *Louisiana*, 83 S.Ct. 1122, 1125 (1963).

[44] On June 10, 1963, the Court agreed to review three new sit-in cases. *Barr* v. *City of Columbia, Bouie and Neal* v. *City of Columbia*, 83 S.Ct. 1690; *Bell* v. *Maryland*, 83 S.Ct. 1691; and noted probable jurisdiction in another: *Robinson* v. *Florida*, 83 S.Ct. 1692.

[45] John P. Frank, *Cases on Constitutional Law* (Chicago: Callaghan & Co., 1952), p. 1032.

to discriminate when he sells his property to a Negro. No such event has occurred in the second case; not only is the store manager entitled to discriminate, but so far as we know, or may know, he wants to discriminate against Negroes and will continue to do so in the future. What becomes visible here is the problem of enforcement, and the problem of enforcement cannot be solved within even the expanded state-action doctrine.

To begin with, the lunch-counter manager will be entitled to take the law into his own hands in order to enforce his acknowledged right to discriminate against whom he pleases— that is, to resort to what the law calls "self-help." It is sometimes assumed that racial discrimination cannot exist without the help of the law, and that the store owners and managers will not resort to the use of force, even if the states give them—as they probably will give them—a greater latitude to do so. Against this optimistic assumption, and the evidence from places like Durham, North Carolina, that supports it, must be placed such events as those of Oxford, Mississippi, and the possibility of similar events in other parts of the South. Will white southerners acquiesce or will they, as they are relentlessly pursued by the federal law, turn vengefully on Negroes when that law gives them the opportunity? In either case, there is surely something wrong with legal principles whose application may provoke violence and that, at the same time, regard that violence as perfectly legal. Yet the meaning of the *Shelley* doctrine as applied to sit-in cases in this manner is that the manager may, under the Constitution, discriminate against Negroes, and may, under both the Constitution and local law, authorize thugs or "bouncers" to use physical force to remove Negroes from his premises.

The way to avoid this possibility, and it is likely that the Court will avoid it, is to forgo a reliance on the *Shelley* rule and to expand the state-action doctrine in another direction, that is, by ruling that the owners or managers of businesses open to the public are acting under color of state law when they discriminate against some members of the public. Then it would not be legal for them to discriminate on the basis of race or color, and they would not be entitled to utilize "self-help." This would solve one aspect of the enforcement problem, for the criminal statute[46] under which Claude Screws, the brutal Georgia sheriff, was indicted would be available to federal prosecutors, and, in addition, there is a civil statute permitting an injured party to bring a damage suit against any "person who, under color of any statute, ordinance, regulation, custom, or usage of any State" deprives him of a right secured by the Constitution or by federal law,[47] including, if the Court adopts this approach, the right to service at a nonsegregated lunch counter open to the public.

The difficulty is that in both criminal and civil actions enforcement of the right will depend on the co-operation of local juries. Even assuming, however, that these juries will act in the worst possible manner and simply refuse to convict or award damages, or even to return an indictment, there is still another way to enforce a federal law against discrimination: an injured party can always petition a federal court for an injunction against the offending lunch-counter manager, and failure to obey an injunction is punishable as a contempt of court, a judgment in which juries play no part. This leaves the problem of what to do with the white customers—for example, the high school students at the favorite soda fountain, or their older brothers at the favorite tavern—who violently object to Negroes joining them at the counter or bar. It is difficult to see how they could be enjoined (unlike the managers, they would not be acting under color of state law and, therefore, would not be acting in violation of a federal law), nor is there a federal statute under which they could be punished.[48] Perhaps the answer to this is to be found in the words of Justice Holmes: "the law does all that is needed when it does all that it can,"[49] and that the Court will have reached the point where it must rely on the demonstrated willingness of most Americans, under

[46] "Whoever, under color of any law, statute, ordinance, regulation, or custom, willfully subjects any inhabitant of any State . . . to the deprivation of any rights, privileges, or immunities secured or protected by the Constitution or laws of the United States . . . shall be fined not more than $1000 or imprisoned not more than one year, or both." 18 U.S.C. 242 (1950 ed.) .

[47] 42 U.S.C. 1983 (1950 ed.) .

[48] The conspiracy provision, 18 U.S.C. 241, protects a citizen in the enjoyment of a federal right, but the federal right here is a right only against those acting under color of law.

[49] *Buck* v. *Bell*, 274 U.S. 200, 208 (1927) .

most circumstances, to obey the law (or, in this case, the spirit of the law).

It should be understood that this approach to the sit-in cases involves the reversal of the holding in the *Civil Rights Cases* of 1883, for the Court held in those cases that the discrimination practiced by inns, theaters, and railroads was not state action. The Court does not casually reverse its constitutional decisions, especially those of such long standing and on which so much depends. Yet, so grave are the implications of *Shelley* v. *Kraemer,* that the Court would nevertheless be adopting the less radical approach if it were to hold that businesses open to the public exercise a public responsibility, and that their acts are state acts.

It is the consideration of what lies beyond the sit-in cases if they are eventually settled on the basis of the *Shelley* rule that is surely troubling more than one of the justices of the Court,[50] just as it has troubled more than one legal commentator. For courts are needed to enforce not only the law of contracts, as in *Shelley,* or the law of trespass, as in the sit-in cases; they are needed to enforce all the laws, including the laws of wills and of charitable trusts. A state may not by law forbid white testators to dispose of their property to Negroes, nor may it forbid the creation of a charitable trust that includes Negroes

[50] "Judicial enforcement is of course state action, but this is not the end of the inquiry. The ultimate substantive question is whether there has been '[S]tate action of a particular character' (*Civil Rights Cases,* 3 S.Ct. at 21) —whether the character of the State's involvement in an arbitrary discrimination is such that it should be held *responsible* for the discrimination.

"This limitation on the scope of the prohibitions of the Fourteenth Amendment serves several vital functions in our system. Underlying the cases involving an alleged denial of equal protection by ostensibly private action is a clash of competing constitutional claims of a high order: liberty and equality. Freedom of the individual to choose his associates or his neighbors, to use and dispose of his property as he sees fit, to be irrational, arbitrary, capricious, even unjust in his personal relations are things all entitled to a large measure of protection from governmental interference. This liberty would be overridden, in the name of equality, if the strictures of the Amendment were applied to governmental and private action without distinction. Also inherent in the concept of state action are values of federalism, a recognition that there are areas of private rights upon which federal power should not lay a heavy hand and which should properly be left to the more precise instruments of local authority." Mr. Justice Harlan concurring in the result of the *Peterson* case and dissenting in whole or in part in the other sit-in cases decided May 20, 1963. 83 S.Ct. 1133–34.

among its beneficiaries. Does this mean that a court may not enforce a will that draws a racial line or appoint trustees to administer a trust the benefits of which are limited to a particular racial or religious group? Even Professor Pollak sees the need to draw a line beyond which *Shelley* should not be extended.

> The line sought to be drawn is that beyond which the state assists a private person in seeing to it that others behave in a fashion which the state could not itself have ordained. The principle underlying the distinction is this: the fourteenth amendment permits each his personal prejudices and guarantees him free speech and press and worship, together with a degree of free economic enterprise, as instruments with which to persuade others to adopt his prejudices; but access to state aid to induce others to conform is barred.[51]

Applied to concrete cases, Pollak's argument means that the host may rely on the police to remove undesired guests, that the lunch-counter manager may rely on the police to remove undesired customers; but that a testator may not rely on a probate court to enforce a provision in a will barring any share in the estate to a child who *in the future* marries outside the testator's faith,[52] because the enforcement of this provision would be to "induce compliance by others with the . . . testator's prejudices."[53] With all respect, I cannot find *in the Fourteenth Amendment* a recognition of a difference between enforcing a will that disinherits a son who has already married outside the faith, and enforcing a will that threatens to disinherit the son if he should, later on, marry outside the faith.

More immediately relevant, however, is the way in which Professor Pollak's distinction works in practice: the father is not permitted to "coerce" his son[54] with respect to a matter of obvious, perhaps even overriding importance to him, but the

---

[51] Louis H. Pollak, "Radical Discrimination and Judicial Integrity: A Reply to Professor Wechsler," 108 *University of Pennsylvania Law Review* 13 (1959).

[52] See *Gordon* v. *Gordon*, 332 Mass. 197; 124 N.E.2d 228 (1955).

[53] Pollak, *op. cit.*, pp. 12–13.

[54] It can be regarded as coercion, of course, only if we assume that the son's attachment to his father's money is such as to overcome his attachment to the woman he would make his bride and to principle.

Kress lunch counter is permitted to call the police to enforce its discrimination against an entire class of citizens.[55] Yet to me, the latter act is more reprehensible, for, unlike Professor Pollak, I am unwilling to say that the father who attempts, even by using his money, to perpetuate the faith of his father is prejudiced; and I am unwilling to say this in part (but only in part) because I do not think I possess the knowledge that allows me to refer to religious belief as prejudice. Beyond this, can we not say that there *is* a difference between behavior based on a love of one's own and of one's own faith, and behavior based on a hatred or dislike of others? Can we not agree that in most cases the perpetuation of religious belief is not contrary to the common good of the United States? Even Justice Douglas once said that Americans "are a religious people whose institutions presuppose a Supreme Being.[56]

Finally, what would be the effect on charitable trusts of the use of *Shelley* in the sit-in cases? Trusts abound in this country,[57] and most of them restrict their benefits to a particular group. What would be the status of a trust endowing an orphanage for poor Methodist children, for instance, or a "senior citizens' home" for Episcopalians, or, for that matter, a school for poor Negro children? This is discrimination. Is it therefore illegal for the state to allow them to exist, or for a probate court to appoint a fiduciary, or, having determined that they are truly charities, for the state to grant them tax immunities? The Court resisted the temptation, or at least, refused the request, to so rule when the *Girard College* case came up for the second time;[58] but it is difficult to see how the Court could apply the *Shelley* rule to the

[55] Pollak, *op. cit.*, p. 14. Pollak's article was written before he was of counsel in the sit-in cases, where he joined in the argument urging the reversal of the trespass convictions.

[56] *Zorach v. Clauson*, 343 U.S. 306, 313 (1952).

[57] It is estimated that charitable trusts value tens of billions of dollars, and that each year sees the addition of trusts worth $4 billion. See Elias Clark, "Charitable Trusts, the Fourteenth Amendment and the Will of Stephen Girard," 66 *Yale Law Journal* 1010 (1957).

[58] 357 U.S. 570 (1958). The first time the case came up, the Court held that it was a denial of the Fourteenth Amendment for officials of the City of Philadelphia to serve as trustees and administer the school set up under the will of Stephen Girard while excluding Negroes from the school, 353 U.S. 230 (1957). But when the Orphans Court substituted "private" individuals as trustees, the Supreme Court refused to review the case.

discrimination involved in the sit-in cases and withhold it from the discrimination involved in charitable trusts. Nor do recent cases provide any confidence that the Court will restrain itself again. In *Burton* v. *Wilmington Parking Authority,* a Negro petitioned for a court order forbidding racial discrimination by a privately-owned restaurant located in space leased from a parking authority that was an agency of the state of Delaware. With three dissenters, and with Mr. Justice Stewart concurring separately, the Court managed to find the required element of state action by "nimbly fetching enough connections to treat the state as the culprit,"[59] while resolutely continuing to insist that private discrimination "does no violence to the Equal Protection Clause" of the Fourteenth Amendment.[60] This prompted Mr. Justice Harlan to protest:

> The Court's opinion, by a process of first undiscriminatingly throwing together various factual bits and pieces and then undermining the resulting structure by an equally vague disclaimer, seems to me to leave completely at sea just what it is in this record that satisfies the requirement of "state action."[61]

It seems obvious that this is a Court that will not easily be satisfied to strike down discrimination only when it is the action of the state, especially when, as time passes, it becomes ever clearer that private discrimination can in fact exist without the support of state laws, and even in the face of state laws, and when the achievement by Negroes of legal membership in the American community is not followed by membership in the ultimate sense.

LAW AND SENTIMENT

> Where is the least student of the law who cannot erect a moral code as pure as that of Plato's law? But this is not the only issue. The problem is to adapt this code to the people for which it is made and to the things about which it decrees to such an extent that its execution follows from the very conjunction of these relations; it is to impose on the people, after the fashion of Solon, less the best laws in themselves than the best of which it

[59] Van Alstyne and Karst, *op. cit.,* p. 57.
[60] 365 U.S. 715, 722 (1961).
[61] *Ibid.,* at 727.

admits in the given situation. Otherwise, it is better
to let the disorders subsist than to forestall them, or
take steps thereto, by laws which will not be observed.
For without remedying the evil, this degrades the laws
too.[62]

Whichever approach the Court adopts in the sit-in cases—the
mechanical application of what appears to be the *Shelley* rule
or the expansion of state action to include managers of businesses
open to the public[63]—the Court will have effected profound
changes in American institutions and will threaten more. To rule
that the local police and courts may not enforce private discrimination is to jeopardize the privacy of clubs, of wills, of trusts,
and theoretically, but so remotely as not to deserve more than a
mention, of homes; and to rule that a local lunch-counter manager is, even if only in some respects, an official of the state whose
conduct in the course of his business is subject to federal control
is drastically to affect the character of the federal system. Changes
of this magnitude are not unprecedented, but, except in other
cases involving Negro rights, school segregation being the best
example, such changes have not in the past been made by courts.
Surely Professor Horn is correct in saying that the *Civil Rights
Cases* rest "upon a theory of American federalism which cannot
be reconciled with that developed and accepted by the Supreme
Court in the great series of cases interpreting national powers"
since 1937,[64] and now that the justice who was least willing to
upset the "federal balance," Justice Frankfurter, is no longer on
the bench, it may be possible for the court to abolish this
anachronism; but the reference to the vast national powers in
other areas—labor relations, for instance, and agriculture—is mis-
leading. The assertion of national power in these areas was made
by the national legislative and executive authorities, organized
by a national political party, and supported by popular majorities—an overwhelming majority in 1936: the Court did not

[62] Jean-Jacques Rousseau, *Politics and the Arts: Letter to M. d'Alembert
on the Theatre,* trans. Allan Bloom (Glencoe, Ill.: The Free Press, 1960),
p. 66.
[63] It is not suggested that these are the only possible rules available to
the Court. Nor is it altogether inconceivable that the Court will decide
against the Negroes.
[64] Robert Horn, "National Constitutional Rights and the Desegregation
Crisis," 10 *Western Political Quarterly* 463 (June, 1957).

initiate these massive changes; it merely accepted them, after first resisting them. These changes were made, and made successfully, with the consent of the governed, expressed in the constitutionally prescribed manner. It is by no means obvious that all of what the Court is trying to do for the Negro has such consent, and to proceed without strong evidence of consent is to ignore, or at least to challenge, the limits of the law.

The law has surely demonstrated its ability to "alter race relations"—indeed, the evidence produced by Jack Greenberg, now director counsel of the NAACP, supports his thesis that "in many places law has been the greatest single factor inducing racial change." But there is little evidence that the law, by working on the "underlying attitudes," can bring about these changes with the "willing consent" of the white persons affected.[65] There is no reason to doubt that the desegregation of the armed forces has led to Negroes being accepted by white soldiers, sailors, and airmen (the complaints of discrimination are lodged mainly against officers); but in the civilian world, the world affected by the school and restrictive covenant decisions, the old attitudes are unchanged, or if changed, only for the worse. According to Morton Grodzins, "racial passions are on the rise and find less community restraint" among the white groups on the fringe of Negro neighborhoods in the large metropolitan areas in the North. This is true even though "segregation is more complete than it ever was for Negro rural residents in the South." There is evidence of some progress, but the preponderant evidence points in the other direction. "The larger evidence is not that of integration [or] intracommunity social gains. Rather it is in the direction of more uncompromising segregation and larger Negro slums."[66] Progress cannot be measured by the number of favorable Supreme Court decisions; we deceive ourselves if we think it can. Indeed, in the case of decisions attempting to promote full Negro membership in the American community, the opposite may be true.

In November, 1962, more than eight years after the school desegregation decisions, the number of Negroes in schools with

[65] Jack Greenberg, *Race Relations and American Law* (New York: Columbia University Press, 1959), pp. 2, 26.

[66] Morton Grodzins, "Metropolitan Segregation," 197 *Scientific American* 38, 40 (October, 1957).

whites in the southern and border states, including Washington, D.C., was 255,367, or 7.8 per cent of the total Negro enrollment; the comparable figure for May, 1960, was 181,020, or 6 per cent. But these figures conceal a significant element of the situation. More than one-third (87,749) of the total number of Negroes in schools with whites are in Washington, where Negroes constitute 83.4 per cent of the total public school enrollment. This means that one-third of the Negroes in "schools with whites" attend schools that, in fact, are almost wholly Negro.[67] Of the remaining two-thirds, the vast majority are in schools in the border states where the situation is similar to that in Washington. Legal desegregation is not desegregation in fact. In the eleven so-called deep South states, containing most of the Negro school population (2,803,882 students), only 12,217 students, or .44 per cent, are in schools with whites.

What is worse, segregation among the inhabitants of Washington and the other cities directly involved in the restrictive covenant suits is probably more pronounced now than it was in 1948, when the decisions were handed down. Whites have simply moved out of the cities; in Washington, for example, the white population declined from 66 per cent of the total in 1948 to 46 per cent in 1960. This exodus is not the result solely of the school and restrictive covenant decisions—various factors having nothing to do with racial problems are at work here—but the decisions certainly contributed to it. If the NAACP's purpose in bringing the covenant suits was to make more housing available

[67] Not counted within this figure are students in those 26 (out of a total of 130) Washington schools that have no white students at all. Of the remaining 104 public schools where Negroes attend with whites, 22 have fewer than 5 white students, and 41 have fewer than 10 white students. The statistics are taken from the *Statistical Summary* published by the Southern Education Reporting Service (November, 1962). One year later the number of Negroes in schools with whites had risen to 9.3 per cent, but the situation was essentially unchanged. For example, Negro enrollment in the schools in Washington, D.C., had risen by 7,156 and the number in schools with whites by 12,249; but the white enrollment in District schools had fallen by 2,338. Negroes, about 57 per cent of the general population of the District in 1963, now constitute 85.7 per cent of the public school enrollment (*Southern School News*, December, 1963). In Louisville, Kentucky, to cite one more example, 73 per cent (1,478) of the Negro high school students attend Central High School. In 1961–62, there was *one* white student in the school (The United States Commission on Civil Rights, *Civil Rights U.S.A./Public Schools Southern States 1962*, pp. 30, 55).

to Negroes, it succeeded (although the demand still exceeds the supply by a wide margin, because the "Negro population always increases faster than the living space available to it"[68]), but it certainly did not succeed in integrating the neighborhoods. In St. Louis, the white population of the area surrounding and including the Labadie Avenue district, the district involved directly in *Shelley* v. *Kraemer,* declined from 82.2 per cent of the total in 1950 to 28.1 per cent in 1960, and Labadie Avenue itself is apparently 100 per cent Negro. In Detroit, the white population of the affected area declined from 77.6 per cent to 12.5 per cent in the same decade, and the 4600 block of Seeboldt Avenue is 100 per cent Negro. The restrictive covenants were replaced at first by "evasionary agreements," but these were short-lived and "of only limited effectiveness," as Jack Greenberg put it. "By and large they leave the housing market subject to other forces."[69] They do indeed, and the result is Negro "ghettos." "The only interracial communities in the U.S., with the exception of a few abject slums, are those where limits exist upon the influx of nonwhites."[70]

The nationwide discrimination against Negroes, manifested in so many ways, does not, of course, preclude a nationwide consent to decisions according Negroes a legal membership in the body known as "the people of the United States." Except in places like Mississippi, Negroes vote with the consent of the governed, their right to a fair trial is acknowledged, as is their right to decent treatment at the hands of the police. What does not appear to have that consent are decisions attempting to force whites to go to school with Negroes or to live in the same neighborhoods with them. The law certainly altered race relations in this country, but it has not been able to abolish racial hatred, distrust, dislike, prejudice, or whatever it is that underlies the racial problem.

Yet it might be argued that the law's inability to overcome racial prejudice has not been demonstrated, that what has been demonstrated is the inadequacy of the law available to federal courts, that these courts have been inhibited by the limited scope

[68] Grodzins, *op. cit.,* p. 37.

[69] Greenberg, *op. cit.,* p. 310. The other information comes from the Census Tracts of the cities involved and from private surveys.

[70] Grodzins, *op. cit.,* p. 37.

of national constitutional rights inherited from the post–Civil War Supreme Court. The solution, for those who continue to argue in this fashion, is new law, a new decision by the Court that authorizes Congress to punish manifestations of racial discrimination wherever it occurs.[71] But racial prejudice is not in itself unconstitutional, and it will manifest itself at least in those places where it is not reached by the law. More to the point is the probability, for which there is some evidence, that, as those places become fewer and fewer, as the Court flushes it from one cover after another, expanding the public sphere as it contracts the private, the prejudice will turn on the Court and on the law itself. The means are available to it; the bigoted have the ballot and the voting booth is still private, and must remain so in a free country. In Alabama, George Wallace is elected governor over the liberal Jim Folsom; in Louisiana, Jimmy Davis defeats de Lesseps Morrison;[72] and in Arkansas, the decent Orville Faubus becomes a racist within a few years, while Dale Alford (on a *write-in vote!*) replaces Brooks Hays in Congress. In Alabama again, the veteran New Dealer Lister Hill is re-elected over the extreme racist, James D. Martin, but only by a margin of less than 1 per cent—even though Martin ran as a Republican. Meanwhile, Ross Barnett has indicated his intention of opposing John Stennis for the Senate in the 1964 Mississippi primary. It may indeed prove to be as true now as it was, or probably was, when Justice Brown said it for the majority in *Plessy* v. *Ferguson* in 1896, that the attempt to eradicate racial prejudice by means of law will "only result in accentuating the difficulties of the present situation," especially when that law is court-made law, made in the absence of support from the legislature, and made with materials—the constitutional words and phrases—that do not readily lend themselves to the solution of the problem, and therefore much of it unable to withstand a sustained search for principle.

"Courts," writes Professor Pollak, "are not all there is to law."

[71] The public accommodations section of the civil rights bill now (January, 1964) awaiting a rule from the House Rules Committee is grounded, uneasily, on both the Commerce Clause and the Fourteenth Amendment. To say nothing more, there is some doubt as to its constitutionality.

[72] On January 11, 1964, Morrison lost again, this time to John McKeithen.

It is imprudent—and it is even nondemocratic—to rely solely on judicial mechanisms. The time has come—it is long since overdue—for our other legal institutions, at every level of government, to assume greater and greater responsibility for the affirmative ordering of a democratic community.

But these other legal institutions are precisely those which—unlike the courts—are intended to be directly responsive to popular will. If they fail to assume responsibility, it is because the majority of the people of the United States have not yet come to terms with the national commitments made in their name.[73]

One recalls Lincoln's words in the First Inaugural:

The fugitive slave clause of the Constitution, and the law for the suppression of the foreign slave trade, are each as well enforced, perhaps, as any law can ever be in a community where the moral sense of the people imperfectly supports the law itself. The great body of the people abide by the dry legal obligation in both cases, and a few break over in each [section of the country]. This, I think, cannot be perfectly cured. . . .

There is support among the majority of the people of the United States for the Court's efforts to promote the Negro's legal membership in the body known as "the people of the United States," and if it is lacking in the case of the effort to promote full membership in this "democratic community," as it certainly appears to be, and as Professor Pollak seems to think, what are we to conclude? How are we to proceed, this country whose government was instituted to secure the rights with which all men are equally endowed by their Creator, *and* whose just powers are derived from the consent of the governed? Do we continue to make commitments? No matter what we do to the law in the process? "With public sentiment," Lincoln said, "nothing can fail; without it, nothing can succeed. Consequently he who moulds public sentiment, goes deeper than he who enacts statutes or pronounces decisions. He makes statutes and decisions possible or impossible to be executed." Lincoln knew that the Supreme Court can mold public sentiment as well as pronounce decisions, and perhaps the contemporary Court is doing so. What

[73] See this volume, p. 181.

it does not appear to be doing in every case, however, is molding the sentiment necessary to the execution of the decisions it pronounces, and one reason for this is to be found in the character of those decisions. Too many of them are "unprincipled," some of them supported by clearly specious arguments, with ostensible reasons that simply cannot be believed. If this is true, its decisions will have to be executed without the consent of the governed, and that, according to the Declaration of Independence, is unjust and, according to the experience of all history, impossible except by terror and violence.

What is true of the Court may also be true of militant Negro leadership. The time is near at hand when it will have won all the legal victories, and it is not impossible that it will then find itself confronted by the same massive, stubborn problem, changed but essentially unchanged, unaffected, or if affected, only for the worse. For, we have it on the authority of James Baldwin that the situation of the Negro in Harlem, which, with continued Negro migration north, will swiftly become the situation of most Negroes in this country, is worse, is more demoralizing, than the situation of the Negro in the South where he started. This is the cruelest aspect of all.

PRINTED IN U.S.A.